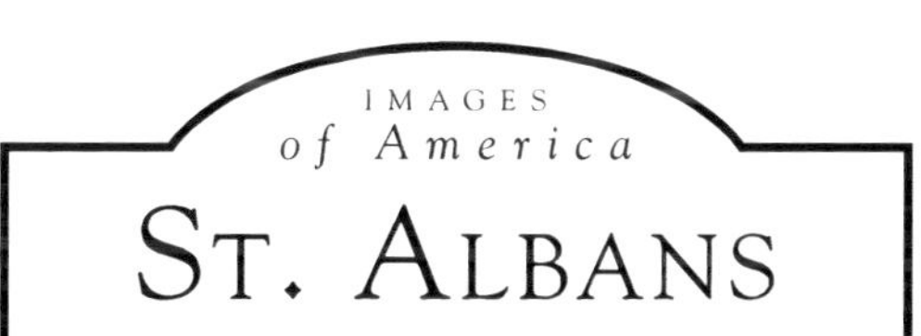
IMAGES
of America
ST. ALBANS

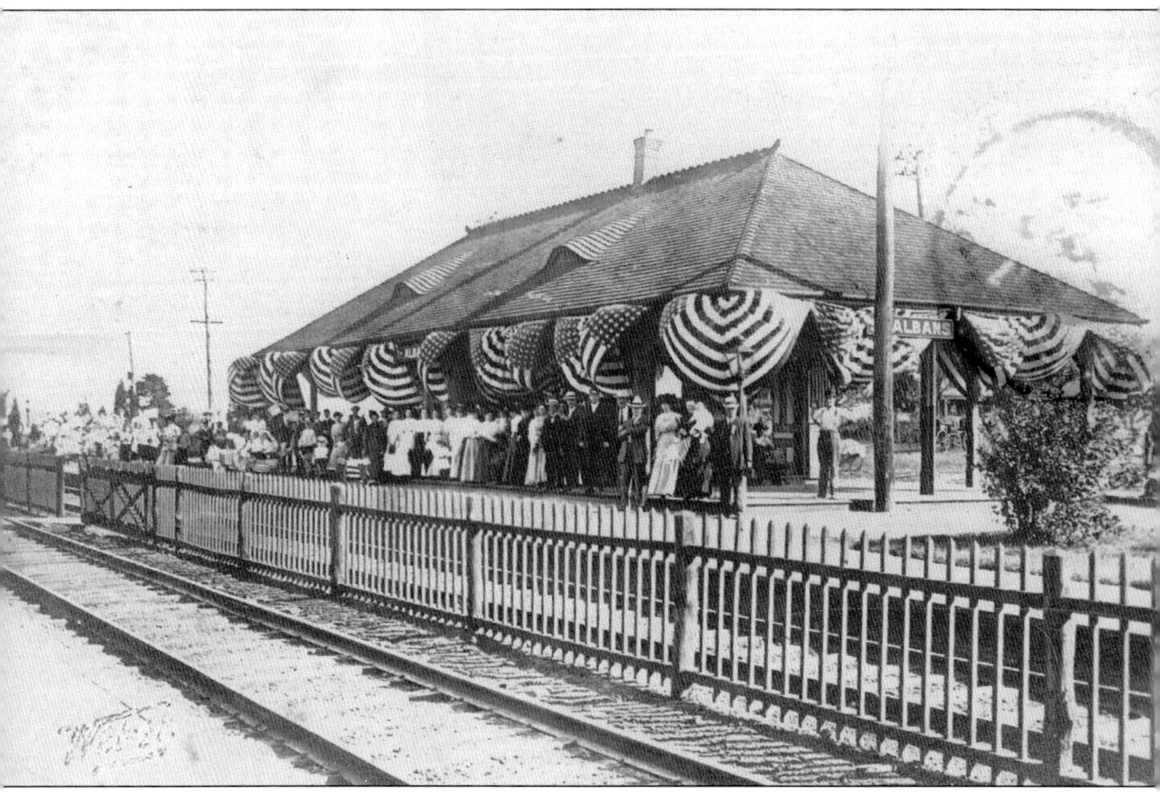

This postcard shows the opening-day ceremony for the Long Island Rail Road's St. Albans station on July 1, 1898. That was the same year Manhattan, Brooklyn, and the Bronx were consolidated with Queens and Staten Island to become New York City's five boroughs. The St. Albans station was originally called Locust Avenue because of its location at Locust Avenue (now Baisley Boulevard), Central Avenue (now Linden Boulevard), and Montauk Street. In 1899, area residents decided to call their community St. Albans after a village in England. (Courtesy of Bob Stonehill.)

On the Cover: Bandleader William "Count" Basie pauses during a rehearsal with pianist/composer/orchestra leader Edward "Duke" Ellington in July 1961. Besides their love of music, both men had ties to southeast Queens. Basie and his wife, Catherine, lived in the Addisleigh Park section of St. Albans since the mid-1940s. Ellington's composer/arranger son, Mercer Ellington, also resided in the affluent community that attracted many African American entertainers and professionals over the years. (Photograph by Don Hunstein, courtesy of Dr. Thomas Manuel, used with permission from Dee Anne Hunstein.)

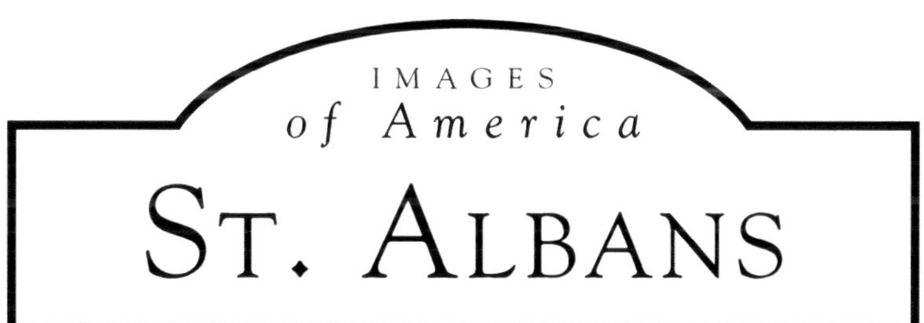

Claire Serant

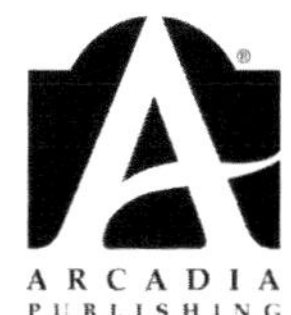

ISBN 978-1-4671-0400-5

Published by Arcadia Publishing
Charleston, South Carolina

Printed in the United States of America

Library of Congress Control Number: 2019936423

For all general information, please contact Arcadia Publishing:
Telephone 843-853-2070
Fax 843-853-0044
E-mail sales@arcadiapublishing.com
For customer service and orders:
Toll-Free 1-888-313-2665

Visit us on the Internet at www.arcadiapublishing.com

For Ronald, Bryan, Brandon, and Blair Garrett;
Lawrence and Ruby Cormier; and Jean Prysock.

Contents

Acknowledgments

It is nearly impossible to contain the history of St. Albans in the confines of this book's 128 pages. However, some wonderful current and former residents came to my aid. Through personal interviews and frequent visits to the Queens Historical Society and Queens Public Library's archives, I was able to highlight some of St. Albans's amazing past. Many, many thanks to Peter B. Antonio, also known as Pete Antell; David G. Berger; Gini Booth; Cassia Campbell; Carl Clay; Billy Cobham; Marcia Comrie; Ruby and Lawrence Cormier; Lillian Crowder; Rev. Edward Davis and his wife, Helen, of the Presbyterian Church of St. Albans; Grace DeSagun, Queens Public Library archives; Rev. Floyd Flake and his wife, Elaine, of the Greater Allen AME Cathedral; Leroy Gadsden, former president of the Jamaica NAACP; Richard L. Gibbs; Eleanor H. Green; John Griffith; Karl Grossman; Lani Guinier; Judith Henry; the Henson Foundation; Angel Hisnanick, my Arcadia editor; Erik Huber, Queens Public Library; Arthur Huneke; the late Clarence Irving Sr.; Leanne J. Jenkins; Charles Kaplan; Philippa Karteron; Beverly Hall Lawrence; Linda Roddy Leavy; Dr. Thomas Manuel, president and founder of the Jazz Loft; Frederick Mays; Jewel Jackson McCabe; Brian McRae; the estate of Rose Morgan; Winifred Morgan; David Morrison; the New York Racing Authority; Paul and Sarah Overs; Robert Pergament; Anita and Olivera Perkins; Julian Phillips; the members of the Presbyterian Church of Saint Albans History Committee; the *Press of Southeast Queens*; Monica Pringle; Jean Prysock and family; Floyd Sarisohn; Adrienne Scarborough, president of the Addisleigh Park Civic Association; Rev. Henry Simmons and his wife, Gayle, of the St. Albans Congregational Church; Archie Spigner; the Spool family; Joe Stephenson; Bob Stonehill; Pamela Blu Webb; and of course, my daughter, photographer extraordinaire Blair Garrett.

INTRODUCTION

Harvard professor and civil rights attorney Lani Guinier was six years old when her Jewish mother and African-American father left Manhattan's Upper West Side to live in a single-family home on a quiet, tree-lined street in Hollis, Queens, in the mid-1950s. However, when city leaders and officials from the US Post Office redrew the area's zip code boundaries to make mail delivery service easier, the Guiniers' modest brick home located near Murdock and 115th Avenue was reclassified to favor the bordering town: St. Albans.

The Guiniers initially startled some neighbors. However, the pair were unfazed by the area's name change and their neighbors' less-than-enlightened racial attitudes. Eugenia and Ewart Guinier had bigger concerns. The homemaker/civil rights activist, along with her college professor husband, wanted a stable community to raise their family that grew from two daughters to three by the time they left St. Albans in the 1980s. The Guiniers were the only interracial family in their immediate neighborhood when they arrived in 1956. Four short years later, an ever-observant 10-year-old Lani Guinier noticed that as darker-skinned couples purchased homes around them, the working-class white families on her block disappeared.

"In 1956, on each side of our house were white neighbors," Guinier recalled. "The people who lived close to 115th Avenue never spoke to us. In May 1957, my sister was born. We had a neighbor who called the police whenever my sister cried in her [first-floor] bedroom. Our windows were open from June to September, and the houses were close to each other. The neighbors called the police several times to say 'a baby was crying and not attended.' My mother assured the officer who showed up that everything was fine. By 1960, my block was black," Guinier said.

Despite less than friendly attitudes, life was fine for the Guiniers. Lani Guinier played chess with friends of Eastern European, Jewish, and Italian backgrounds on her front porch and played piano in her living room. She was a Brownie in the Girl Scouts and frequently accompanied her mother on trips to 204th Street and Linden Boulevard to patronize a local supermarket. Routine medical appointments were kept nearby with Dr. Goffman, the family's doctor. As a student at Public School (PS) 136 Q on 115th Avenue, Lani was finally allowed to cross Murdock Avenue with her parents' permission. Ewart Guinier had two sisters who lived in St. Albans, which made for convenient family gatherings.

Looking back, there were several reasons for the area's white flight. St. Albans always had a few black families scattered throughout the town. However, a 1948 federal and state lawsuit ended the practice of racial covenants that prevented blacks from purchasing homes in better neighborhoods, such as St. Albans's more prestigious Addisleigh Park section. Adam Clayton Powell Jr., the first African American from New York elected to Congress, used his tenure from 1945 to 1971 to advocate for blacks to obtain better-paying civil servant jobs. Soon, black migration from other New York neighborhoods such as Brooklyn's Bedford-Stuyvesant, the Bronx, and Harlem changed the homeowner landscape in southeast Queens. Black city bus drivers, correction officers, postal workers, police officers, nurses, subway workers, and teachers gained access to better housing, jobs, and schools. Black residents appreciated the work of the Jamaica branch of the National Association for the Advancement of Colored People (NAACP), with Paul Gibson Jr. and St. Albans residents William H. Booth, Guy R. Brewer, and Roy Wilkins, to name a few, fighting to empower African American residents at home and across the nation as the civil rights movement took center stage in America's political and social consciousness. Numerous civic, political, and social groups, along with area churches, are credited with getting newcomers and longtime residents involved in their southeast Queens community.

At the same time, Jim Crow–weary southern blacks bolted to the Big Apple in droves. Many ultimately found their way to southeast Queens. From the early 1950s throughout the 1960s, white St. Albans residents were bombarded with numerous flyers and visits from unscrupulous real estate agents who convinced worried homeowners to flee, recalled Richard Greene, a longtime local African American realtor. Today, St. Albans, which is situated near John F. Kennedy International Airport, has once again gained the attention of developers. Growing numbers of ethnically diverse families with middle-class roots are interested in the predominantly African American and Caribbean American neighborhood as a place to raise the next generation.

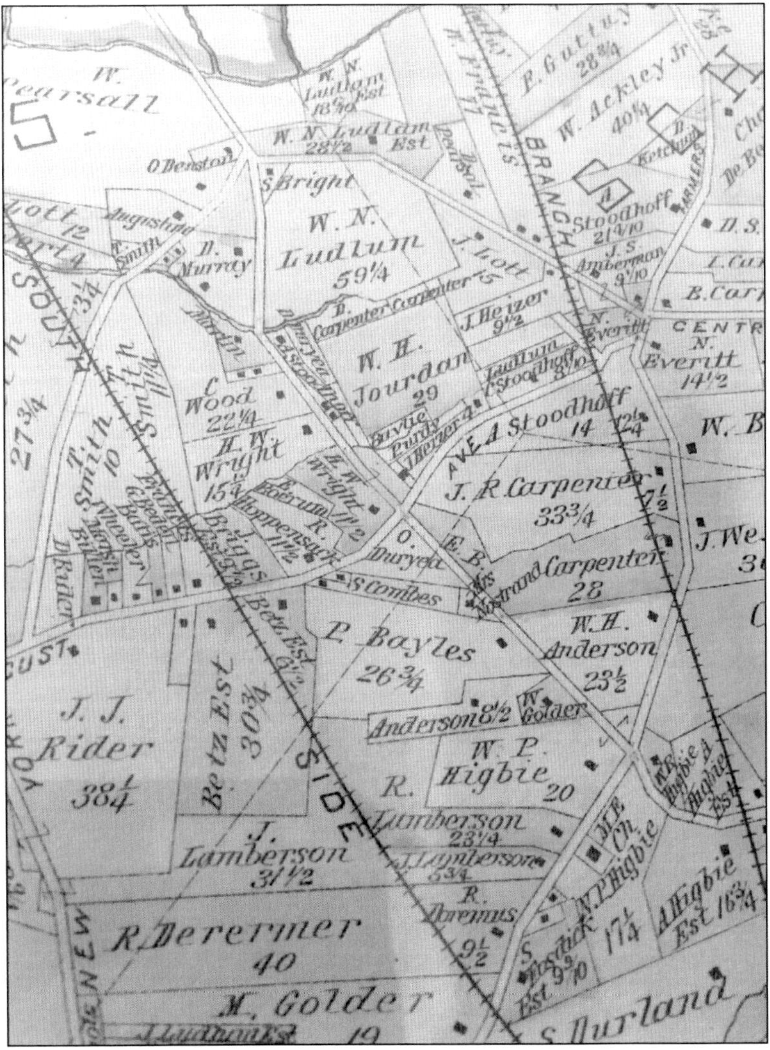

This 1891 map from the *Atlas of Borough of Queens County* shows a partial view of land owned by local property owners W.H. Anderson, P. Bayles, J.R. Carpenter, and N. Everitt.

One

The Early Years

Verdant meadows that stretched miles beyond the edge of colonial Jamaica enticed members of the Remsen family to leave their Brooklyn home in 1735 to live in southeast Queens County. The Jamaica settlers benefited from a 1656 land grant that allowed Daniel Denton to obtain 10 acres near Beaver Pond from Native Americans.

By May 1744, the Remsens were joined by four like-minded families: the Everitts, the Hendricksons, the Ludlums, and the Stoothoffs. Those settlers, who were mostly of Dutch and English descent, appreciated the status and freedom that land ownership gave their growing families. Jacob Remsen was the first person to have a title to land outside of the village of Jamaica, in 1735.

More families followed, such as the Oldfields and the Higbies. The steady sale of land parcels that ranged from $700 to $1,000 per acre attracted other families and turned the outskirts of Jamaica village into a thriving farm community. The major roadways that connected the new area to Jamaica's Fulton Street were given unusual monikers—Lazy Lane and Freeman's Path—which were later known as Linden and Farmers Boulevards respectively. The families carved out new identities in their rustic surroundings and did so with help from enslaved Africans and indentured servants. Many notable families, like the Remsens, began freeing enslaved Africans and indentured servants as early as 1819. By 1827, slavery was abolished in New York. Meanwhile, southeast Queens's long and expansive unpaved roads allowed the new farmers to travel to and from Jamaica on horseback, and venture, if needed, into Hempstead, Long Island, to sell bushels of corn, grapes, potatoes, and other goods to the public. The pastoral area was in stark contrast to Jamaica Village, with its wooden buildings that stood along Fulton Street, which later became known as Jamaica Avenue. The heartiness of the newcomers was tested in March 1888 when the nation's northeast experienced a major blizzard. New York City residents dug out from 50 inches of snow. Despite the setback, rural living in southeast Queens still appealed to the adventurous.

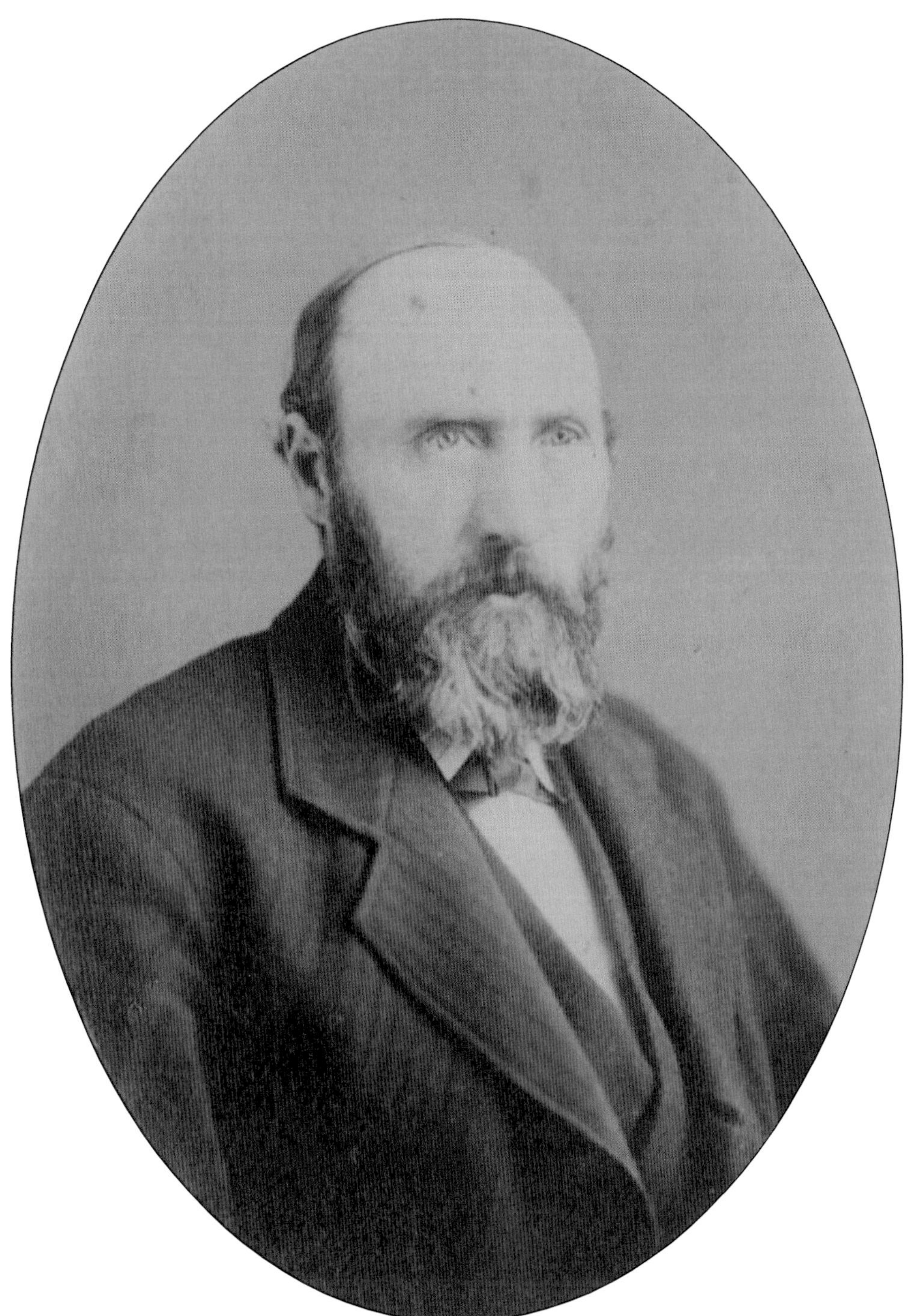

Steely-eyed Abraham Remsen came from a huge family from the Netherlands that established roots in America first in Brooklyn and later in Queens. There are streets named after the Remsens throughout Brooklyn, Queens, and parts of Long Island. A Remsen homestead in southeast Queens was located on what is today 199th Street and Linden Boulevard. The Remsen family owned that property for 200 years. (Courtesy of Queens Public Library archives.)

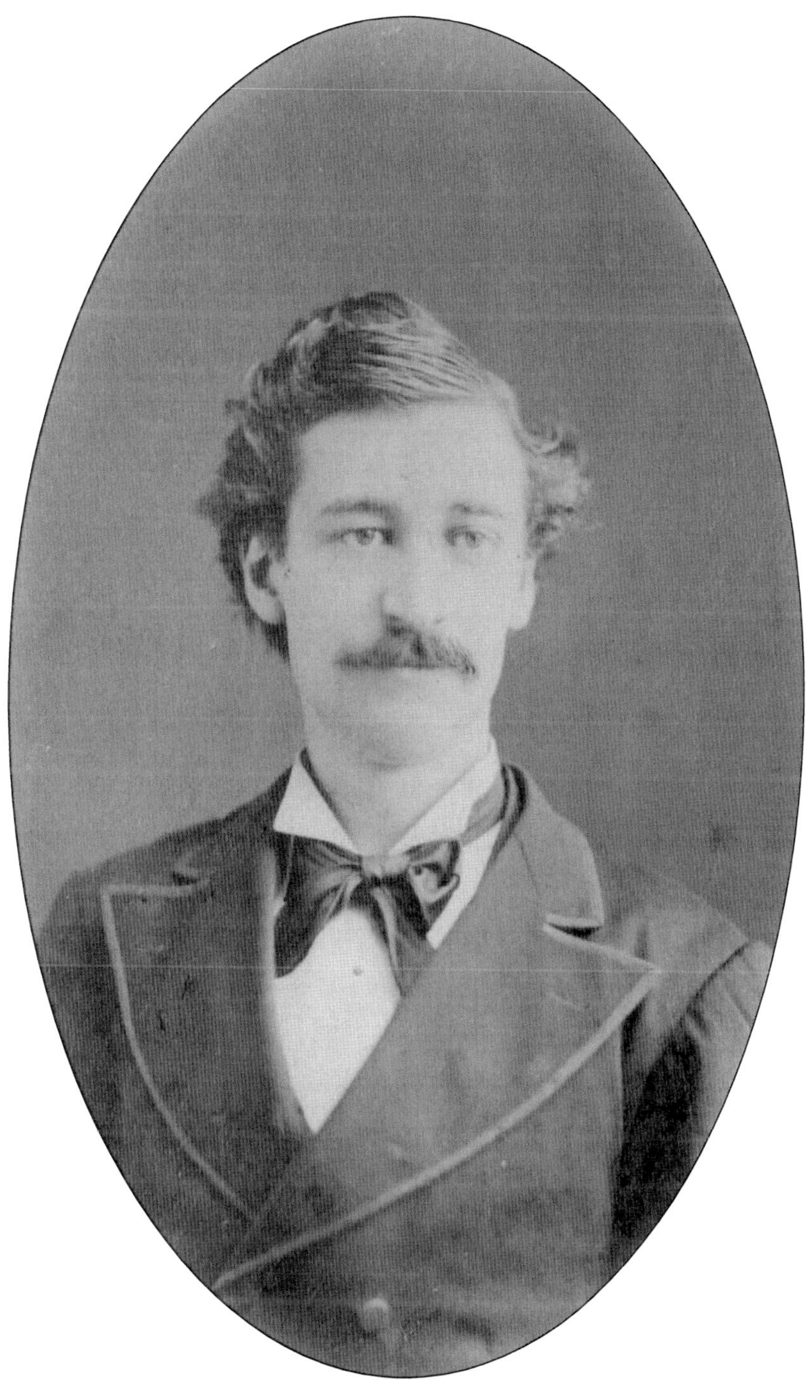

Benjamin Everitt, a relative of August Everitt, established the first general store in St. Albans. Without his family's store, early settlers would have to trek to the village of Jamaica or Springfield to purchase food or household items. The Everitts' store is featured on a mural that celebrates St. Albans history at the community's Long Island Rail Road (LIRR) station. New York City has two streets with different spellings bearing the Everitt name: Everitt Place near Linden and Foch Boulevards, and Everett Place near Farmers Boulevard. (Courtesy of Queens Public Library archives.)

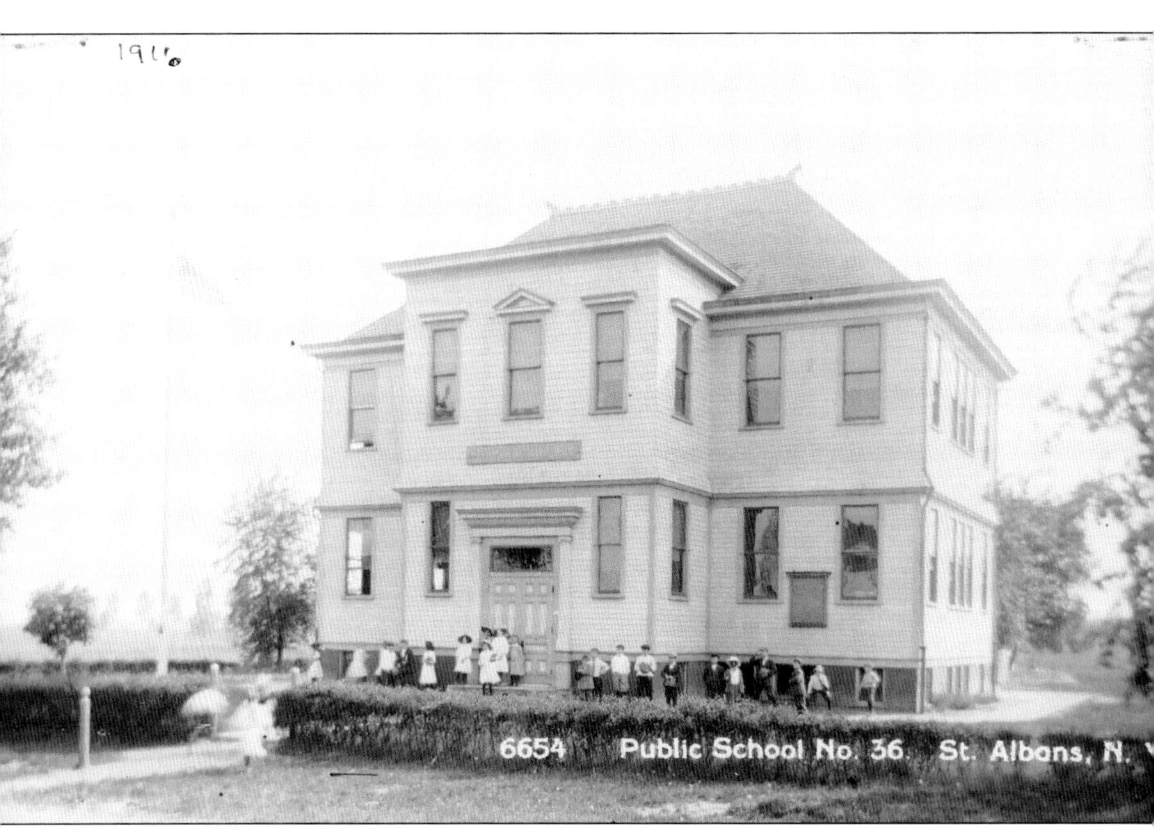

PS 36 students stand outside of their school in a 1916 postcard. It appears girls were instructed to stand on the left side of the wooden building as their male counterparts lined up on the right side, possibly returning from recess. The area's first school was built in 1893. (Courtesy of Bob Stonehill.)

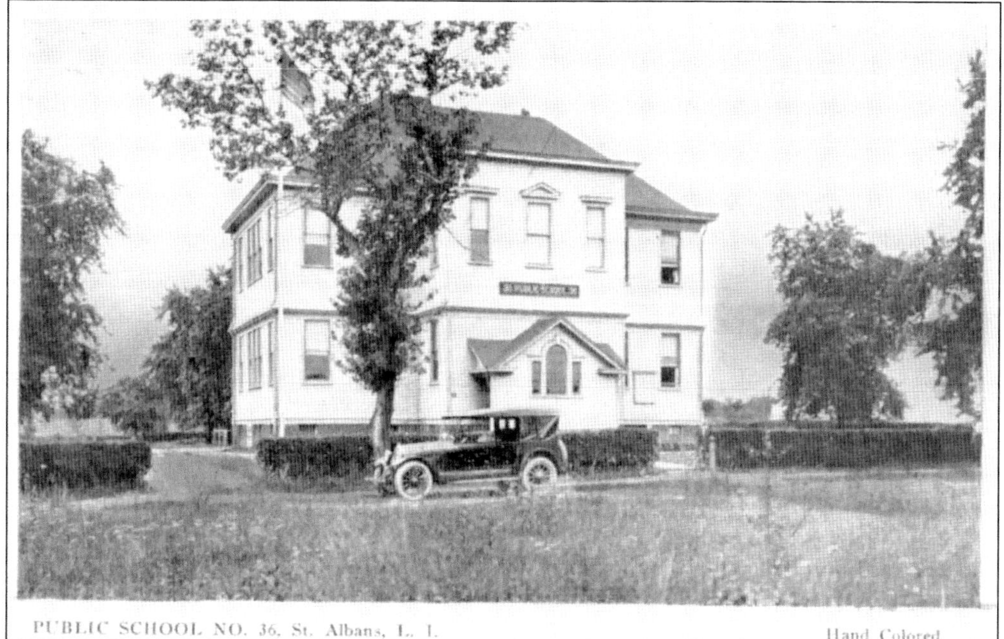

This color postcard shows the exterior of PS 36's wood-frame building with a car parked outside. The windows to the right are wide open and without protective window guards that would be required today by school officials. (Courtesy of Bob Stonehill.)

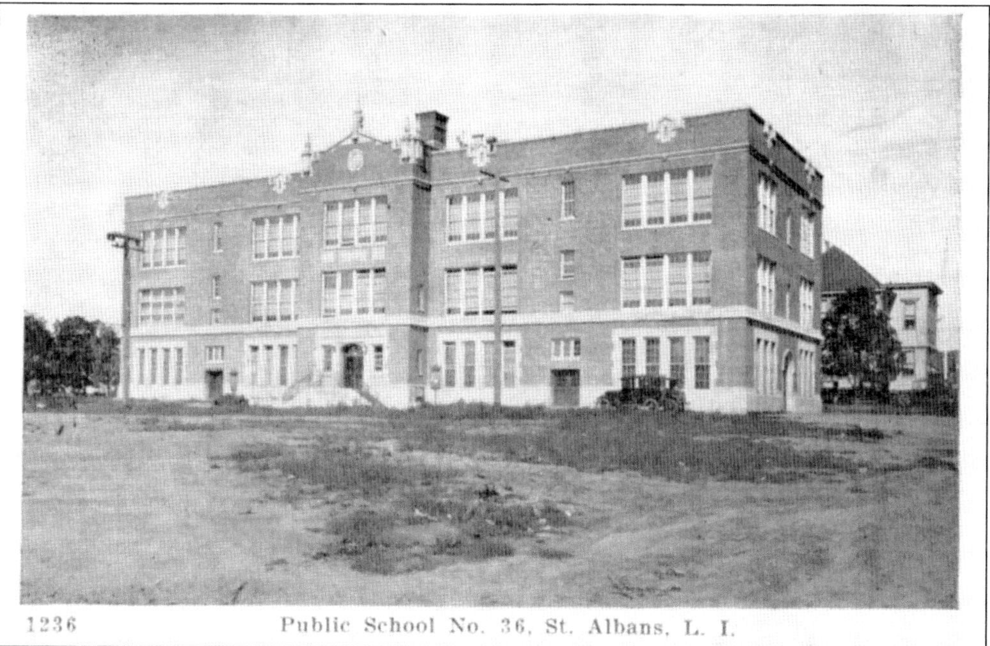

In 1923, PS 36, a new brick schoolhouse, was built on land that was first occupied by a two-story wood structure. Five years later, another grade school, PS 136 on 115th Avenue, opened in 1928. Today, PS 136 is also known as the Roy Wilkins School and is named after the late civil rights leader and former executive director of the NAACP who resided in St. Albans. (Courtesy of Queens Public Library archives.)

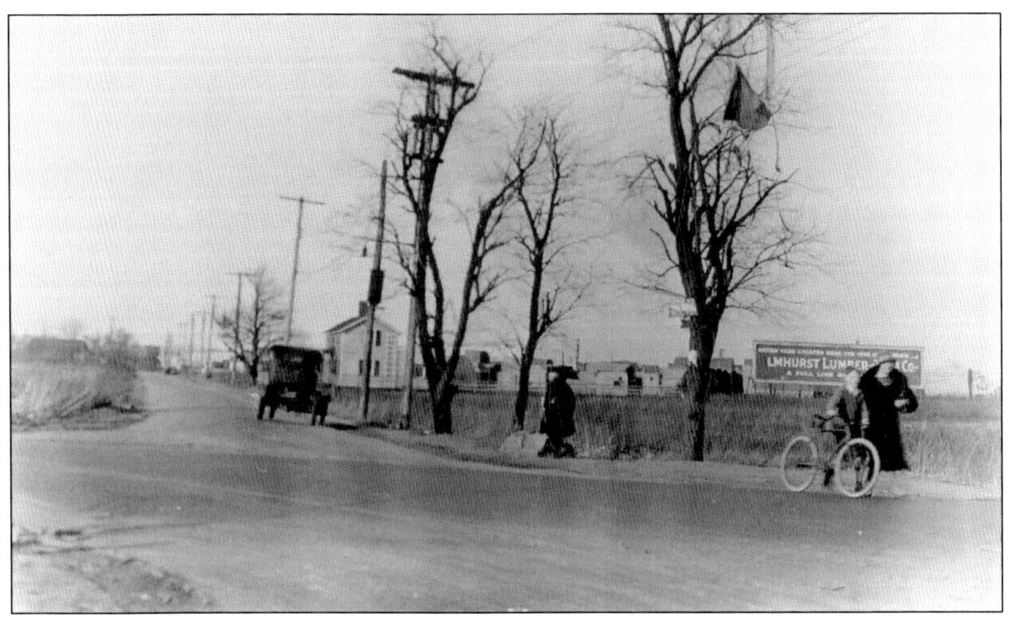

This is a 1920s photograph of a street scene near Farmers Avenue (now Farmers Boulevard) and Central Avenue (Linden Boulevard). The wide roadway and sparse buildings indicate that more development is underway for the area. A lumber company advertised its services on the major thoroughfare to attract customers. (Photograph by Frederick J. Weber, courtesy of Queens Public Library archives.)

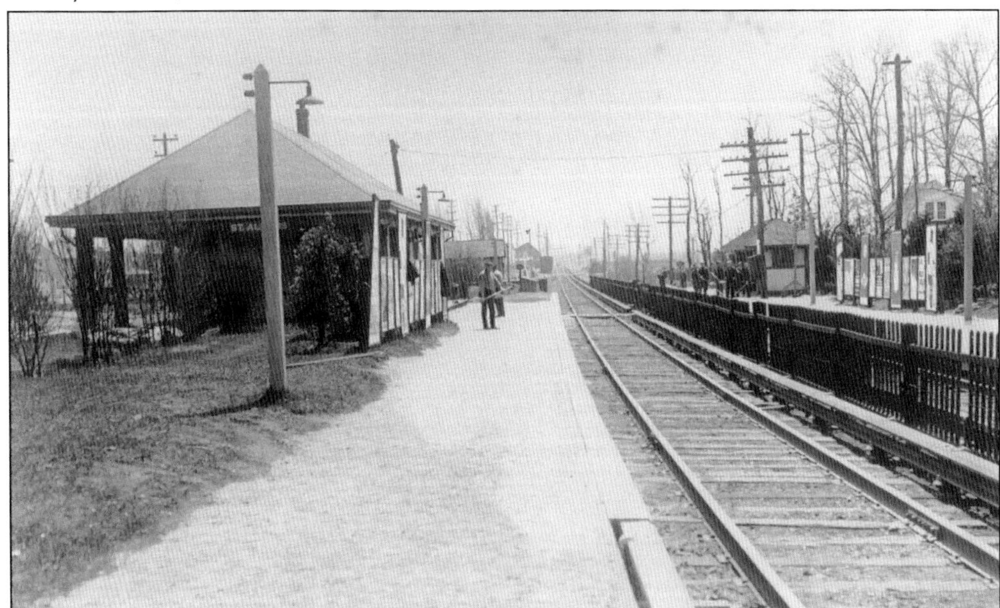

This is a 1925 photograph of the St. Albans train station. St. Albans commuters wanted a better way to get to Jamaica, Brooklyn, and other parts of Nassau County, and were thrilled to have their own LIRR station. Since 1872, the LIRR operated a Cedarhurst branch that passed through St. Albans. However, in July 1898, residents celebrated the new train station that required a stop at the southwest corner of Central Avenue (Linden Boulevard) and Montauk Place. The ground level station was electrified in 1925. (Courtesy of Arthur Huneke.)

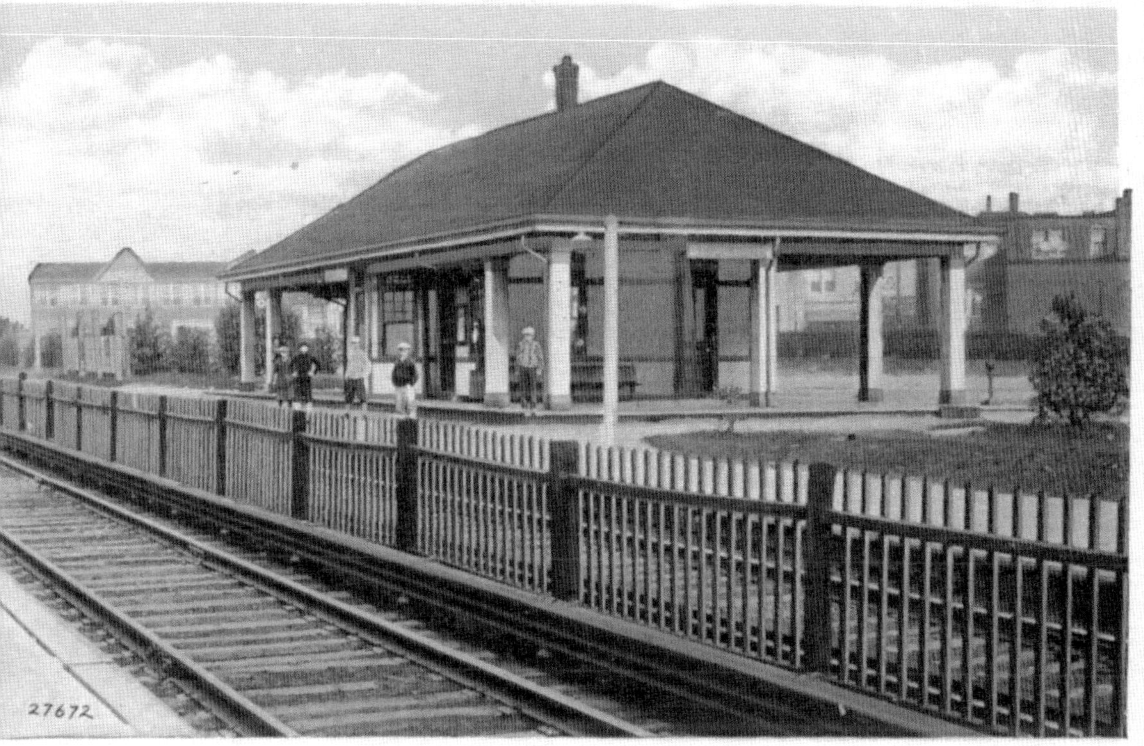

This 1928 postcard shows commuters waiting at the St. Albans train station. By 1935, the ground level station was razed to make way for an elevated structure that featured one large platform and two tracks. (Courtesy of Bob Stonehill.)

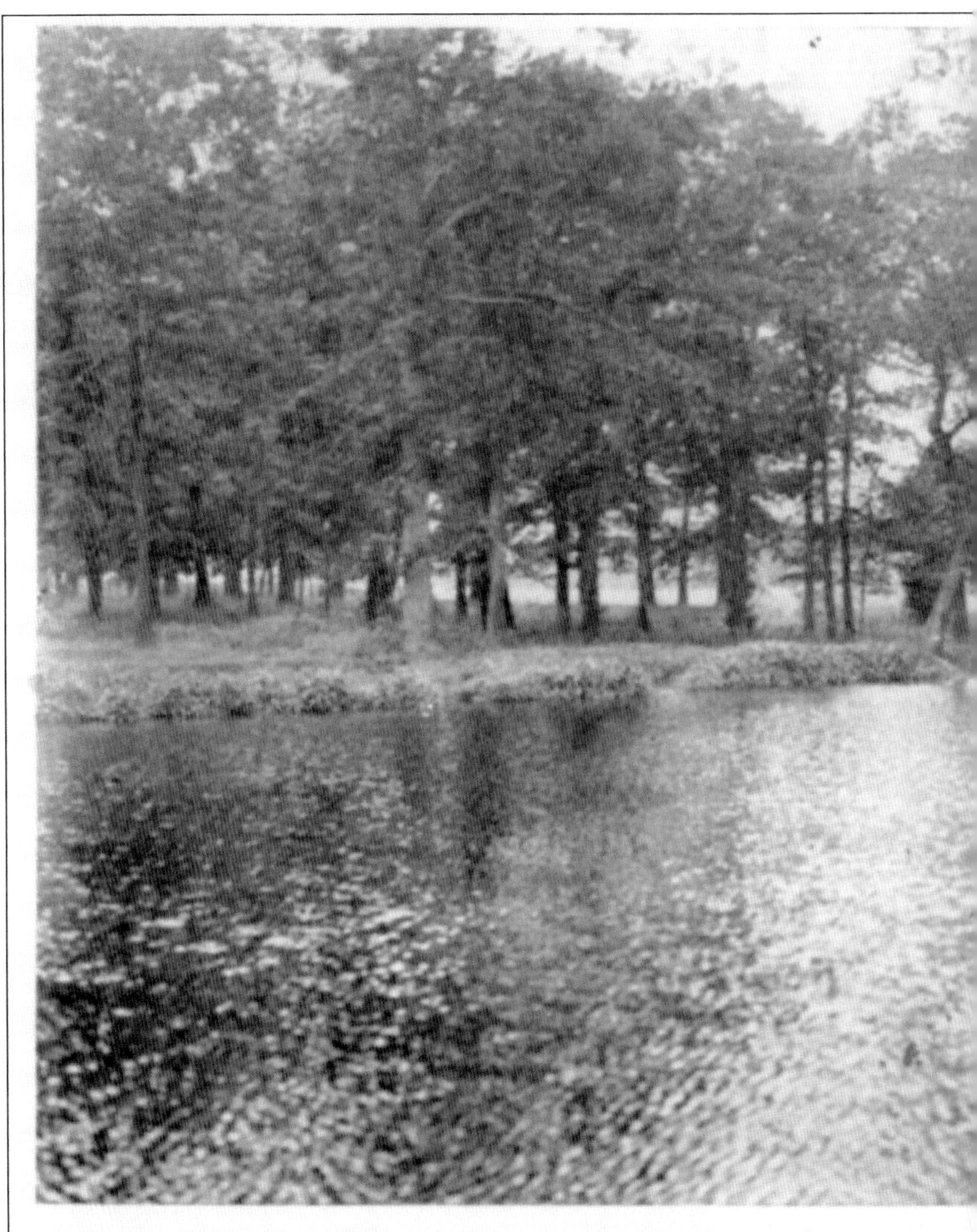

In 1915, Albert Warren "A.W." Tillinghast (1876–1942) designed two 18-hole courses that were part of the St. Albans Golf and Country Club. The 125-acre property attracted wealthy men from Brooklyn, Queens, and Manhattan who played golf and tennis and sat in the facility's clubhouse. Yankee slugger Babe Ruth perfected his golf game there. Tillinghast created attractive golf courses across the nation including at Bethpage State Park in Farmingdale, Long Island. St.

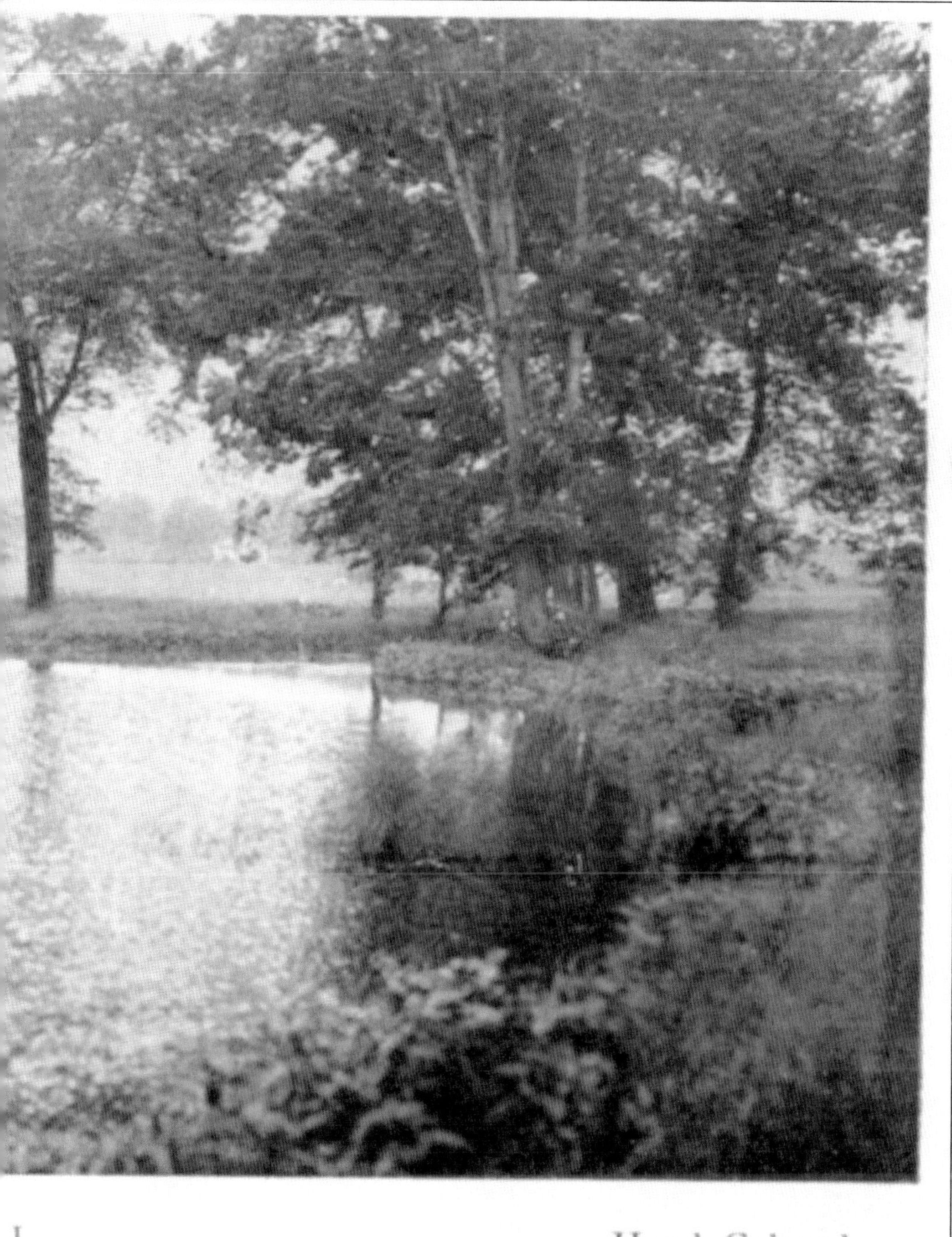

Albans lost its golf course when the facility closed shortly after the stock market crash of 1929. This undated postcard shows the tranquil pond that stood on the grounds. Babe Ruth enjoyed the Queens club's amenities so much that locals and autograph seekers thought he lived in the area. (Courtesy of Bob Stonehill.)

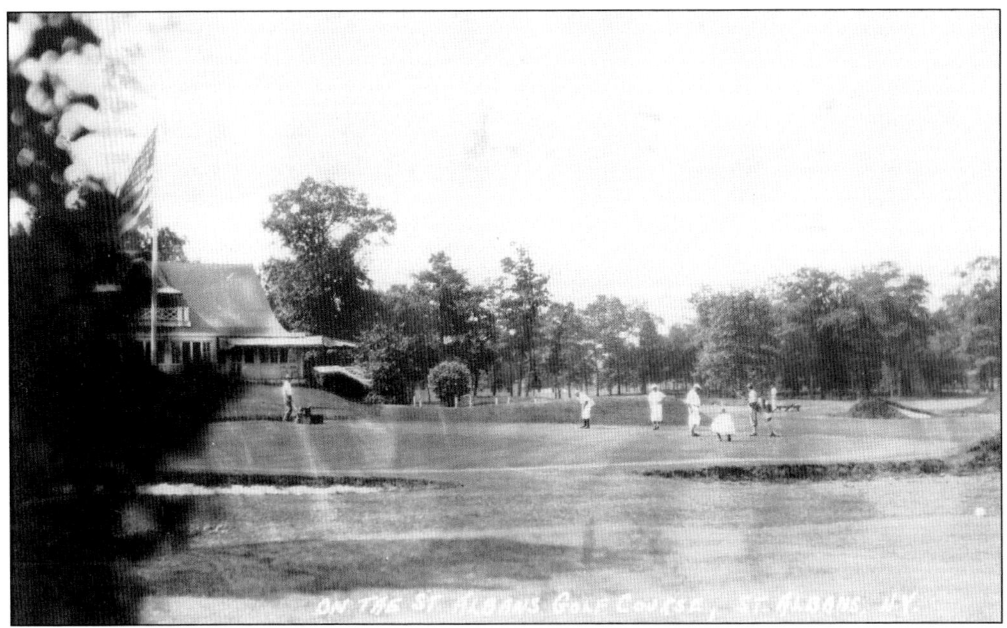

This is a long view of the St. Albans Golf and Country Club from an undated postcard, including a partial view of the clubhouse. (Courtesy of Bob Stonehill.)

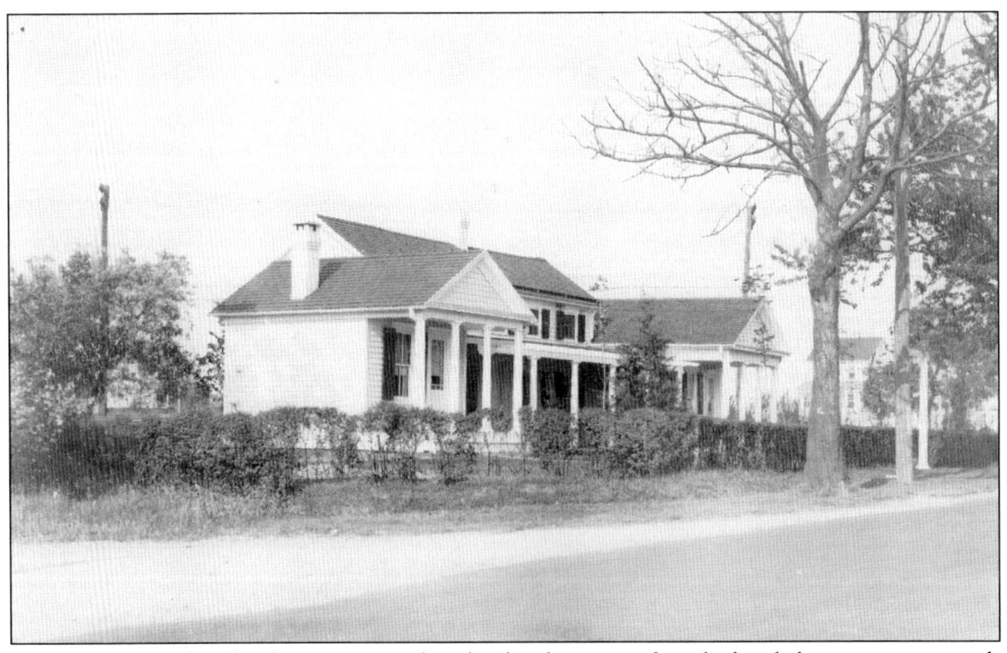

As more Queens farmland was converted to the development of single-family homes, many wood-frame structures were built on major roadways to attract families. The Howsard family home on 180th Street and Linden Boulevard is shown here. The dwelling represents the construction boom the borough experienced in the 1920s and 1930s. (Courtesy of Queens Public Library archives.)

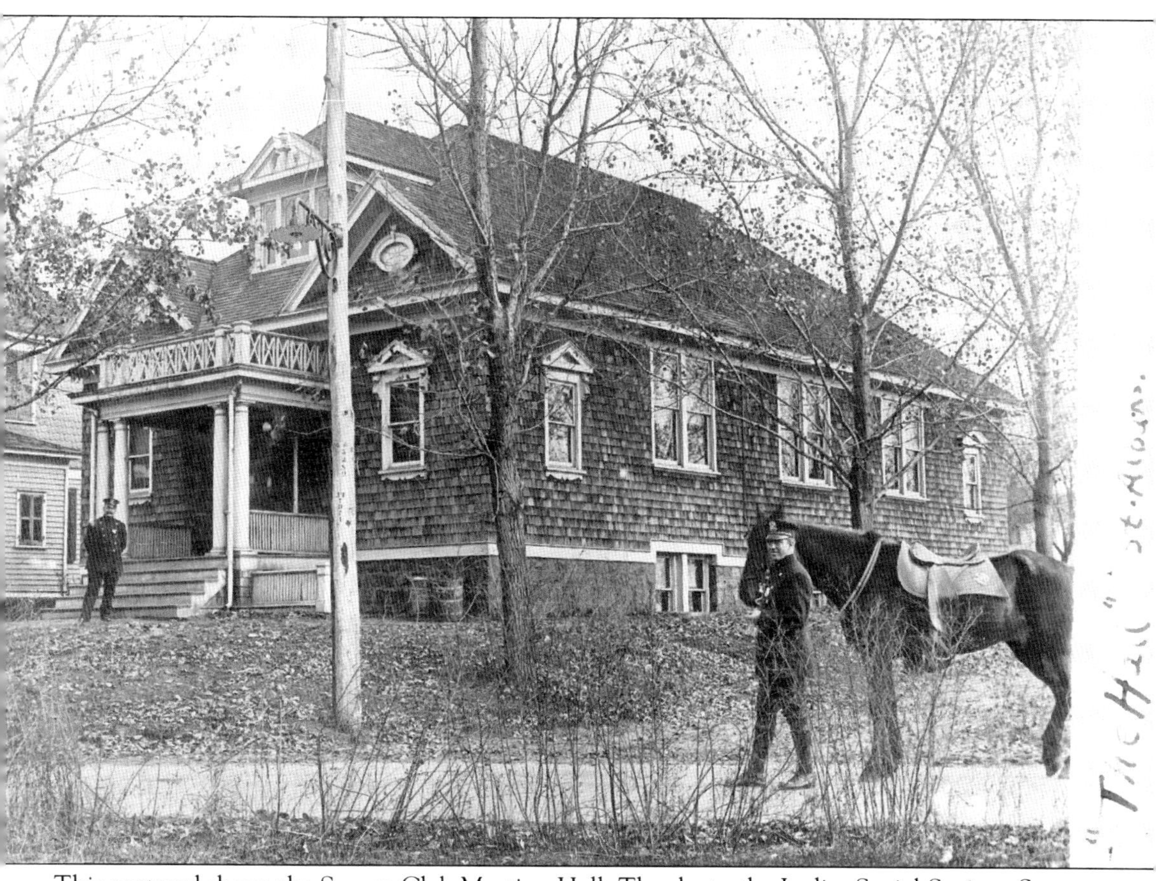

This postcard shows the Square Club Meeting Hall. Thanks to the Ladies Social Society, St. Albans had this meeting place near Linden Boulevard where locals attended prayer meetings and held ping pong parties and other events. Vigorous fundraising allowed the volunteers to purchase John Hendrickson's property for recreational and religious space. The hall was so successful that it was incorporated as the St. Albans Social Club Inc. The club's first officers were Isabelle Wells, president; Louisa Everitt, vice president; Adella Kuchman, secretary; Ella Smith, treasurer, and Agnes Husson and Aletta Carpenter, directors. The women were also credited with establishing the Presbyterian Church of St. Albans. By October 1907, they helped raise funds for the new edifice. The Ladies Social Society was established in 1900 and incorporated two years later. Other social organizations followed. The St. Albans Civic Improvement Association was the first of its kind when it was established in 1907. Charles Simpson, the group's first president, came up with the idea for the association in 1903. The St. Albans Improvement Association started in 1906 as a nonpartisan, non-political group interested in the town's progress. By 1927, the association had 650 members from the 2,200 families that resided in town at that time. (Courtesy of Bob Stonehill.)

1

1907 Jan 6.

St Albans Jan 6, 1907

A meeting of the residents of St Albans for the purpose of organizeing a Presbyterian Church held to-night in the Hall, was called to order by Mr. B. A. Everitt who asked that a permanent Chairman be elected.

On motion of Mr. John Baylis Rev. J. H. Hobbs of the Jamaica Presbyterian Church was chosen

On motion of Mr Everitt William Rylance was elected Secretary

After the singing of a hymn scripture reading and prayer, the Chairman stated the object of the meeting, and as a member of the committee on Church Extension of the Presbytery of Nassau made a statement as to the steps necessary to be taken in petitioning Presbytery to organize a Church.

In order to obtain a general discussion as to the desireability of organizeing such a church a motion was made by Mr Everitt and seconded that a committee be appointed to take the necessary steps in obtaining signatures to a petition to Presbytery a discussion followed in which the sentiment of those present was that the Church should be organized and the motion was carried unanimously

The Chairman called for nominations and appointed

This January 6, 1907, letter shows that St. Albans property owners John Baylis, a Mr. Everitt, William Rylance, and the Rev. J.H. Hobbs of the Jamaica Presbyterian Church met to discuss the establishment of a Presbyterian church in their community. Rylance was a well-known farmer who sold a large part of his land to James A. Roberts, head of the Greater New York Homes Company, in the 1903–1907 land boom. (Courtesy of the Presbyterian Church of St. Albans History Committee.)

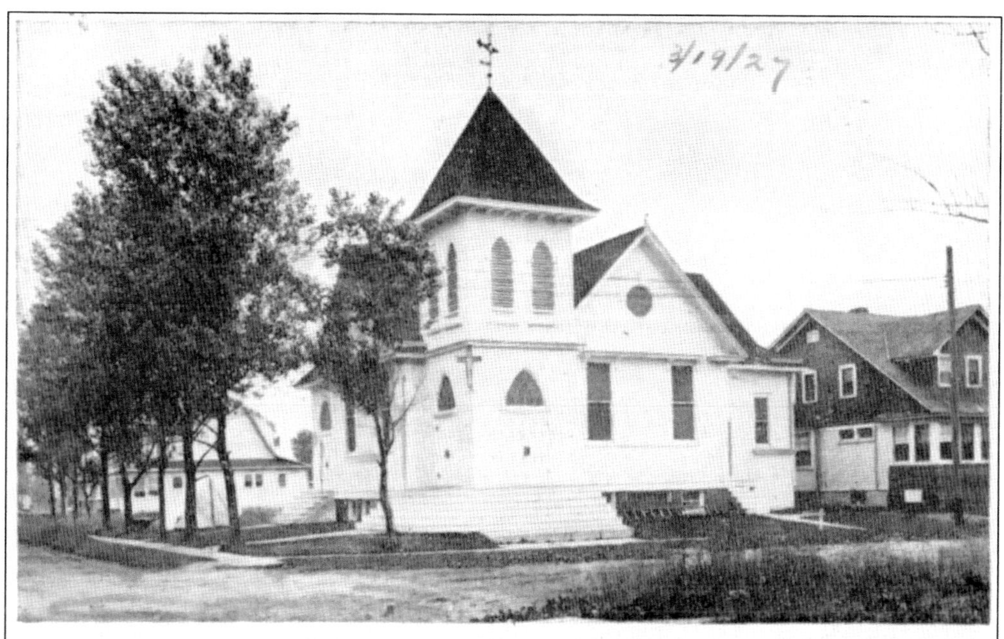

This 1927 postcard shows the town's first house of worship, the Presbyterian Church of St. Albans. The church, located on 190th Street and St. Marks Avenue (now 119th Avenue), has served the community for 113 years. Eager congregants traveled to the church by horse when it first opened. The Rev. E. Frank Lee was pastor. Brooklyn realtor James Nevis donated the land where the church still stands. (Courtesy of Bob Stonehill.)

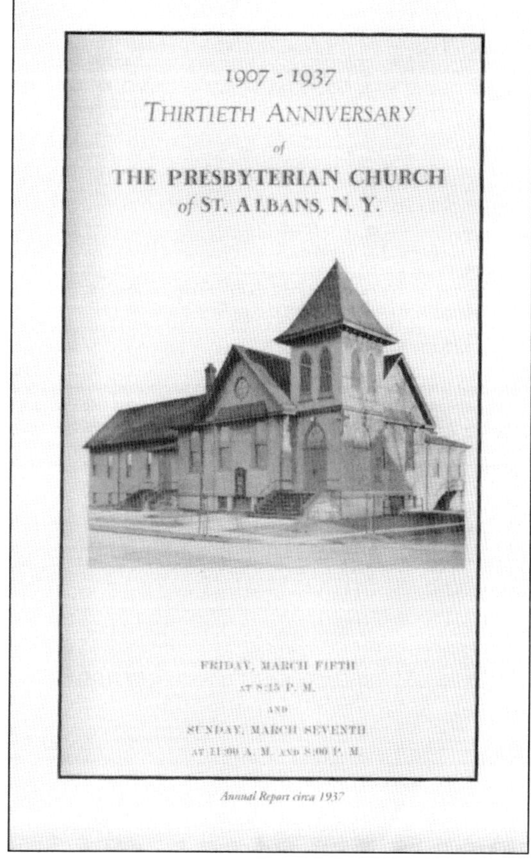
1907 - 1937

THIRTIETH ANNIVERSARY

of

THE PRESBYTERIAN CHURCH

of ST. ALBANS, N. Y.

FRIDAY, MARCH FIFTH

AT 8:15 P. M.

AND

SUNDAY, MARCH SEVENTH

AT 11:00 A. M. AND 8:00 P. M.

Annual Report circa 1937

This program highlights the 30th anniversary of the Presbyterian Church of St. Albans. The stately edifice stands in the midst of a residential neighborhood. (Courtesy of the Presbyterian Church of St. Albans.)

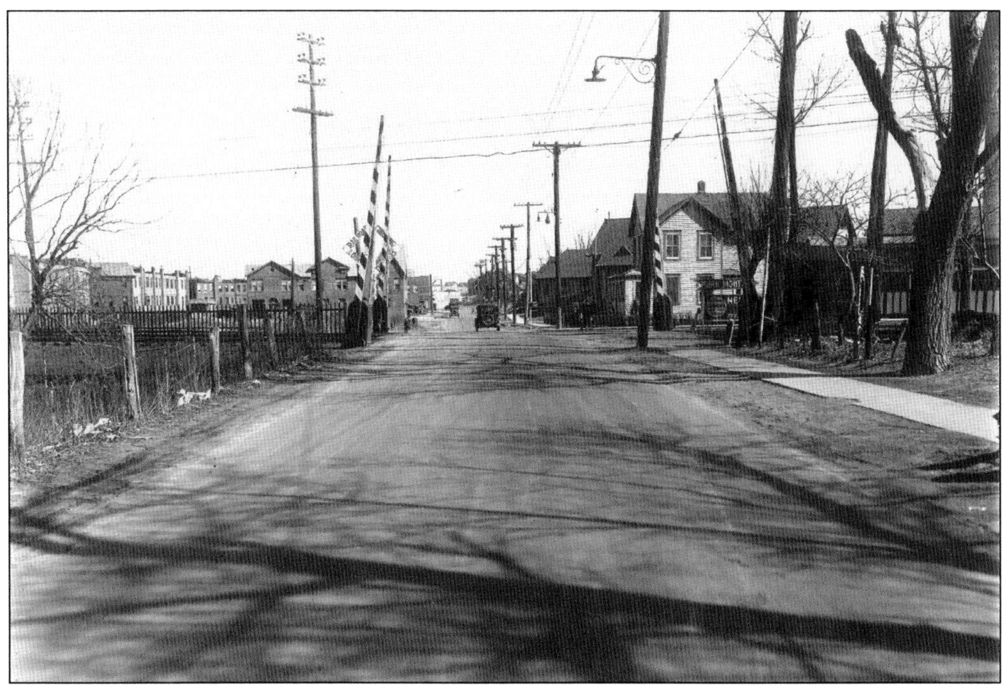

This is a view of the street-level rail crossing near the St. Albans train station at Locust Avenue (Baisley Boulevard) looking east. The homes that surround the crossing indicate that the suburban community was attractive to families who wanted to be within walking distance of the train station. (Courtesy of Queens Public Library archives.)

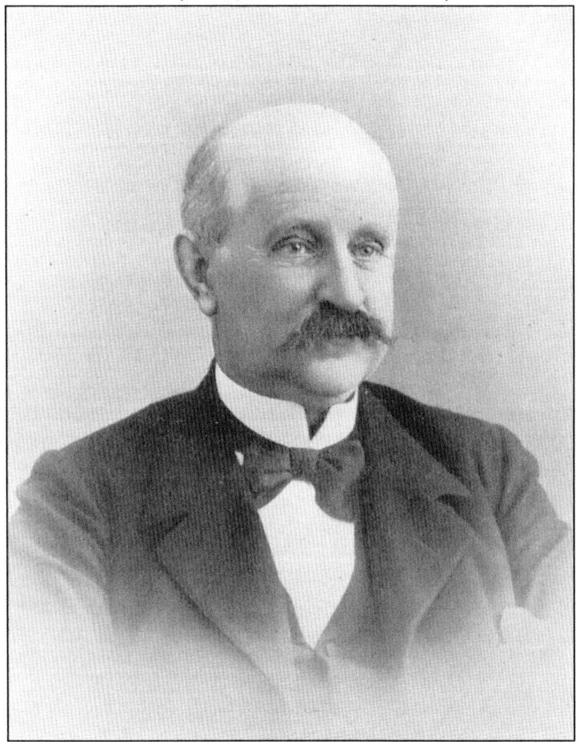

John R. Carpenter started a lumber company in Jamaica in the 1800s. He also owned a large farm near Farmers and Central Avenues. Carpenter lived in a farmhouse opposite 119th Avenue that was destroyed in a 1924 fire. The Carpenter homestead was described as a Dutch farmhouse that was typically found on Long Island in the 17th and 18th centuries. (Courtesy of Queens Public Library archives.)

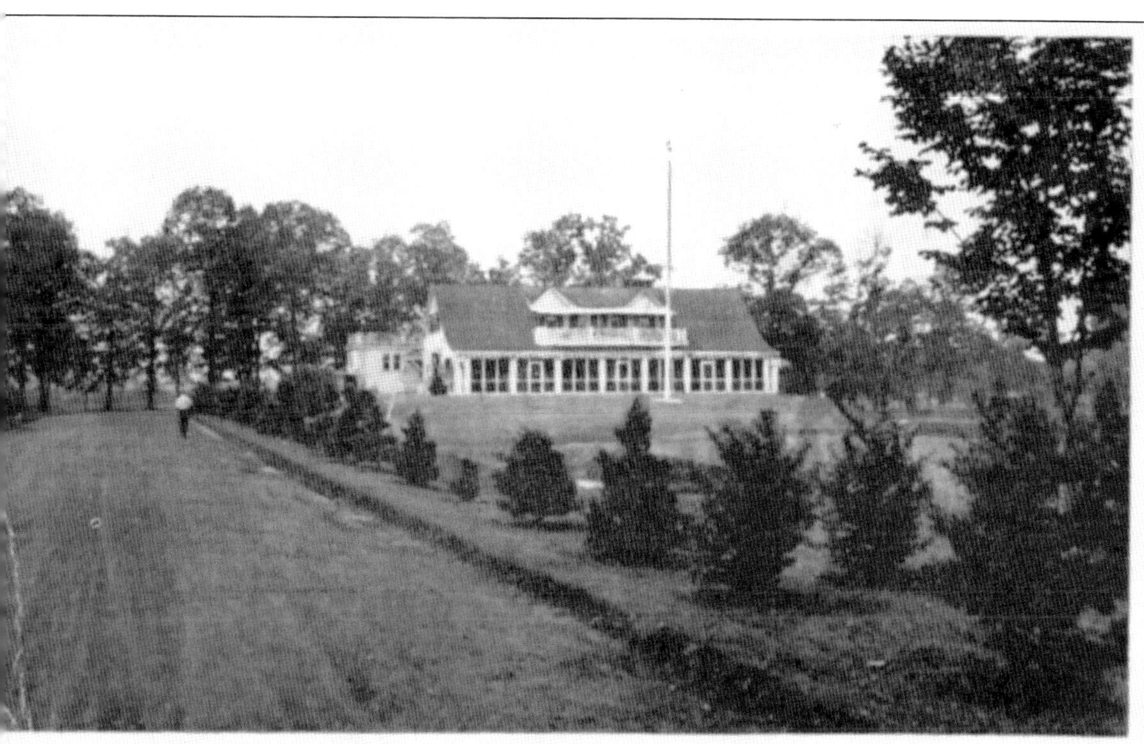

This postcard shows the lush surroundings of the St. Albans Golf and Country Club. The golf club's well-manicured lawns were a perfect setting for affluent members who wanted peaceful surroundings not far from their business activities in Manhattan or Brooklyn. Many private events were held at the exclusive facility, and the guests enjoyed the clubhouse view. (Courtesy of Bob Stonehill.)

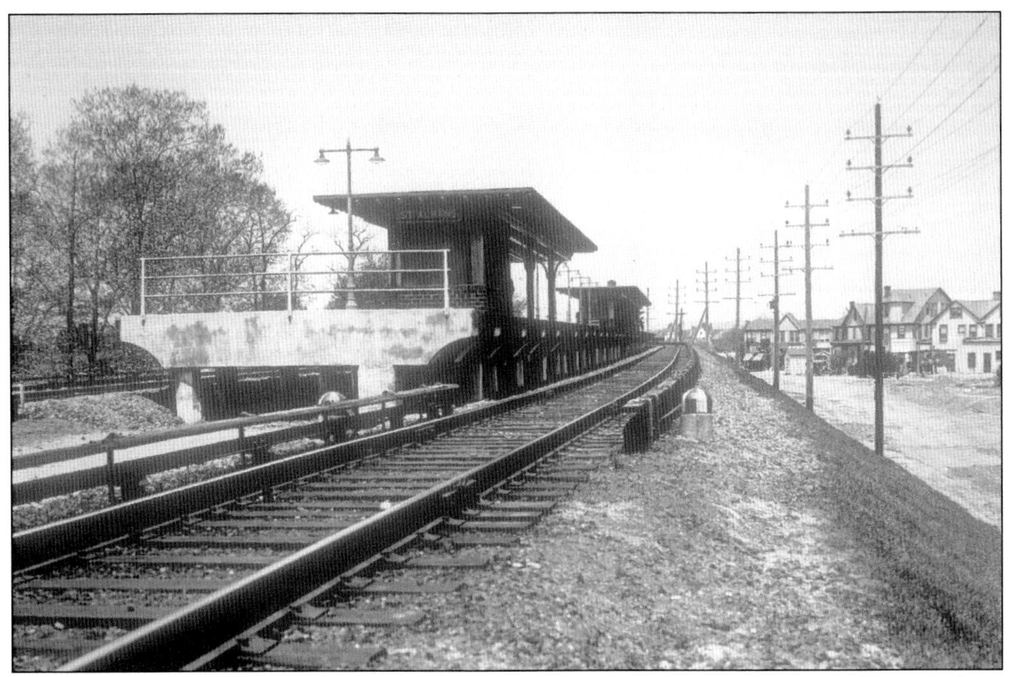

In 1935, an elevated St. Albans railroad station helped alleviate ground-level traffic woes along Linden Boulevard. Commuters and the surrounding community benefited from the upgrade. (Courtesy of Dave Morrison.)

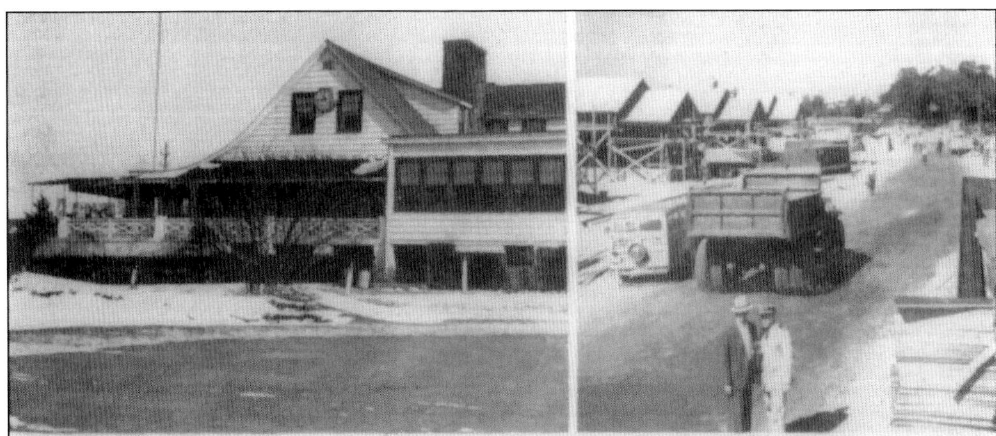

ST. ALBANS GOLF CLUB . . . Compare these photographs with the masthead above to see just how much the hospital has grown. At the left is the original clubhouse which stood on the 117-acre tract that once was a community recreational center. The photo on the right show construction getting underway, in 1943, on the greens where businessmen of St. Albans congregated to relax with their putting irons.

This is another look at the two-story St. Albans Golf and Country Club. During the Great Depression, the club's membership dwindled along with its finances. The federal government later seized the property in 1942 and established the St. Albans Naval Hospital on the site in 1943. The vast property bordered Central Avenue (now Linden Boulevard), Merrick Road (Merrick Boulevard), and Locust Avenue (Baisley Boulevard). (Courtesy of *St. Albans Life*.)

Two

A Naval Hospital Reigns

As the nation tried to right its economic course after the Great Depression, the US government took over the underutilized St. Albans Golf and Country Club property. In its place, the St. Albans Naval Hospital was built to provide enlisted men and women and military retirees along with their dependents access to medical care and other services. The naval hospital was commissioned in January 1943, and construction was completed in 1950. The facility had several amenities such as a bowling alley, movie theater, a 300-seat non-sectarian chapel, a commissary store known as the Exchange, and a barbershop.

The hospital provided medical care primarily to World War II, Korean War, and Vietnam War service persons. In 1943, First Lady Eleanor Roosevelt visited. She wrote: "There are so many wards that it was impossible to cover them all, but I hope I visited those that had casualties back from overseas." In January 1944, some 3,942 wounded patients were treated at the naval hospital, which had more than 42 wards and additional temporary wooden barracks that could be seen from Merrick Boulevard. The following year, the facility experienced a spike in patients—about 5,200. The institution operated for 30 years and closed in June 1974.

For the most part, the naval hospital coexisted with homeowners from the surrounding area. However, there were grumblings in local newspapers about neighbors' complaints of rowdy servicemen on Linden Boulevard. The naval hospital was a welcome addition to St. Albans because it was a source of jobs for several hundred civilians from southeast Queens and Long Island. Military personnel patronized St. Albans commercial strips. Local newspapers were especially delighted when Pres. Harry S. Truman made a surprise visit to the naval hospital in October 1950. One newspaper, *St. Albans Life*, reported that the "daily press and radio apparently knew nothing of the chief executive's visit, but the town was 'buzzing' after seeing policemen putting up 'No Parking' signs along Linden Boulevard. The crowd on the street saw President Truman's light grey hat inside his car as it traveled to the naval hospital to visit wounded service personnel."

Years later, when the federal government decommissioned St. Albans Naval Hospital, the vast property was turned over to the Veterans Administration (VA), which eventually established the St. Albans Community Living Center as an extended living facility for veterans of all ages. The facility offers sub-acute rehabilitation and palliative and hospice care, among other programs.

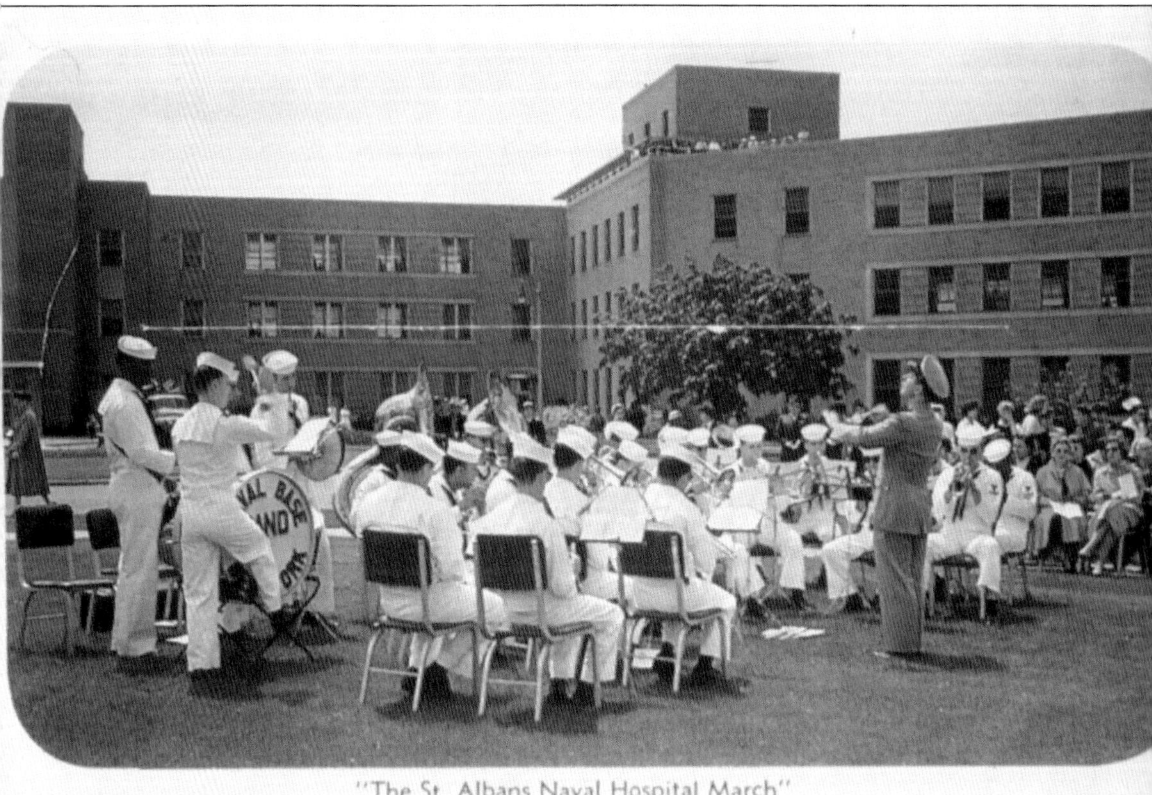

This naval band is playing "The St. Albans Naval Hospital March." The song was written by Lt. Col. Alf Heiberg, who was the first commander of the US Air Force Band from 1941 through 1944. (Courtesy of the National Library of Medicine.)

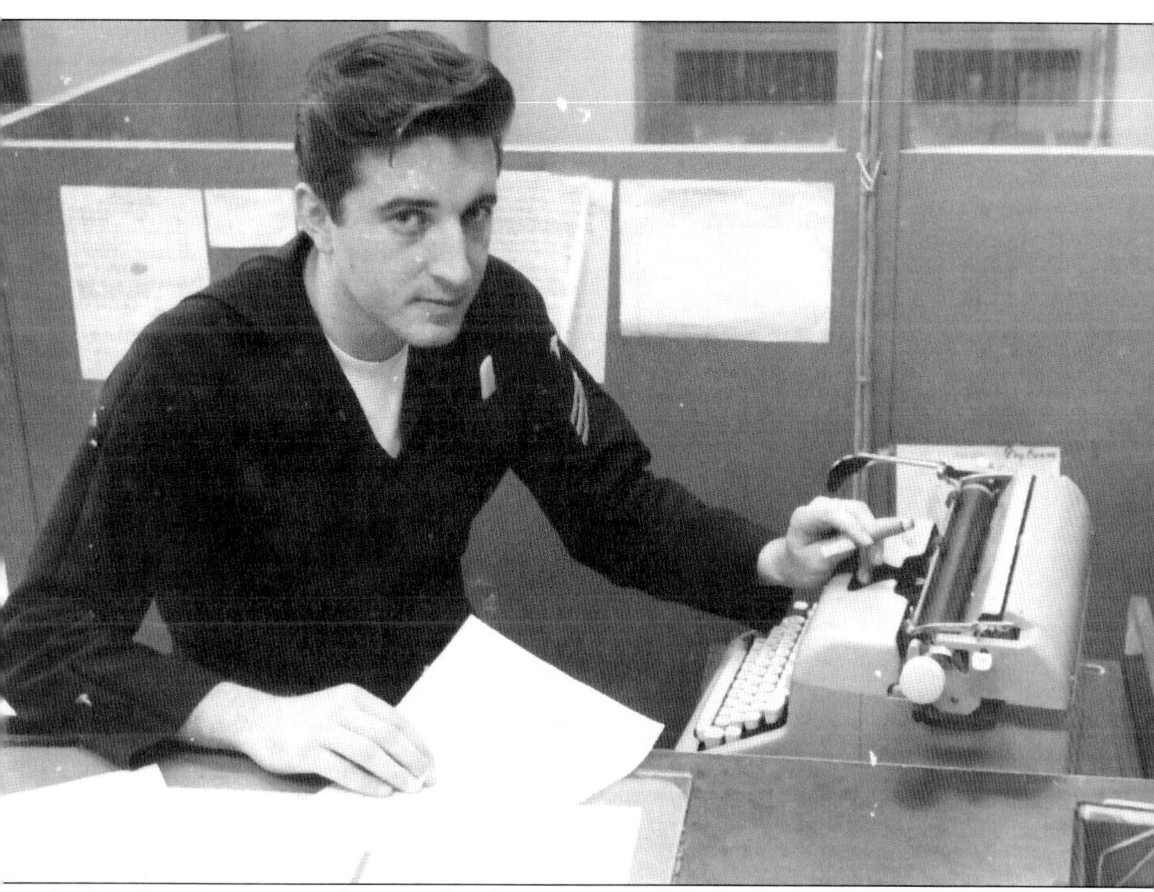

Paul F. Overs Jr. was one of many enlisted service personnel who worked at St. Albans Naval Hospital during the Vietnam War. The son of Dr. Paul F. and Helen (Michler) Overs Sr. of Elyria, Ohio, he graduated from Howe Military Academy in Indiana and joined the US Navy in November 1961, training as a hospital technician. He was assigned to St. Albans Naval Hospital from 1962 to 1968. This photograph was taken in an office of the hospital's emergency room. (Courtesy of Sarah Overs.)

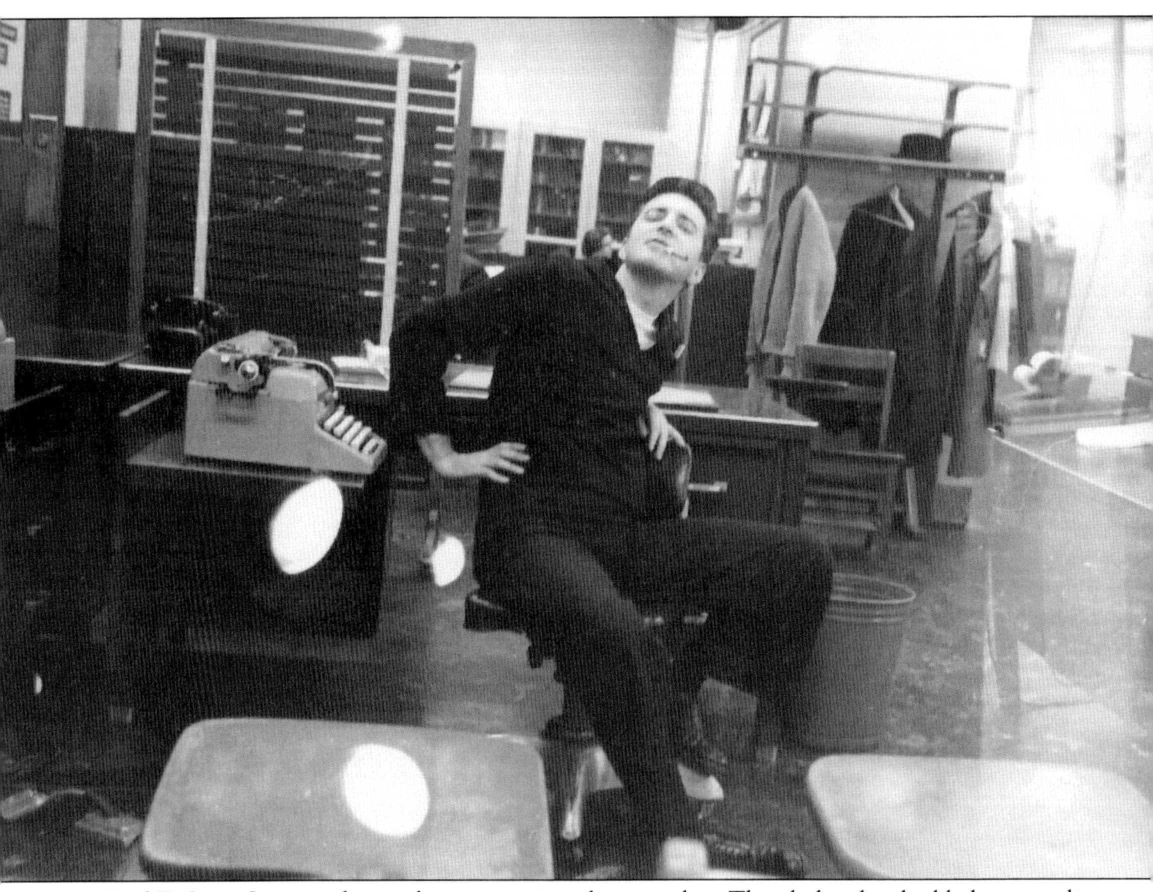

Paul F. Overs Jr. poses for a volunteer service photographer. The clerk, who doubled as a medic, dispensed medication and drew blood for patients with measles, mumps, and other ailments. Overs also took down patient information in the emergency room. He recalled hearing about William Henry Cosby Jr., better known as Bill Cosby. The Philadelphia native joined the Navy in 1956 and was trained as a hospital corpsman. By the time Overs arrived at St. Albans, Cosby had released his first comedy album. When Overs was not at work, he enjoyed libations at two local watering holes that catered to military patrons—the Castle and Sig and Eddie's—both on Linden Boulevard. Overs died in 2018. (Courtesy of Sarah Overs.)

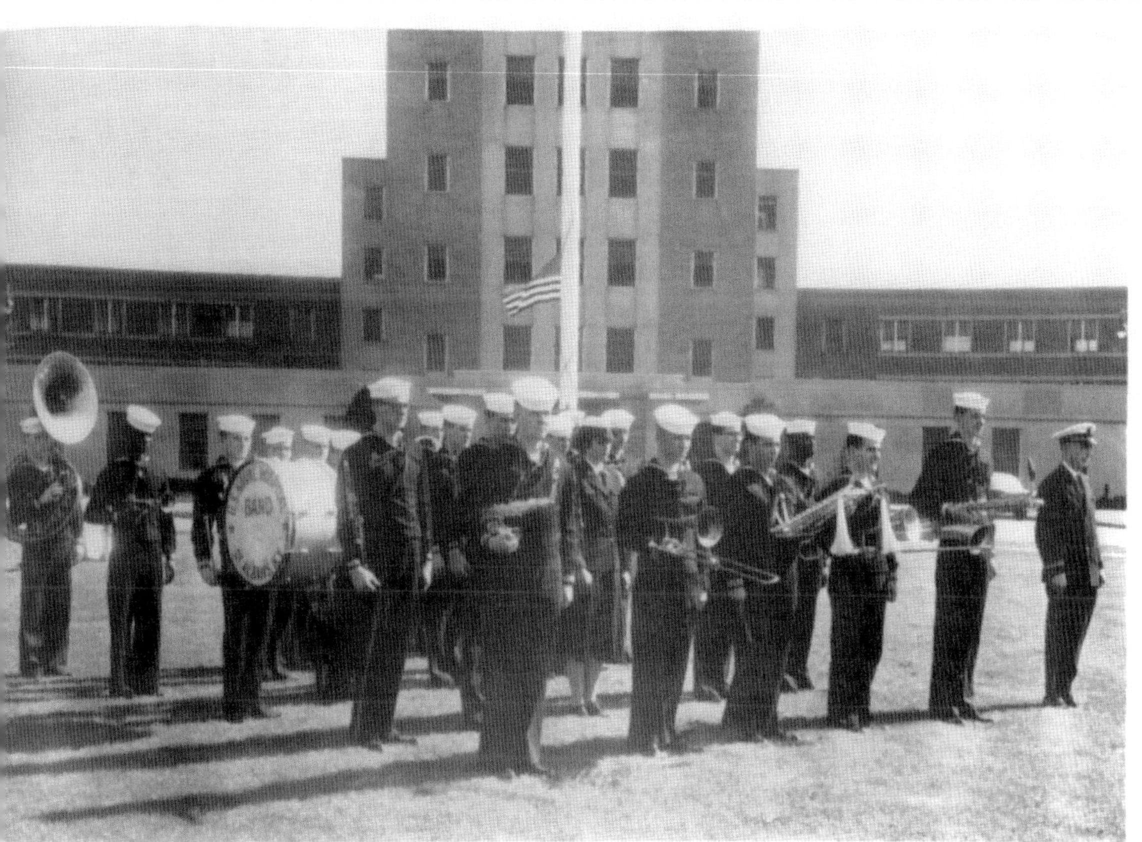

The St. Albans Naval Hospital Band

Members of the St. Albans Naval Hospital Band stand at attention before a performance at the facility during the 1940s. A lone enlisted servicewoman can be seen with her male counterparts. (Courtesy of Queens Public Library archives.)

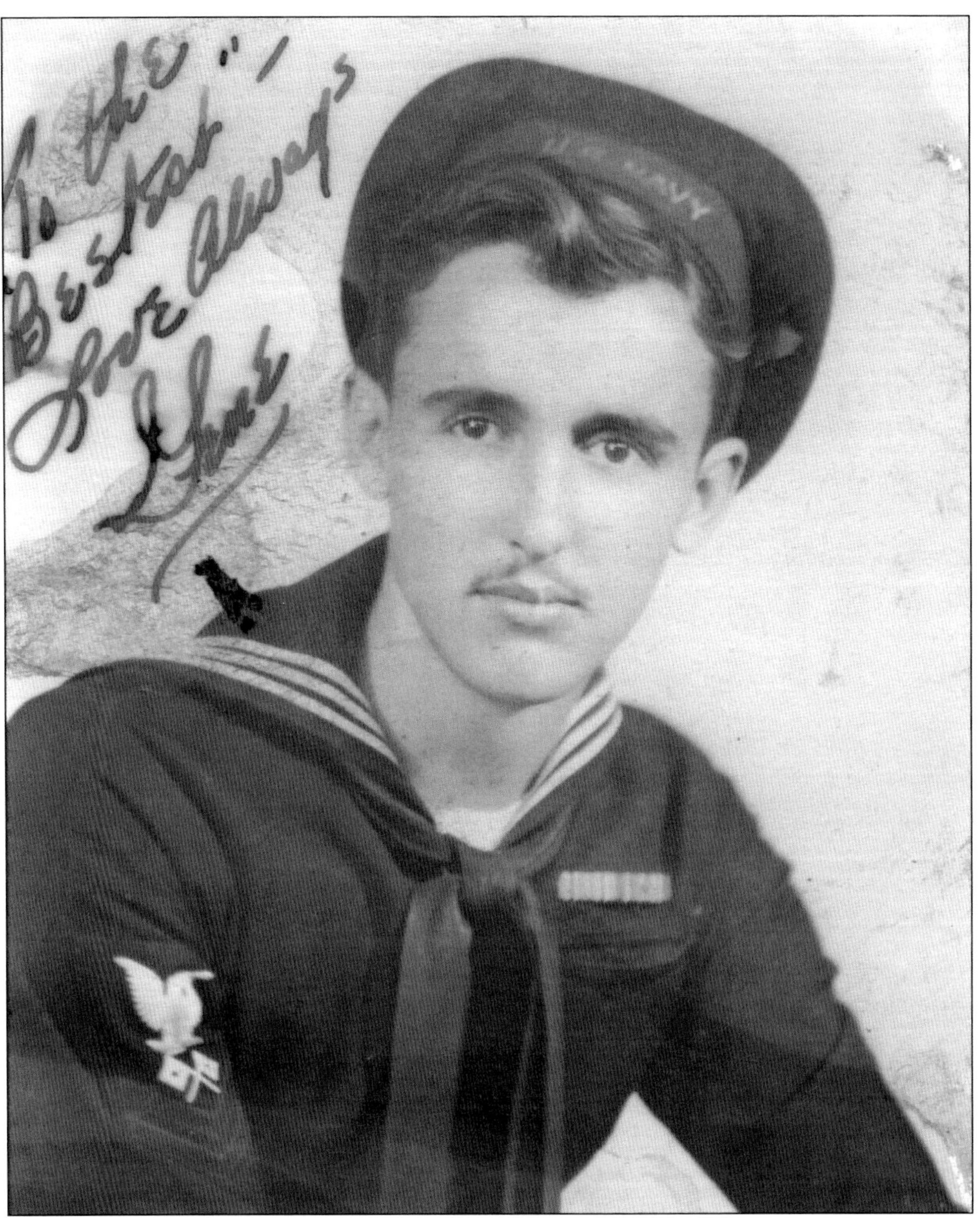

Gene W. Jenkins (1926–1996) from Lubbock, Texas, was 21 years old when he joined the US Navy in 1942. He ran flags as a signalman with the Naval Armed Guard on ships like the USS *Midway*, which traveled back and forth from Liverpool, England, to Normandy, France, during World War II. A bout with tuberculosis sent Jenkins to St. Albans Naval Hospital to recover from 1947 to 1948. During that time, he picked up a Kodak Brownie camera and documented his friendships with other military men in the facility's tuberculosis unit. (Courtesy of Leanne J. Jenkins.)

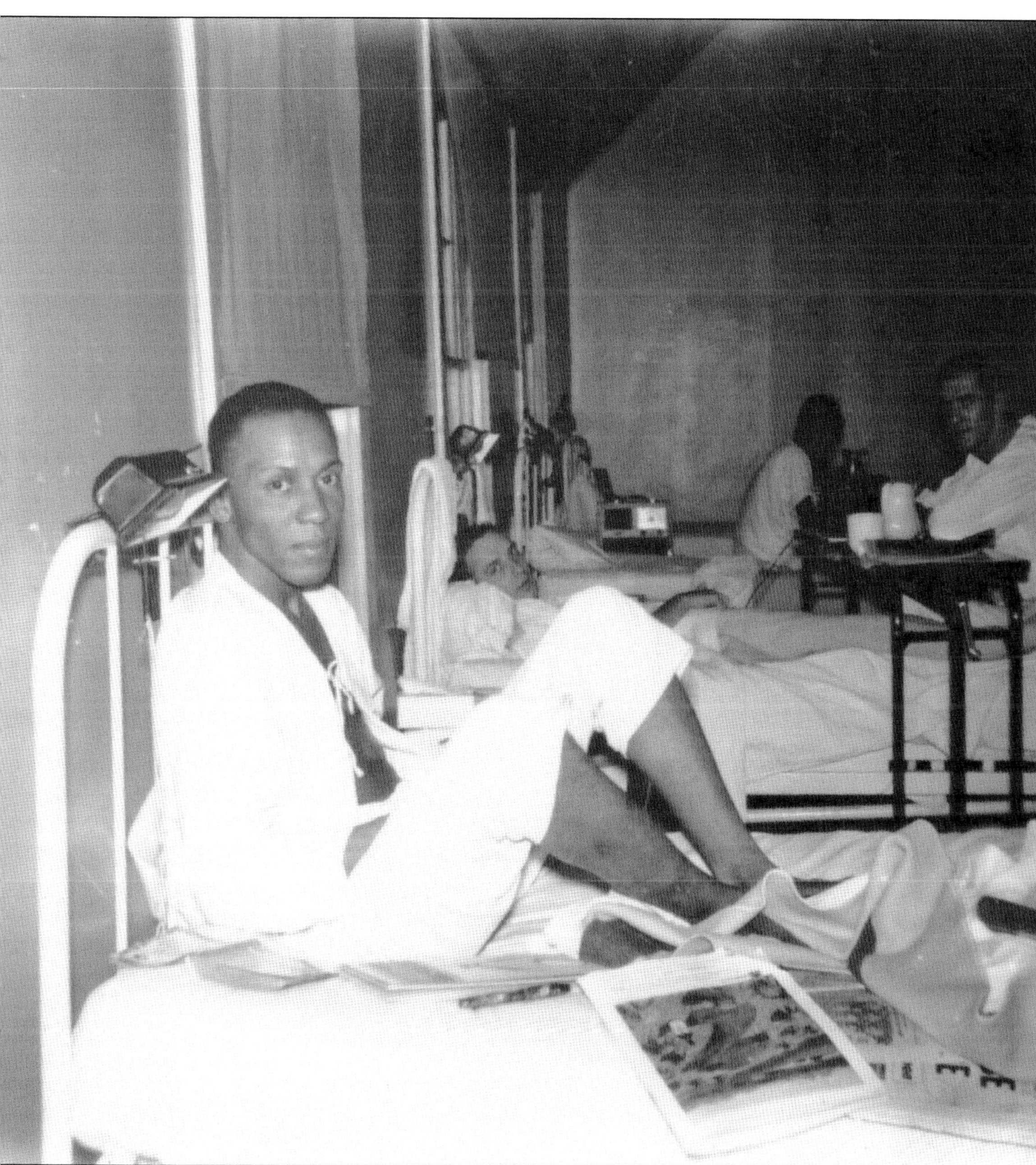

Deacon Payne sits on a bed inside the naval hospital's tuberculosis unit. Payne was one of several African American servicemen and women who were treated in integrated facilities at the naval hospital during World War II. (Photograph by Gene W. Jenkins.)

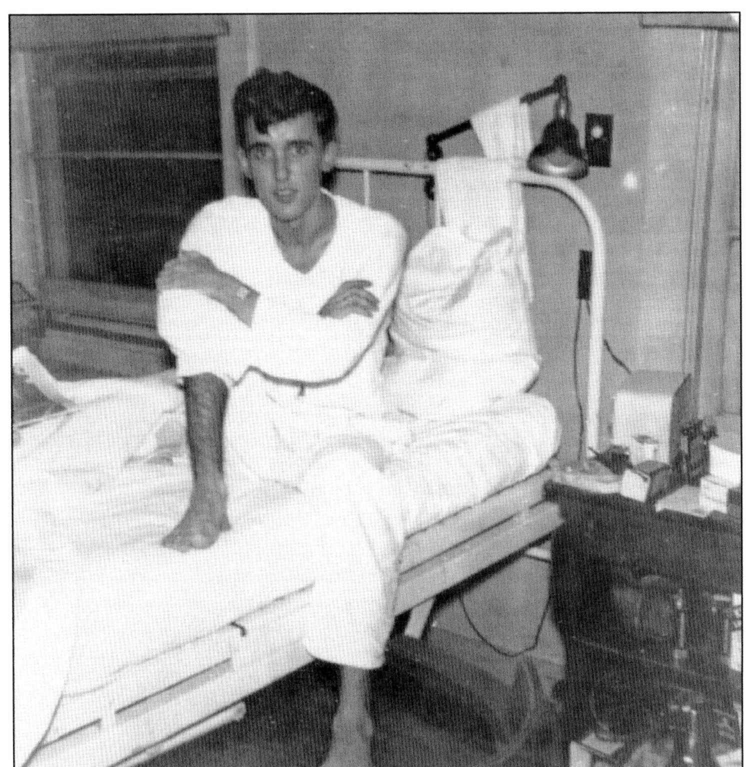

Amateur photographer Gene Jenkins poses for his own picture inside the tuberculosis unit. Jenkins took more than 100 war-related photographs. (Courtesy of Leanne J. Jenkins.)

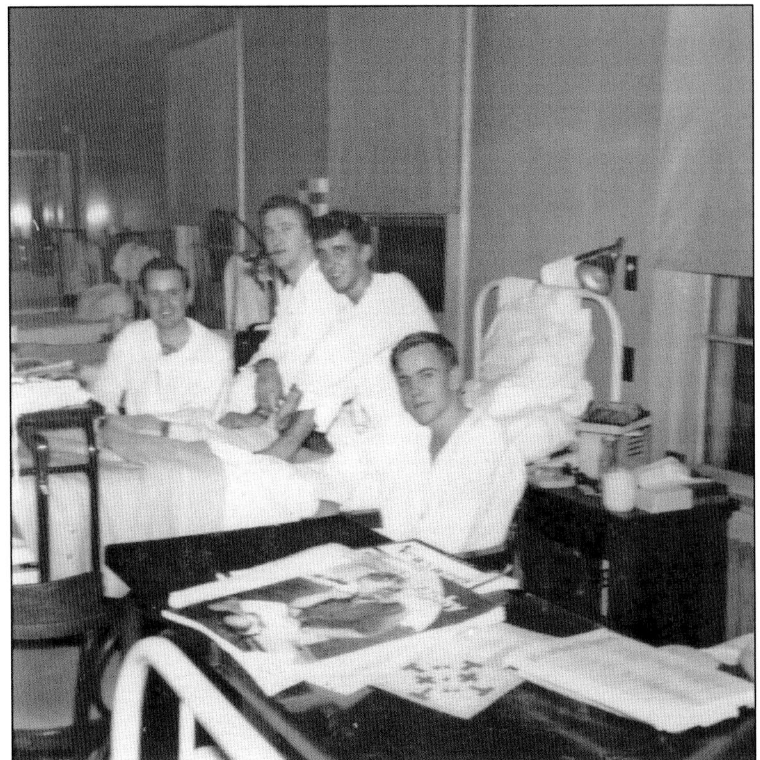

Servicemen housed alongside Gene Jenkins in the tuberculosis unit are seen here. Tuberculosis is an infectious disease that typically affects the lungs and other body parts. (Courtesy of Leanne J. Jenkins.)

The identity of this smiling serviceman is unknown. Doctors urged patients who were infected with TB bacteria and were not sick to still seek treatment. (Photograph by Gene W. Jenkins.)

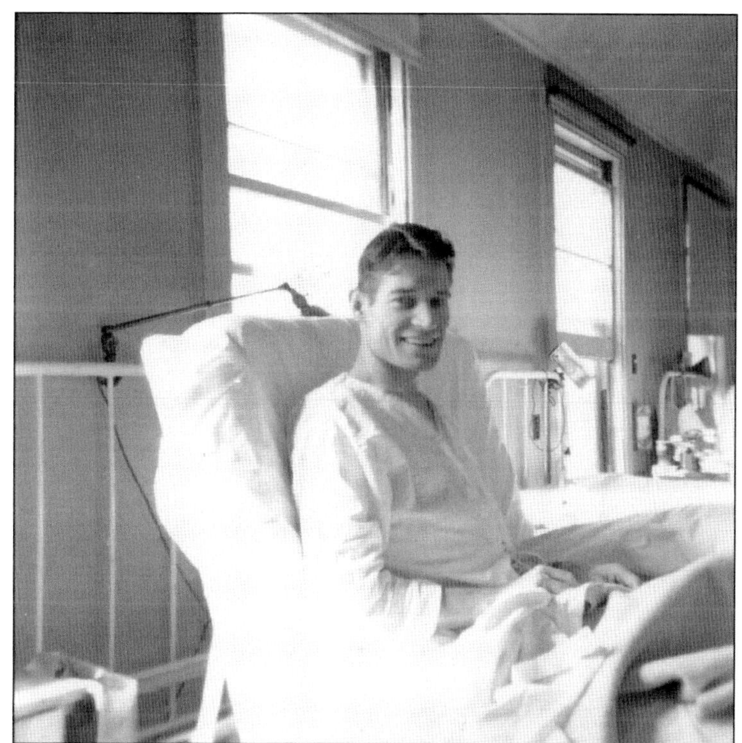

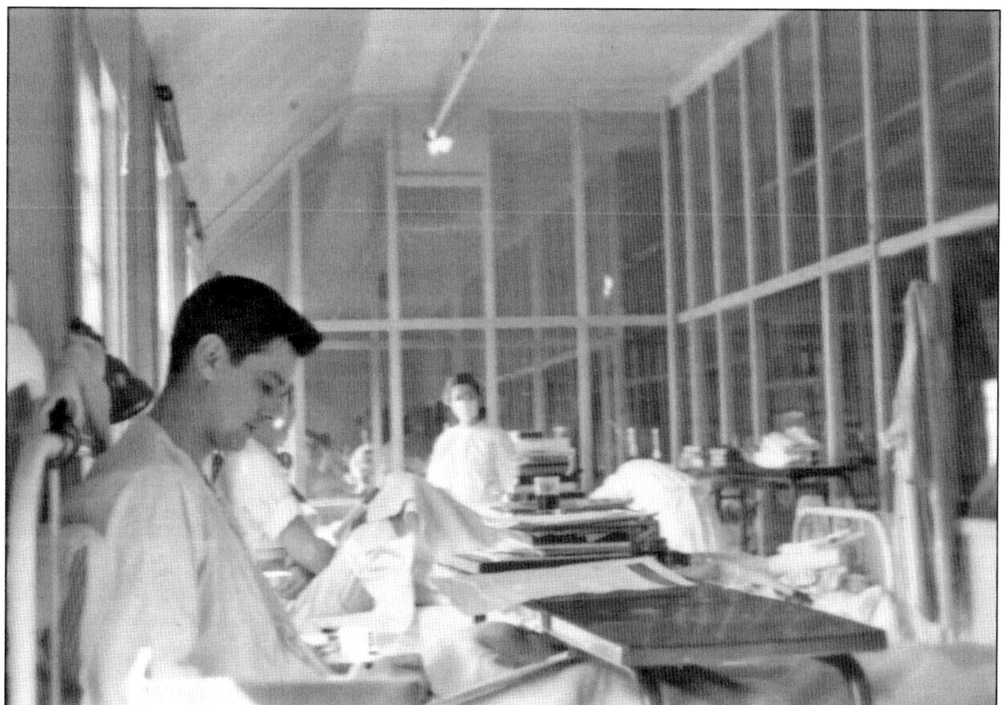

A patient waits for medication to be distributed by a masked nurse. He appears to be writing a letter or completing a crossword puzzle to pass the time in the tuberculosis ward. (Photograph by Gene W. Jenkins.)

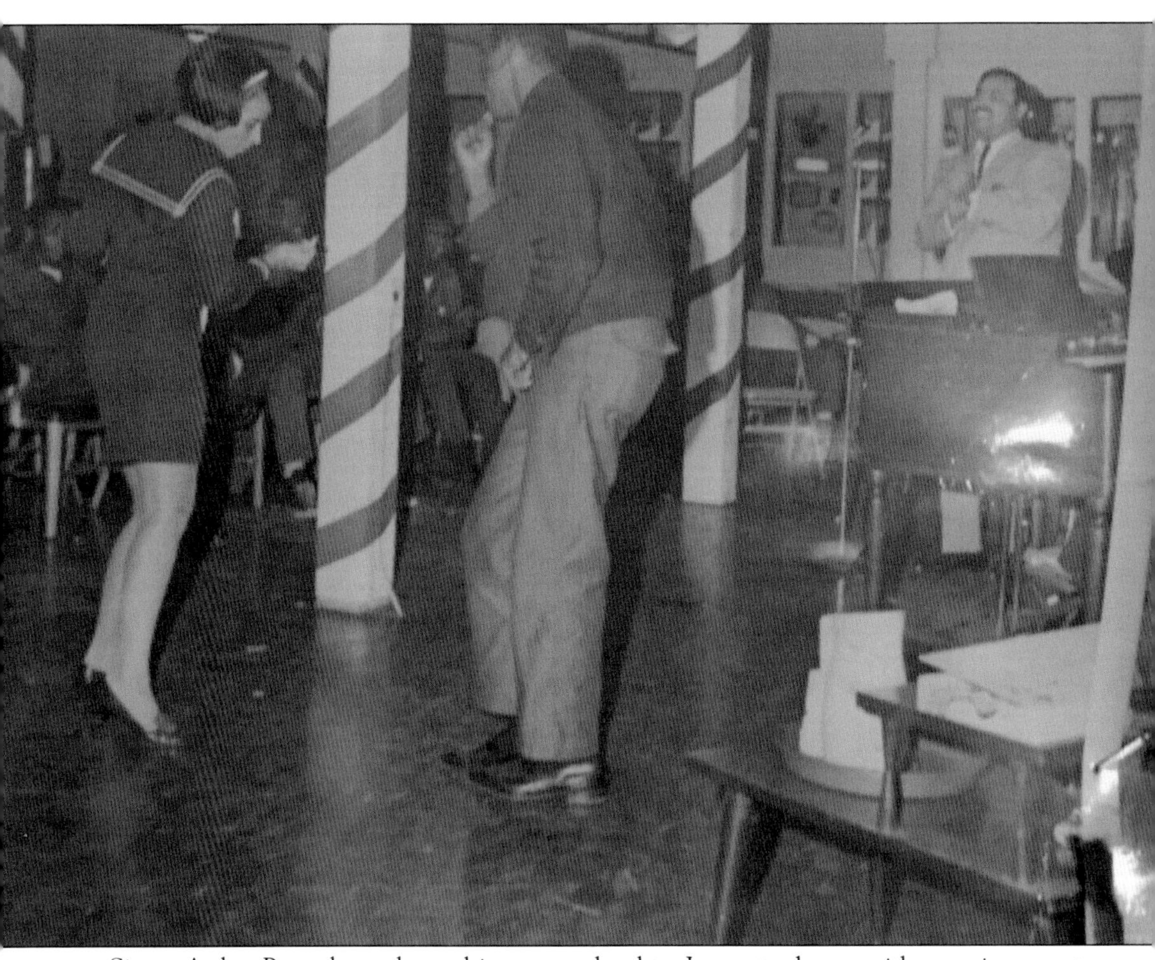

Singer Arthur Prysock watches as his teenage daughter Jeanartta dances with a serviceman at a Valentine's Day celebration held at the naval hospital in the 1960s. The Prysocks lived near Foch Boulevard and supported many community events. (Courtesy of Jean Prysock.)

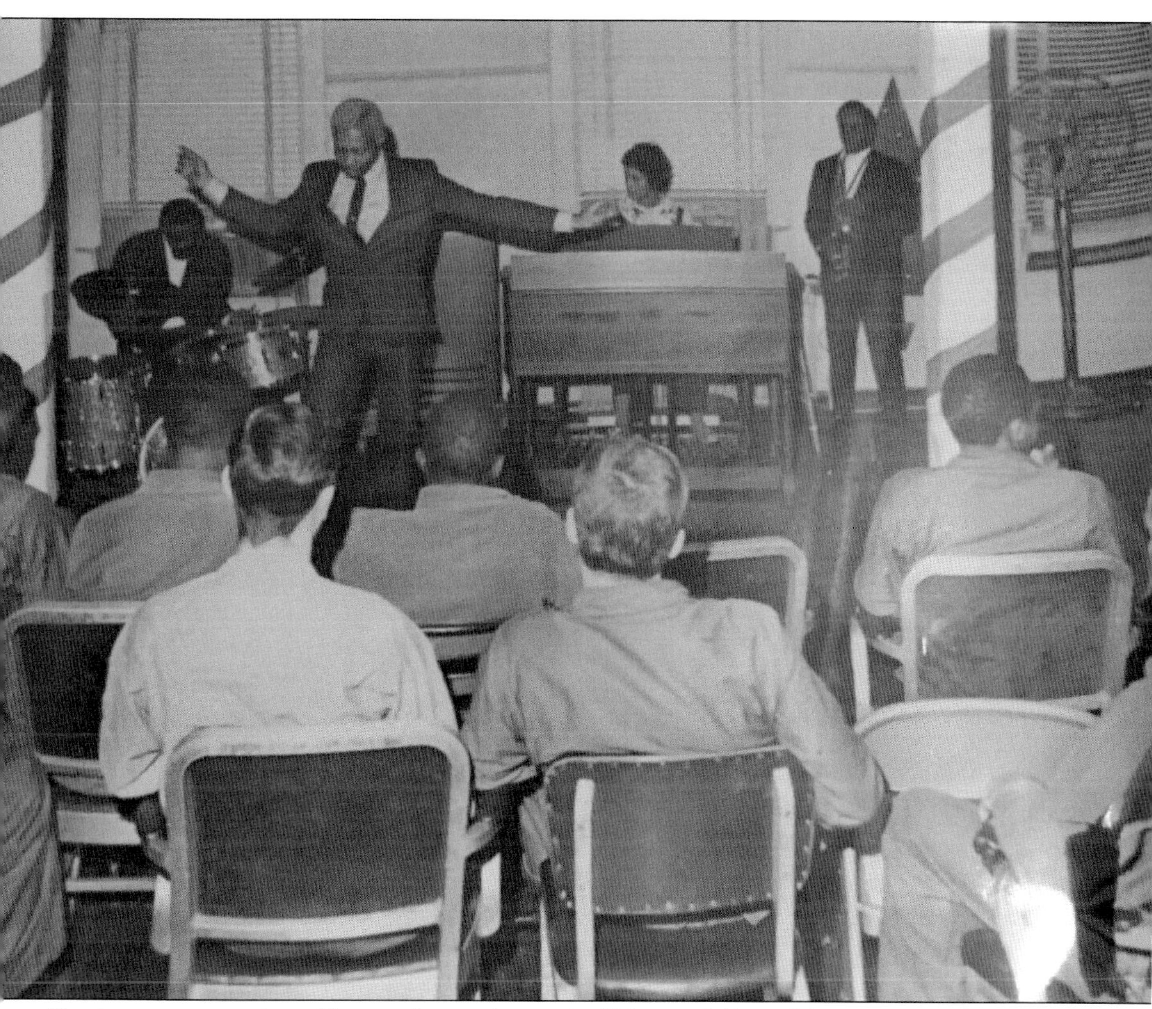

Servicemen are captivated by a performer during the Valentine's Day celebration. Special events were planned by the naval hospital's welfare and recreation department. It booked entertainers and theatrical performances along with other events at the facility. (Courtesy of Jean Prysock.)

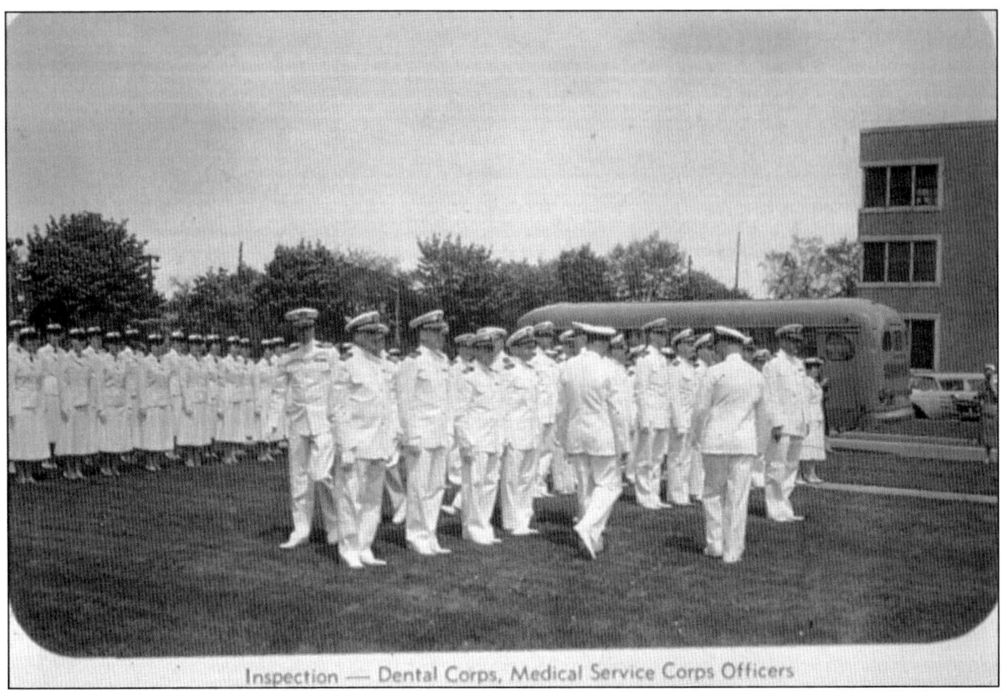
Inspection — Dental Corps, Medical Service Corps Officers

Uniformed officers from the Dental and Medical Service Corps walk outside of the main entrance of the St. Albans Naval Hospital during a commanding officers' inspection. (Courtesy of the National Library of Medicine.)

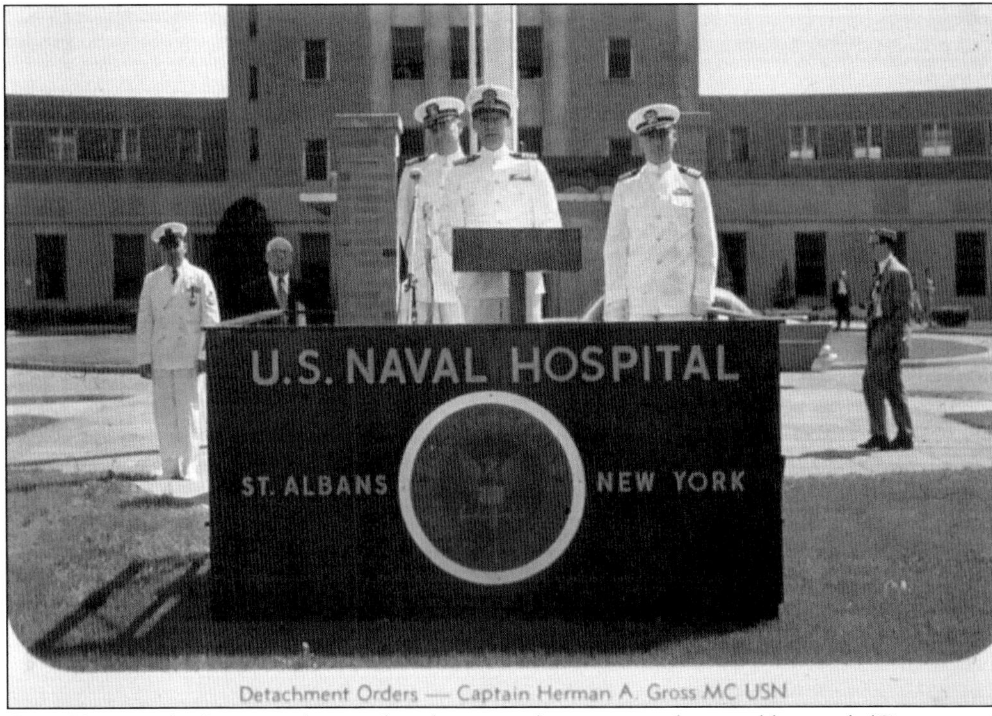

Detachment Orders — Captain Herman A. Gross MC USN

Capt. Herman A. Gross speaks at a detachment orders event at the naval hospital. (Courtesy of the National Library of Medicine.)

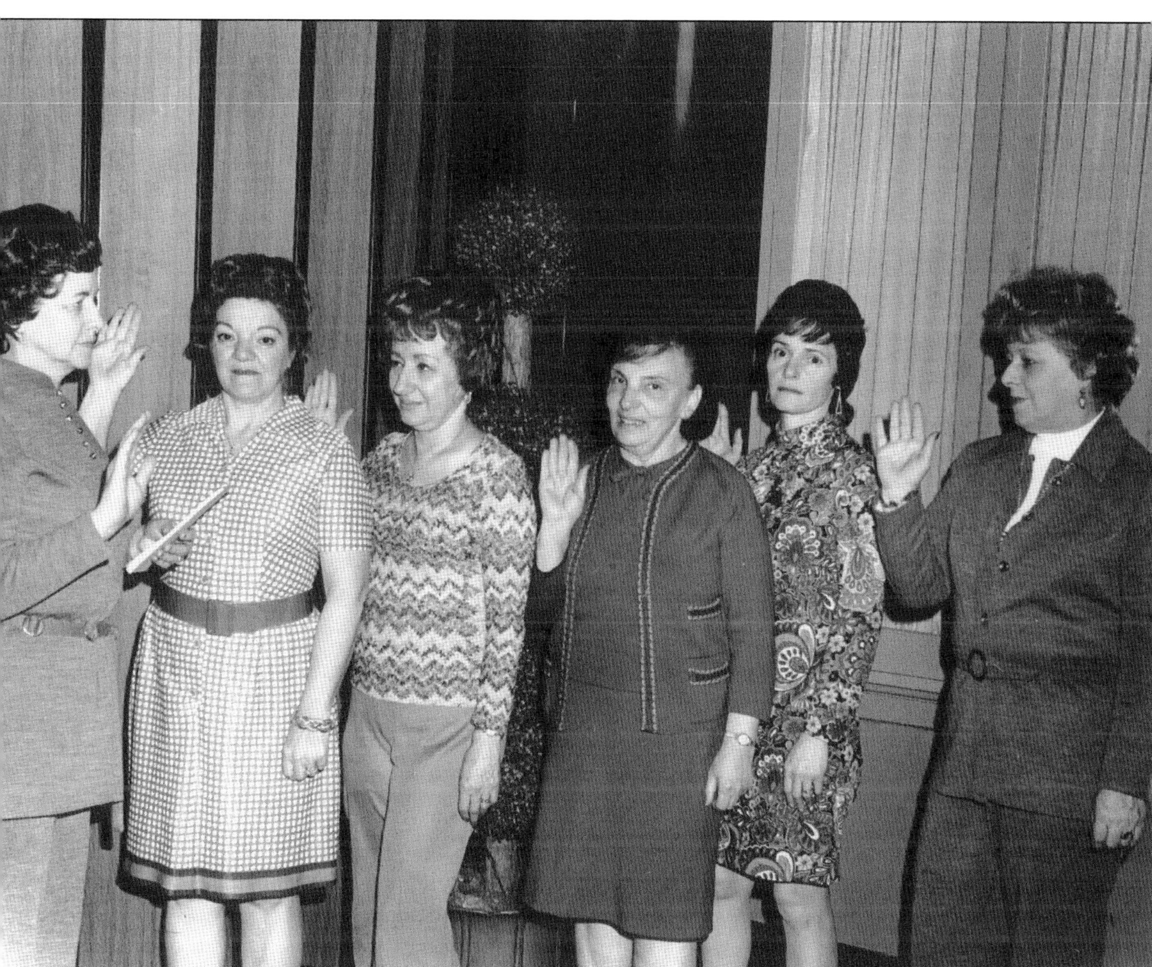

This April 1972 photograph shows the wives of Army Reserve officers at the Officers Club at St. Albans Naval Hospital during an installation ceremony for new officers. From left to right are Donna Bavetta, state first vice president; Thelma Severance, first vice president; Emillie Frank, president; Helen Applebaum, public relations; Billy Doyle, second vice president; and Beryl Brandmark, chaplain. (Photograph by Joseph A. Ullman, courtesy of Queens Public Library archives.)

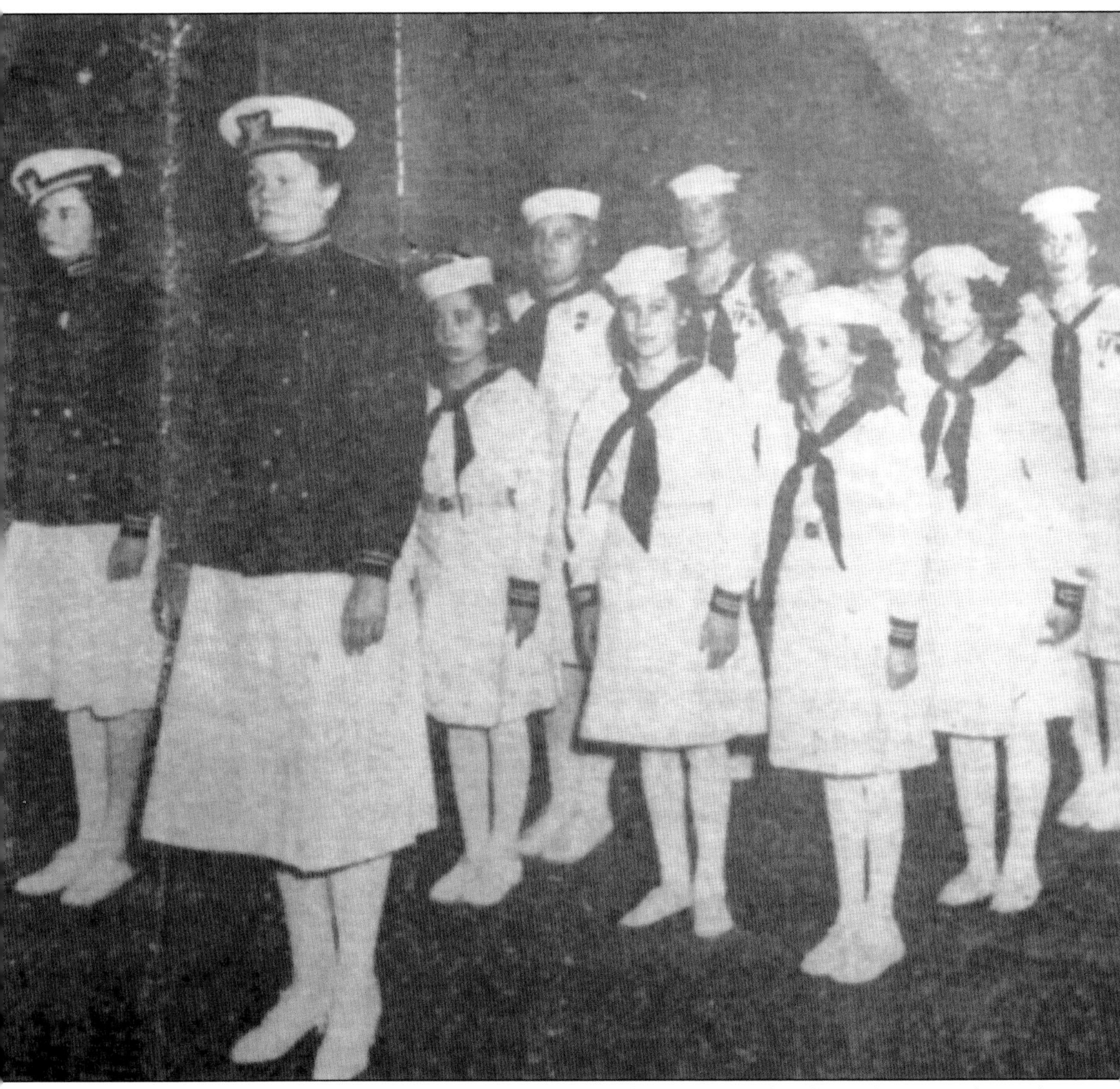

Female students from PS 147 in St. Albans show their support for the military in the 1950s. Members of the American Sailorettes of Battalion 14 posed for this photograph, which appeared in *St. Albans Life*. Among the young faces was Linda Roddy, daughter of the newspaper's publisher, Roger Roddy. (Courtesy of Linda Roddy Leavy.)

Three

Addisleigh Park and Its Jazz Past

Edwin H. Brown, an attorney and real estate developer, is widely credited with planning and building the first homes in Addisleigh Park in the early 1900s. Nearly a century later, when research consultant Jane Cowan wrote a report on Addisleigh Park for the Historic Districts Council in New York City, she mentioned a 1926 *New York Times* article that credited Brown with designing the neighborhood and pointed out that he had "land and house restrictions of the highest type." That meant Addisleigh's white middle- and upper-income residents were expected to abide by "strict racial covenants that forbade the area's white homeowners from selling their properties to African-Americans."

It did not work. Somehow, African American musician/composer Fats Waller of "Ain't Misbehavin" and "The Joint is Jumpin' " fame purchased an attached one-family home on Sayres Avenue that overlooked parkland that was later named St. Albans Memorial Park. Waller moved to the area in the late 1930s and lived there until he died in 1943. Years later, a *New York Times* article repeated local lore that a white policeman who was involved in a dispute with his neighbors sold his home to Waller.

The growing numbers of darker-skinned homeowners led to two separate lawsuits. In 1942, Henry M. and Madeline Neely, who lived at 112-29 175th Street, wanted to sell their home to an African American couple. The Neelys were sued over the racial covenants, but they believed that the majority of homeowners had not signed the covenant, thus making it invalid. The lawsuit reached New York State Supreme Court justice Thomas J. Cuff, who ruled against the Neelys, who instead leased their home to an African American family for more than four months.

In February 1947, the *New York Times* reported on the racially charged climate in Addisleigh. The headline read, "Court Grants Writ Barring Sale of Home in Queens to a Negro." Sophie Rubin, of 112-03 177th St., wanted to sell her home to Samuel Richardson, an African American candy store owner. Rubin's disgruntled neighbors Harold F. Kemp of 112-59 177th St. and Joseph H. Lutz of 112-20 177th St. had other plans. They filed a lawsuit against Rubin for violating the area's restrictive covenant. Queens Supreme Court justice Jacob H. Livingston granted an injunction that prevented Richardson from buying the home. Richardson's attorney, Andrew D. Weinberger, and Rubin's attorney, Paul Silverstein, countered that the restrictive covenants were "unconstitutional and violated public policy of the state and the nation."

The next year, everything changed. In May 1948, the US Supreme Court heard a landmark case, Shelley v. Kraemer. J.D. and Ethel Shelley were an African American couple from Missouri who were unaware that the St. Louis home they purchased in 1945 had a restrictive covenant. Justices on the nation's highest court agreed that courts could not enforce racially restrictive covenants because they violated the 14th Amendment of the US Constitution. That legal precedent allowed Samuel Richardson to purchase his Addisleigh Park home.

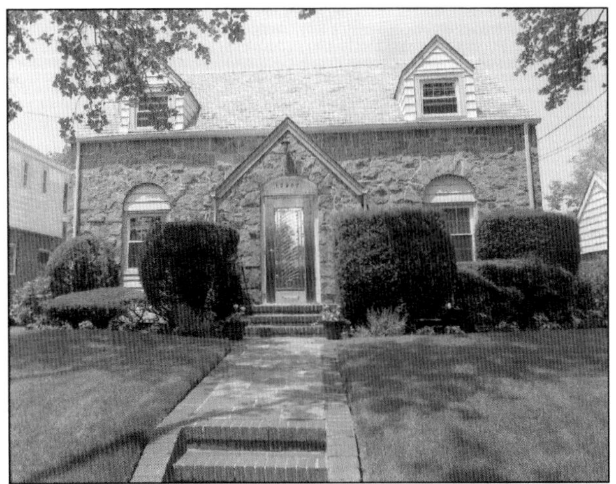

"The First Lady of Jazz," Ella Fitzgerald (1917–1996), lived in this Addisleigh Park home after she married her second husband, bassist Ray Brown (1926–2002), in 1947. By 1953, the globetrotting couple, who had adopted a son, were divorced. The couple continued to collaborate professionally after their divorce. Area residents described Fitzgerald as a nice woman who did not drink alcohol but kept it for guests—mainly jazz musicians, who walked from their homes to hang out with her. (Photograph by Blair Garrett.)

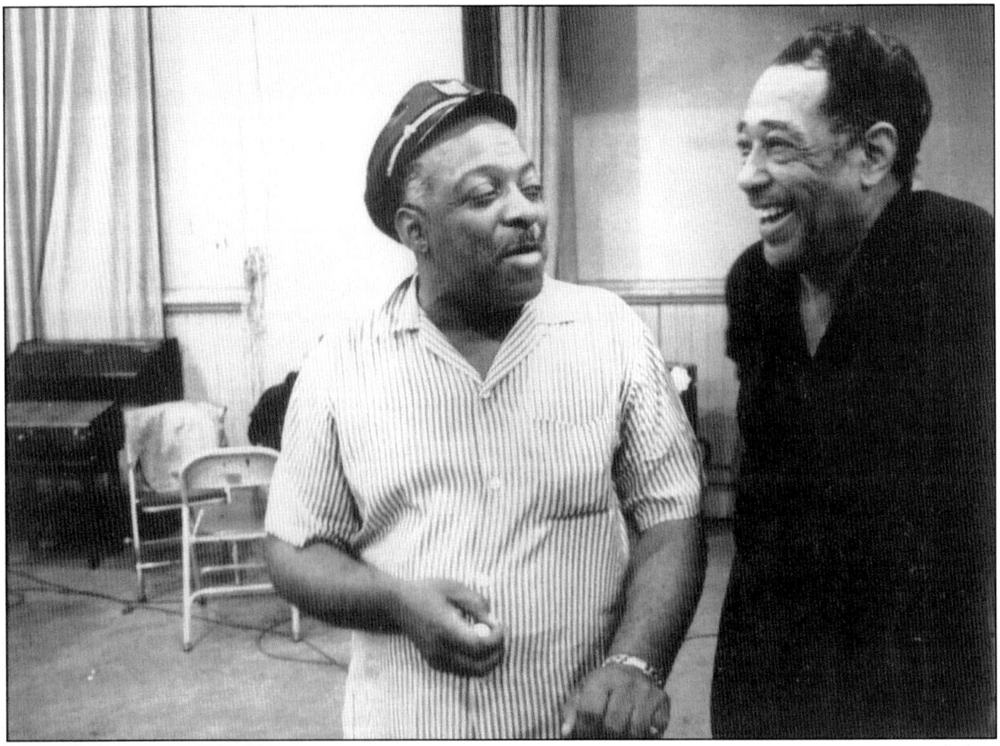

Jazz pianist, composer, and bandleader Count Basie (left, 1904–1984) is pictured with his contemporary Duke Ellington (1899-1974) in July 1961. Basie and his wife, Catherine (1914–1983), a former dancer, were well-known as gracious hosts who shared their huge pool with friends and the public for private events and summer parties that often included neighborhood kids. Former city councilman Archie Spigner lives in an Addisleigh Park home where Basie's pool once stood. "It gives me pleasure to know my home is located in a place that brought Count Basie and others so much joy," Spigner said during a 2016 interview. New York City Board of Education officials renamed Benjamin Schlesinger Intermediate School 72, located on Guy R. Brewer Boulevard in Jamaica to honor the Basies. Catherine & Count Basie Middle School 72 stands as a constant reminder of the couple's civic and charitable contributions to the world. (Photograph by Don Hunstein, courtesy of Dee Anne Hunstein.)

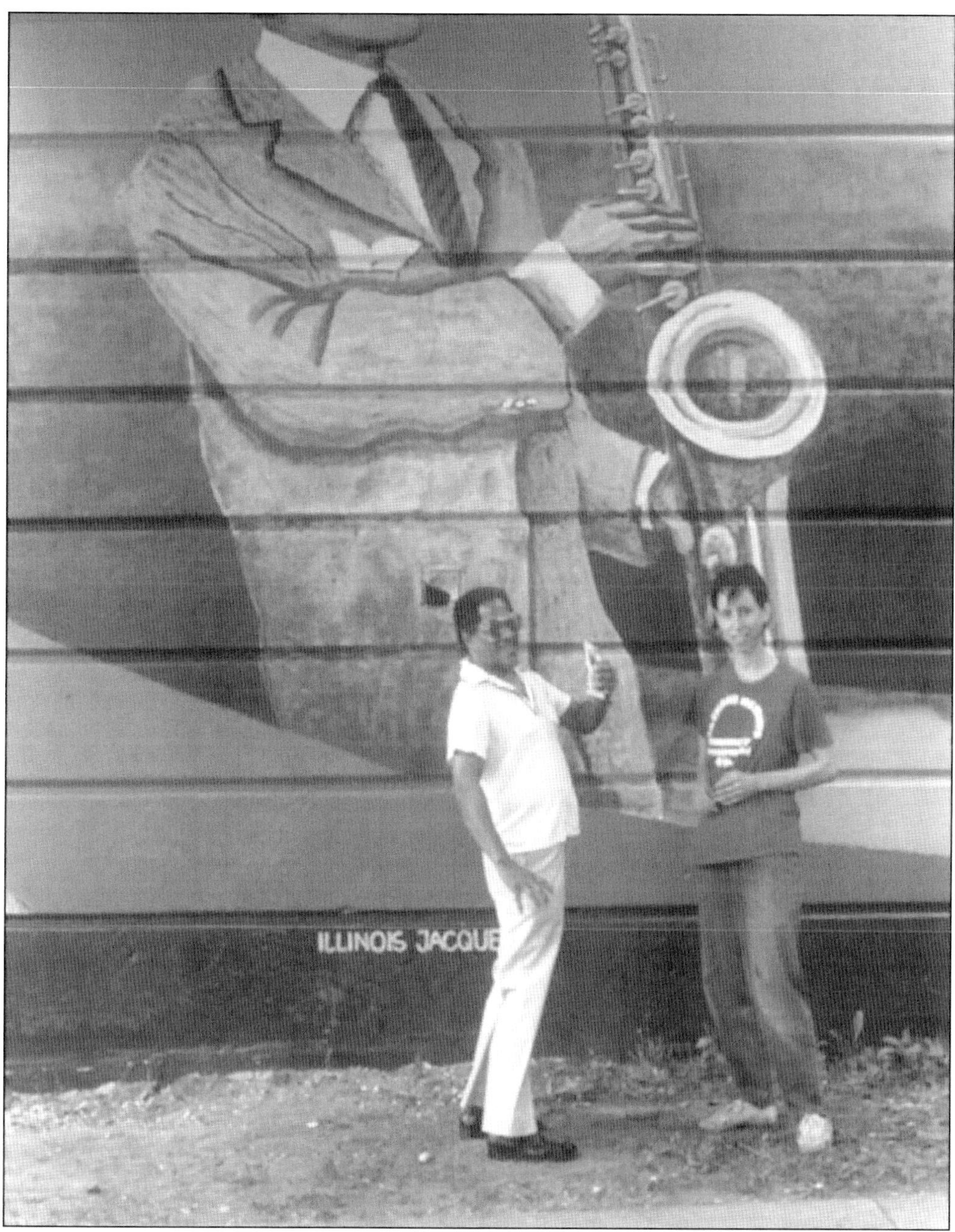

Tenor saxophonist and composer Jean-Baptiste Illinois Jacquet (1922–2004) was a fixture in Addisleigh Park. He was a member of Count Basie's band from 1945 to 1946 and performed with numerous jazz and swing artists, including fellow St. Albans residents Wild Bill Davis (1918–1995) and Lester Young (1909–1959). Jacquet is known for his solo on "Flying Home" and other songs. He intensely watched as artist Joe Stephenson drew his image for this St. Albans Greatest mural. He offered suggestions about how his instrument was held, Stephenson recalled. Jacquet lived next door to his eldest brother, trumpeter Russell Jacquet (1917–1990). The Louisiana-born siblings were known for encouraging younger musicians in the neighborhood to perfect their craft. (Photograph by Catherine Symne, courtesy of Joe Stephenson.)

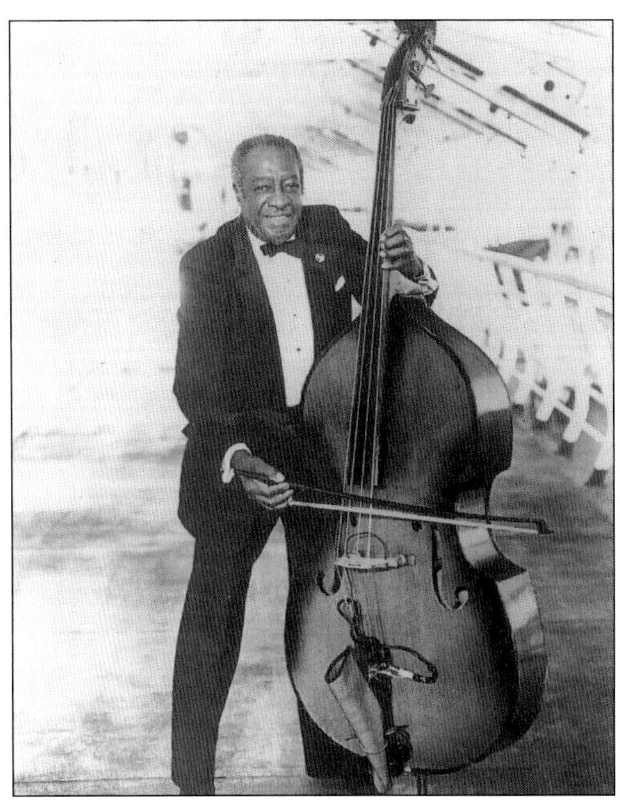

Milt Hinton (1910–2000), better known as the "Dean of Jazz Bassists" or "the Judge," lived on 113th Avenue and Marne Place with his wife, Mona, from the 1950s until his death in 2000. Besides his obvious love of music, Hinton was an avid photographer who chronicled his peers during his journeys. David G. Berger and Holly Maxson curate the Milton J. Hinton Photograph Collection, which has over 60,000 photographs. Hinton was a longtime member of St. Albans Congregational Church on Linden Boulevard, which is within walking distance of his home. (Courtesy of Dr. Tom Manuel.)

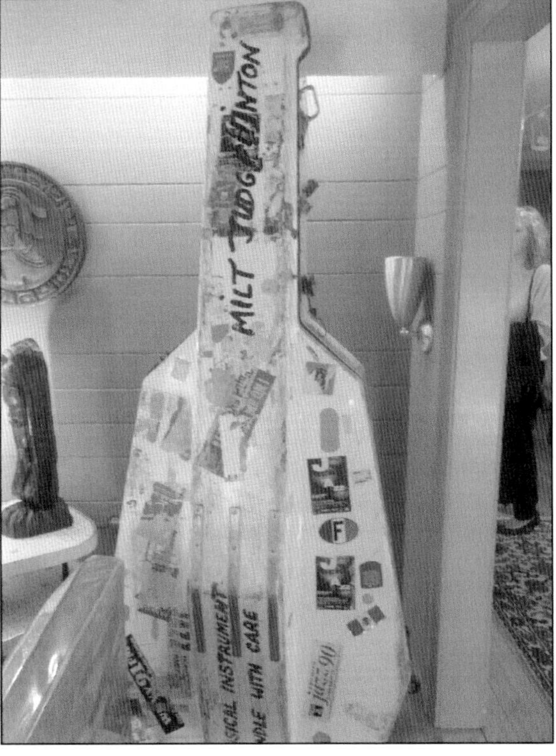

This upright bass case covered with stickers from all over the world belonged to Milt Hinton. The case is now displayed at the Jazz Loft, a museum and event space that features educational programs about jazz music in Stony Brook, Long Island. (Photograph by Blair Garrett.)

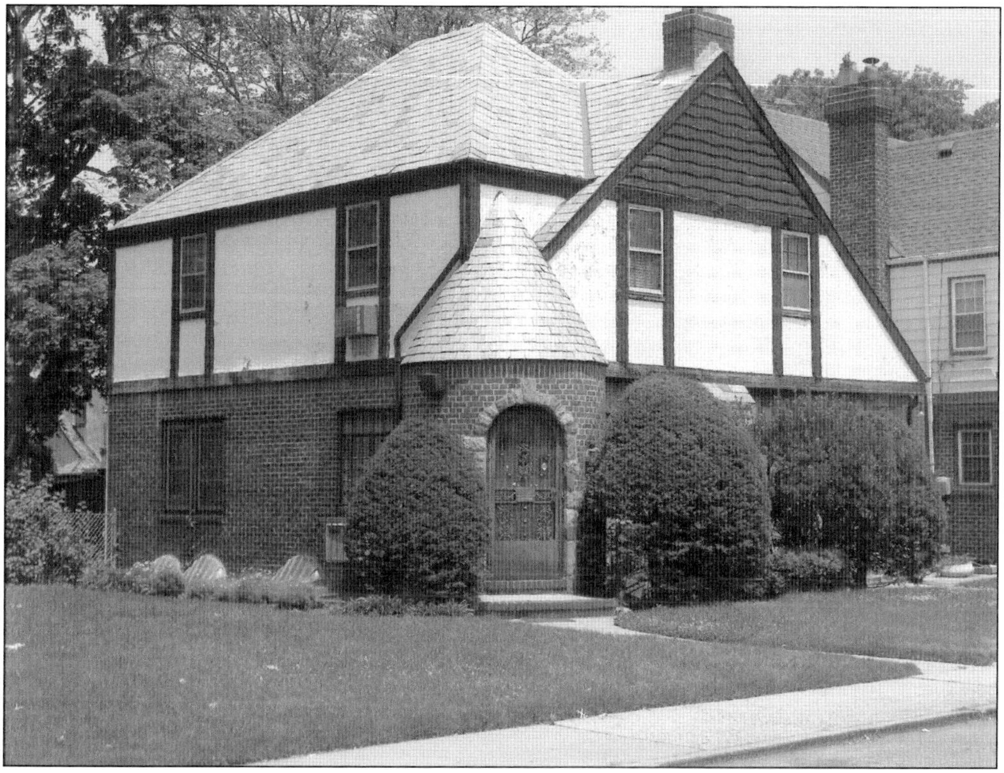

This stately Tudor home was where Mona and Milt Hinton lived for many years. Edmonia "Mona" Caesar Clayton Hinton (1919–2008) was a bookkeeper and business advisor for her husband on the road. She later returned to school and graduated from Queens College. When she ceased traveling with her husband, Mona became a public school teacher who often tutored students in her home. She was a close friend of Catherine Basie, and the two, along with other wives of New York musicians, raised funds for several charitable organizations in their spare time. (Photograph by Blair Garrett.)

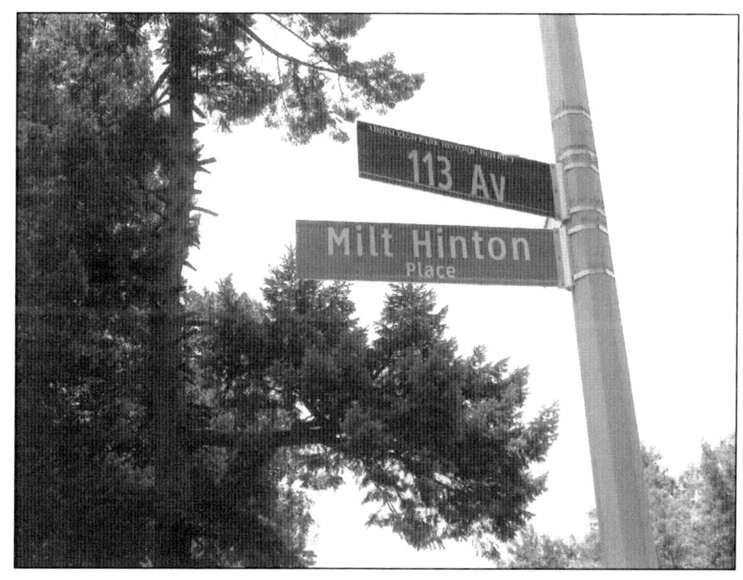

Milt Hinton touched the lives of so many people over the years during his time living in Addisleigh Park that after he died, local officials and neighbors agreed to have the street near his home named after him. Hinton's beloved neighborhood became a historic district in 2011. (Photograph by Blair Garrett.)

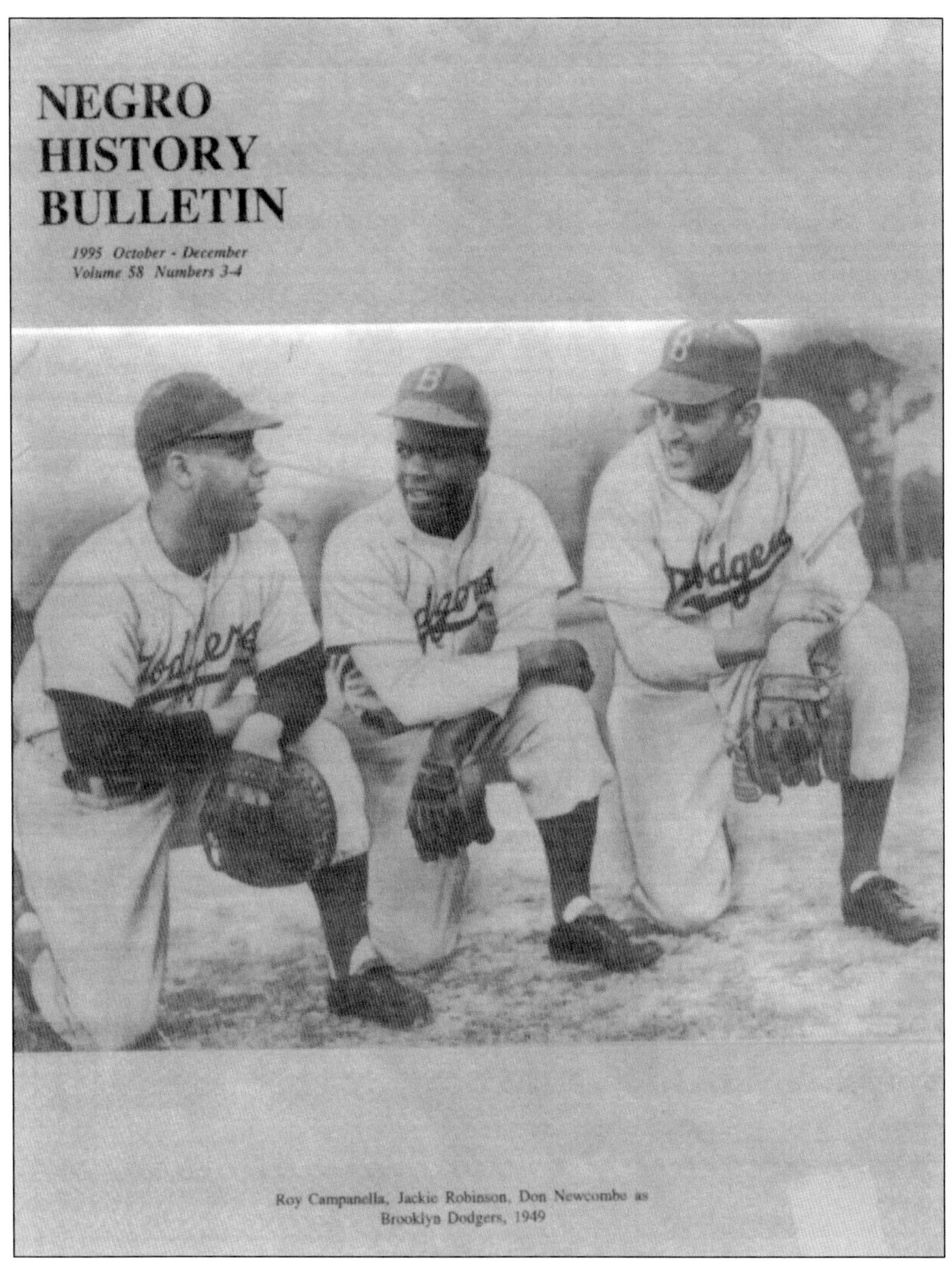
NEGRO HISTORY BULLETIN

1995 October - December
Volume 58 Numbers 3-4

Roy Campanella, Jackie Robinson, Don Newcombe as Brooklyn Dodgers, 1949

Addisleigh Park residents and Brooklyn Dodgers Roy Campanella (left) and Jackie Robinson (center) talk with teammate Don Newcombe in a 1949 photograph. Decades later, the image was used on the cover of a 1995 *Negro History Bulletin* magazine. (Courtesy of Queens Public Library archives.)

Roy Campanella's home today looks as charming as it did when the baseball great lived there with his family. Philippa Karteron, whose parents purchased the dwelling after Campanella, recalled seeing one of Campanella's sons, Roy Jr., in her backyard playing basketball not too long after the family moved. Karteron has that same attachment with Addisleigh Park. Although her family no longer lives in the former Campanella home, she still resides in the community. (Photograph by Blair Garrett.)

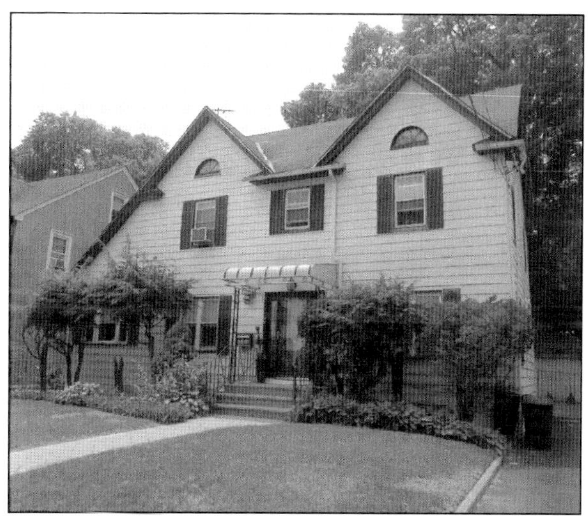

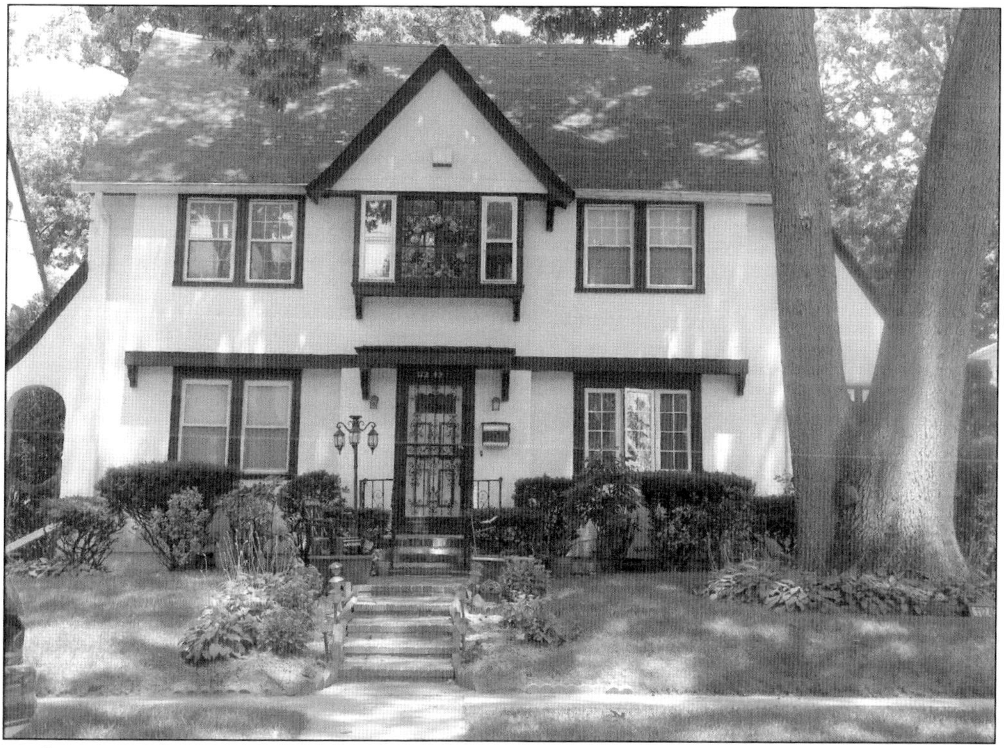

Looking at this striking Tudor home, one can almost imagine the beautiful singer-dancer and actress Lena Horne (1917–2010) coming home from a long day at a movie studio or Broadway performance. The Brooklyn native was among the first wave of African American entertainers to move to Addisleigh Park. Lena Mary Calhoun Horne was also active in civil rights and donated her time to several charities. Her signature song was "Stormy Weather," from the 1943 movie of the same name. Horne played Glinda the Good Witch in the all-black musical film *The Wiz* in 1978. She was inducted into the Big Band and Jazz Hall of Fame in 1991. Her feisty spirit led her to work with First Lady Eleanor Roosevelt on anti-lynching laws and other civil rights activities. One of Horne's famous sayings summed up her attitude about being African-American: "You have to be taught to be second class, you're not born that way." (Photograph by Blair Garrett.)

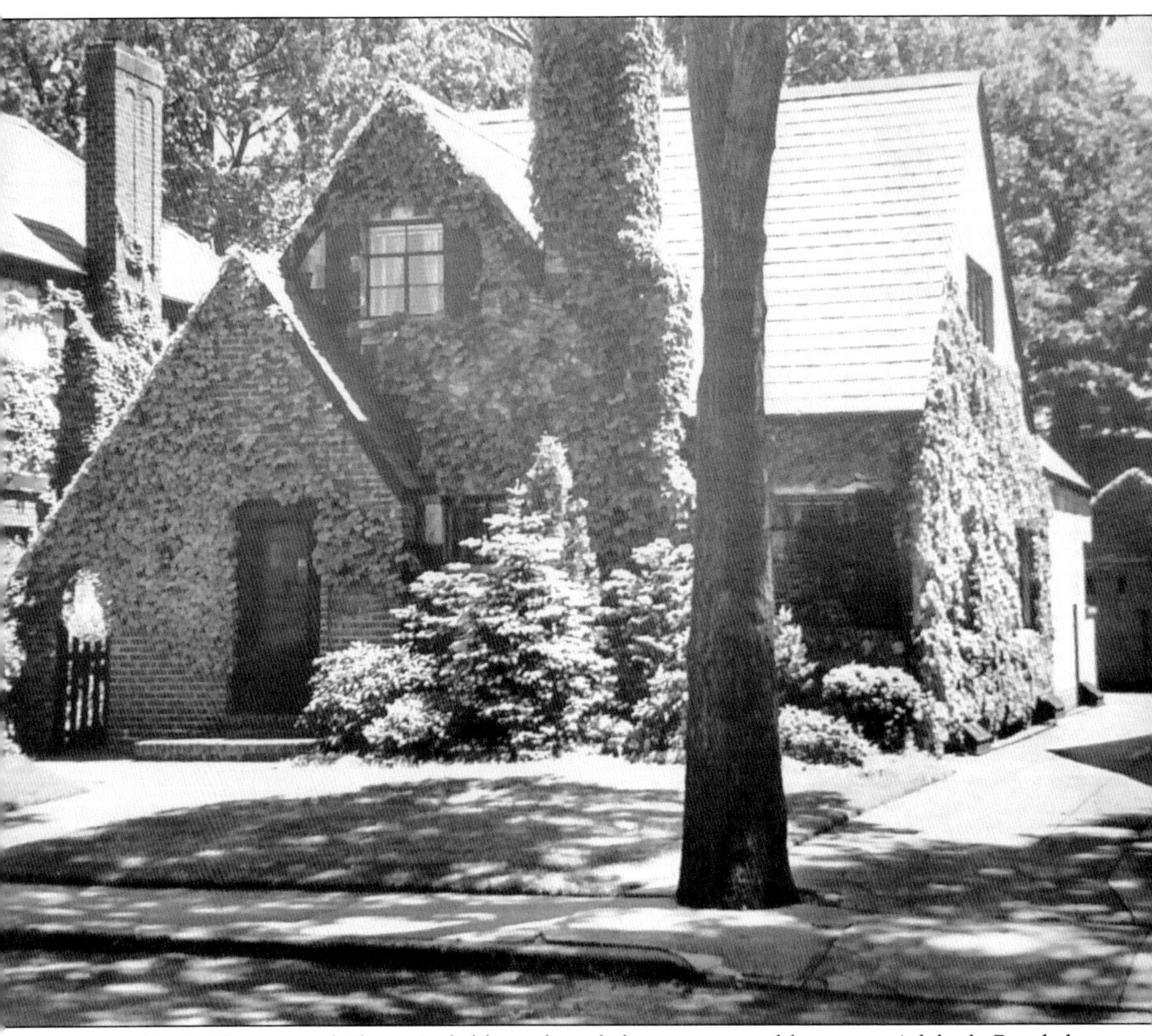

In 1946, Thomas and Eloise Cofield purchased this ivy-covered home on Adelaide Road that was across the street and two homes down from Catherine and Count Basie. Thomas Cofield was a manager/owner of Cofield Motor Company, a luxury sports car dealership in Manhattan. The Cofields were active members at St. Albans Congregational Church. A 1959 *Jet* magazine photograph showed a happy Eloise Cofield standing with church leaders as they raised $2,500 toward the church building fund. (Courtesy of Brian McRae.)

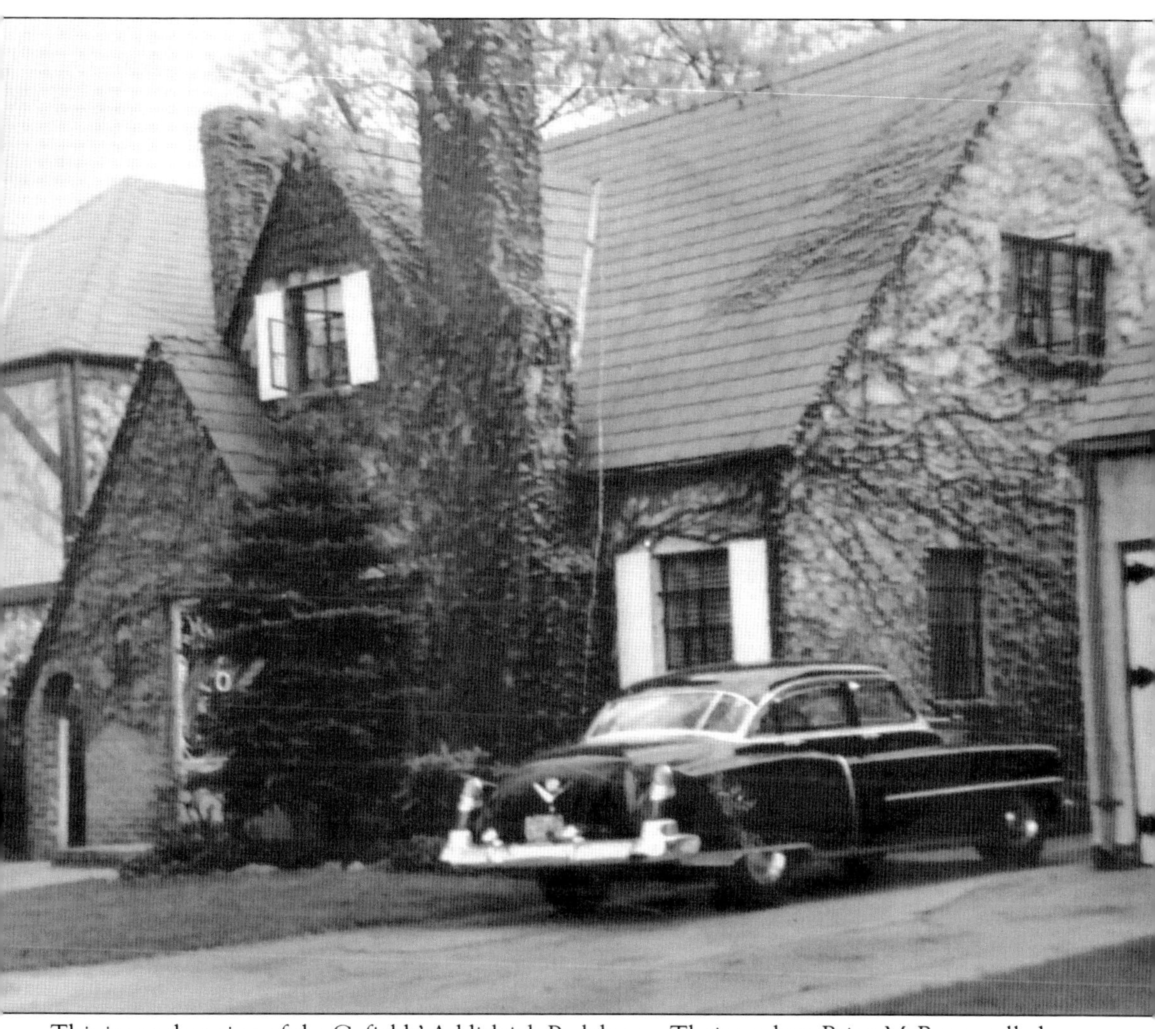

This is another view of the Cofields' Addisleigh Park home. Their nephew Brian McRae recalled that his aunt and uncle knew the Basies well. "My family was invited to parties the Basies held in the 1950s. They met Duke Ellington there several times," said McRae, whose late father, Ivan McRae, was a Tuskegee Airman who lived in the greater St. Albans neighborhood for many years before moving to Hempstead and then Suffolk County. "It [Addisleigh Park] was always a nice neighborhood," McRae said. (Courtesy of Brian McRae.)

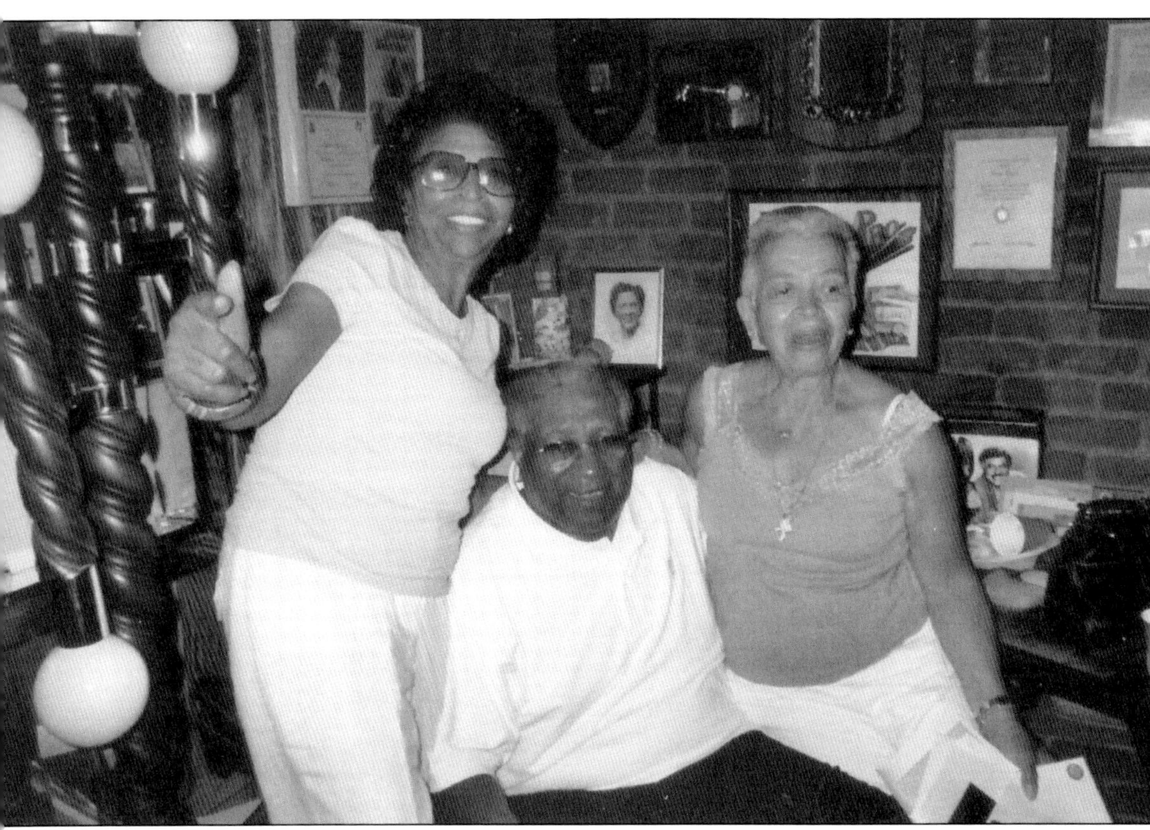

Historian Clarence L. Irving Sr. is pictured with his partner Lillie B. Crowder (left), and Jean Prysock, the wife of singer Arthur Prysock, enjoying a fun time celebrating at a birthday party held in Jean's honor. (Courtesy of Lillie B. Crowder.)

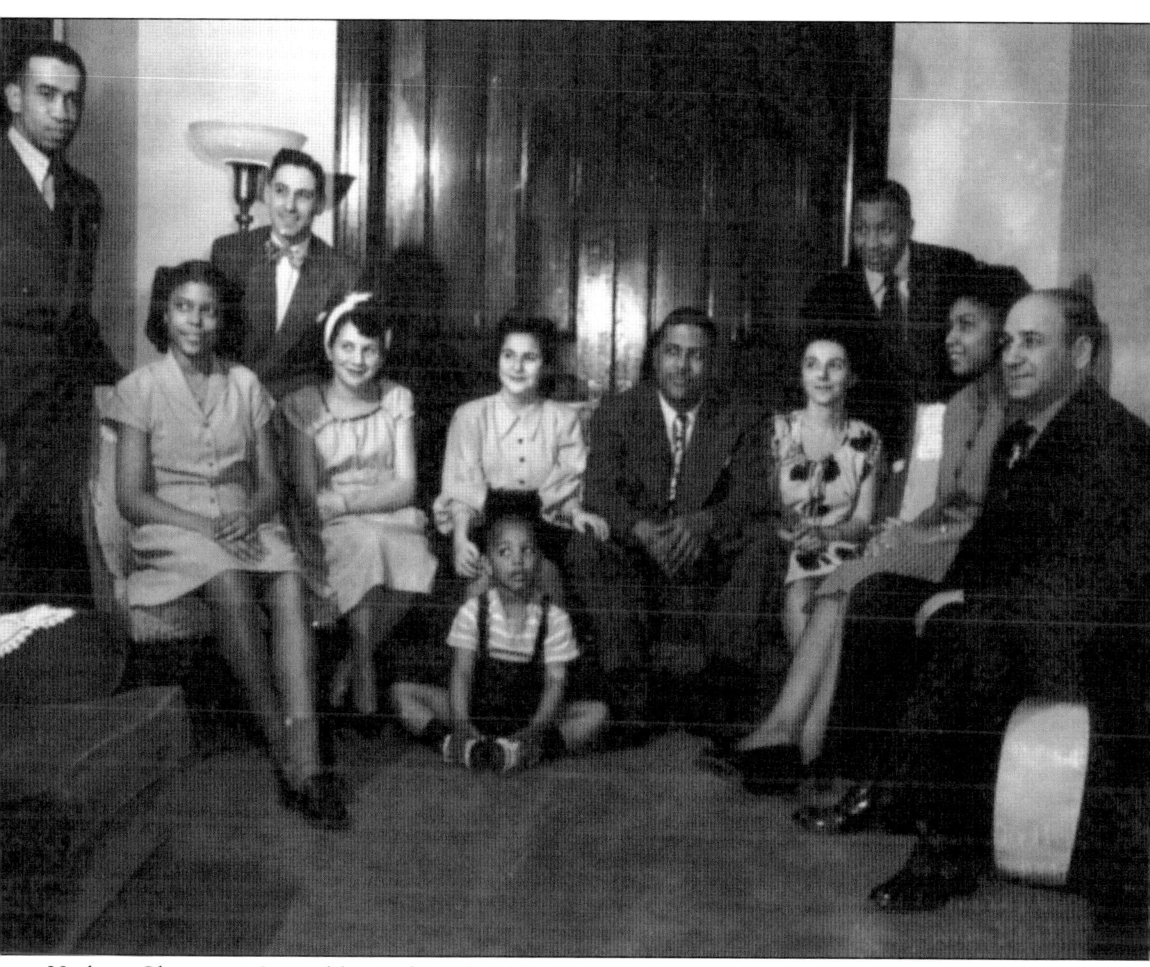

Herbert Christmas Sr. and his wife, Arlee, are seen in this 1946 or 1947 photograph in their Addisleigh Park home. The Christmases lived on 113th Street and co-owned Allied Custom Hatters, a Harlem millinery, with Julius Kutscher, who is also pictured here. Years later, the Christmases' eldest daughter, Joan, married historian Clarence L. Irving Sr. He lived in Addisleigh Park from the 1960s until 1977. Joan Christmas died in 1993. Irving died in 2014. (Courtesy of Lillie B. Crowder.)

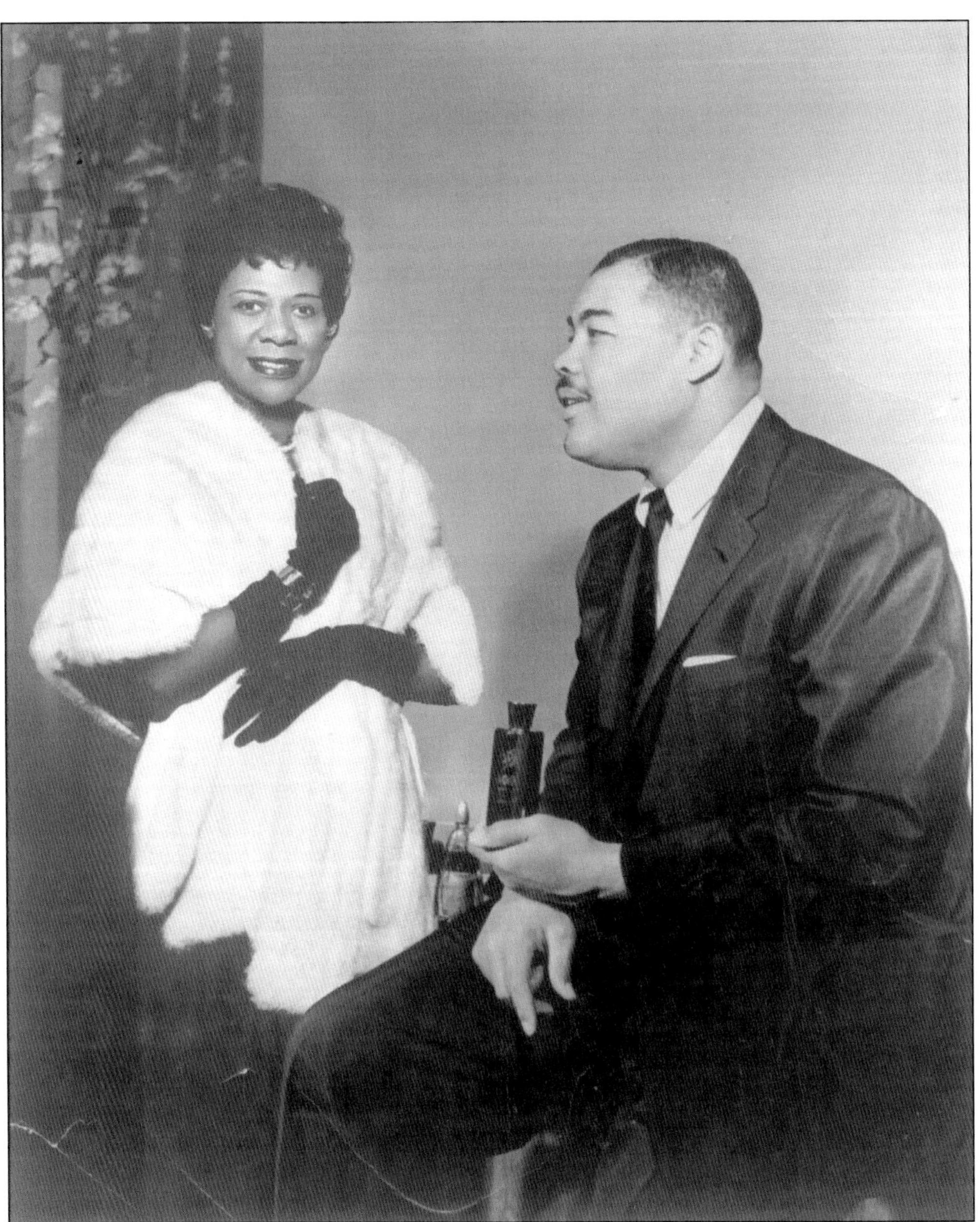

Fur-clad beauty entrepreneur Rose Meta Morgan (1912–2008) poses in the Addisleigh Park home she shared with her husband, heavyweight fighter Joe Louis, in 1955. Morgan, a talented Chicago hairdresser, was invited to the Big Apple by singer-actress Ethel Waters in 1938. Morgan saw opportunities to expand her services to African American women who wanted to be pampered and purchase cosmetics in an upscale salon. Rose Morgan's House of Beauty was established in Harlem in the mid-1950s. Morgan later diversified her business, adding a charm school, dressmaking, and a wig salon. She was married to Joe Louis (1914–1981) for two years. Louis was heavyweight champion from 1937 through 1949 and retired from boxing in 1951. Morgan later became a founder of Freedom National Bank, a black-owned commercial bank, in 1965. (Courtesy of the Rose Morgan estate.)

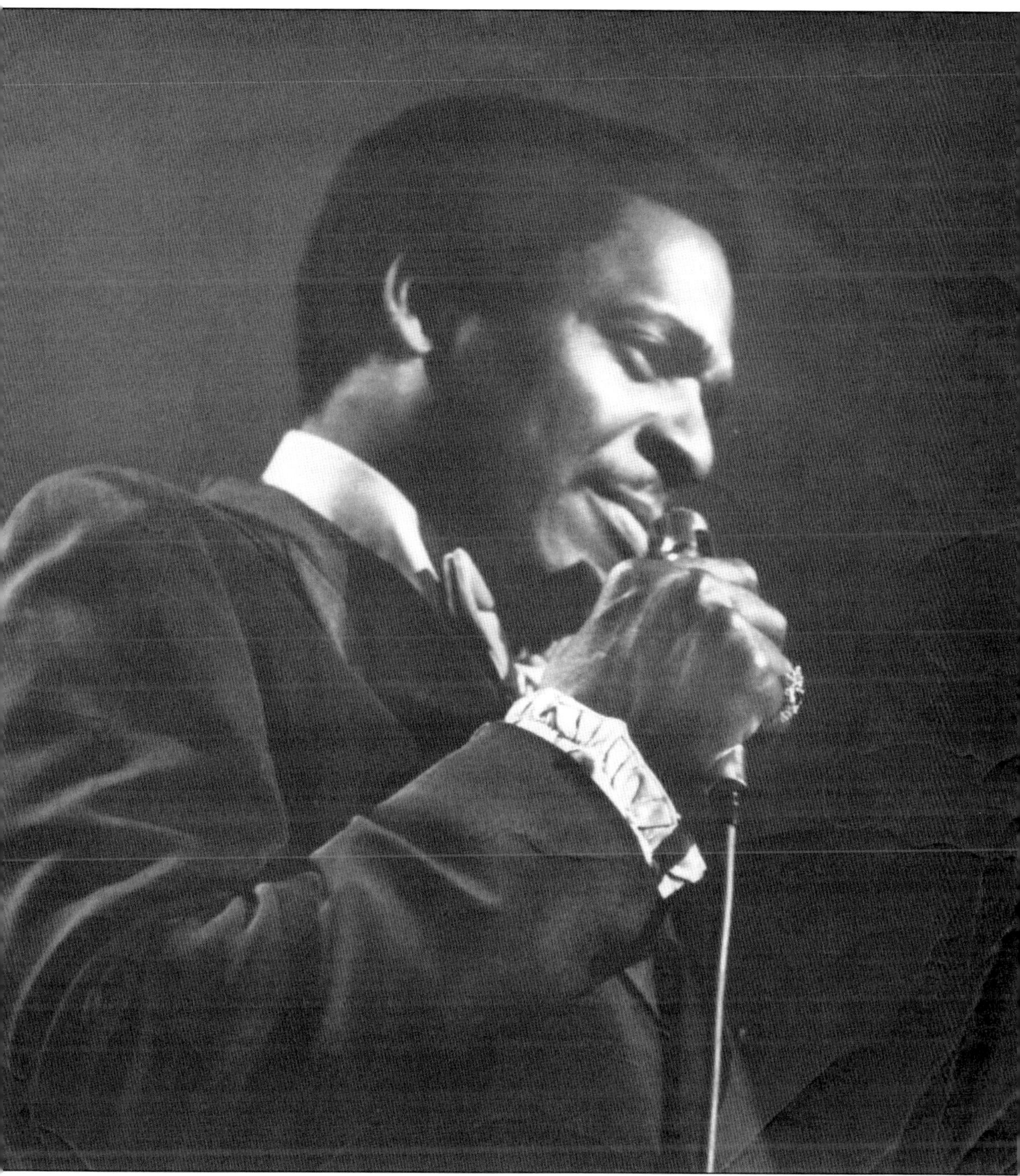

Singer/songwriter Benjamin Franklin Peay, better known as Brook Benton (1931–1988), is best known for his smooth baritone voice that could interpret any gospel, rock and roll, or rhythm and blues song. The South Carolina native first came to New York as part of a gospel group. He returned home and joined the R&B group the Sandmen, and decided to change his name. When the Addisleigh Park resident was not performing, Benton wrote songs for entertainers Nat King Cole and Clyde McPhatter. (Courtesy of Lillie B. Crowder.)

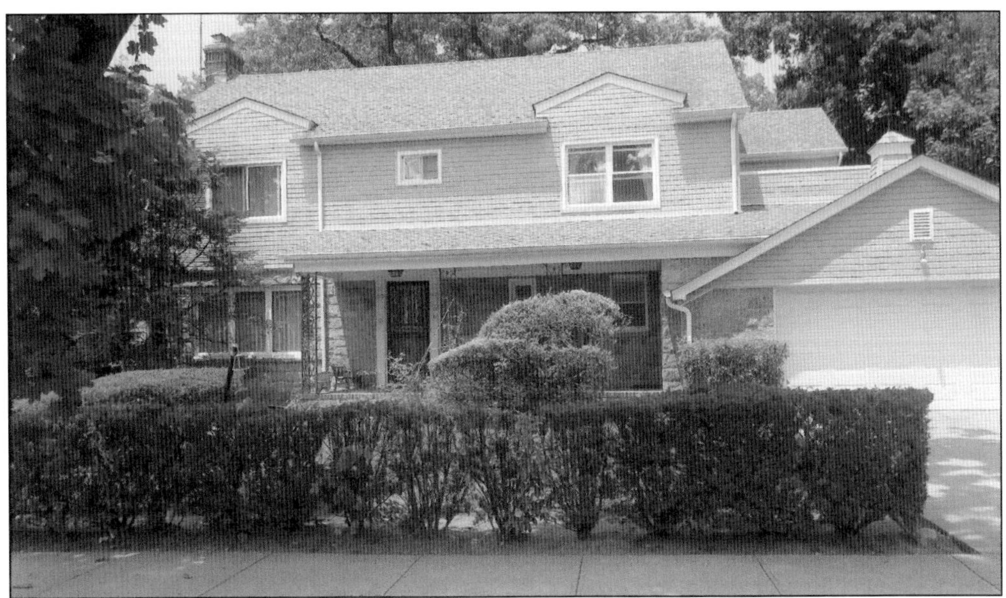

Visitors to Addisleigh Park often point out the house with the light blue trim and gray stone front where Brook Benton once lived. Among Benton's popular songs were "A Million Miles from Nowhere" (1959); "Baby (You've Got What it Takes)," a duet with Dinah Washington (1959); and "Rainy Night in Georgia" (1970). (Photograph by Blair Garrett.)

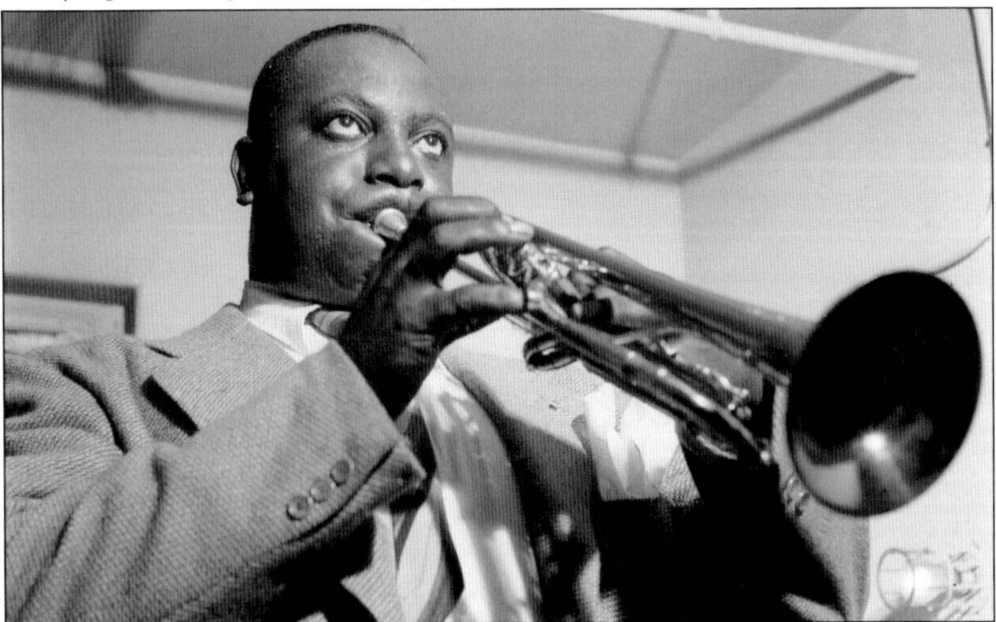

Jazz trumpeter and band leader Charles Melvin "Cootie" Williams (1911–1985) and soul singer James Brown (1933–2006) had more than music in common. Williams first lived in a stately English Tudor home at 175-19 Linden Blvd. where Brown later resided. Williams performed with the Chick Webb Orchestra and worked with other band leaders, including Duke Ellington, Benny Goodman, and Fletcher Henderson. Williams co-wrote the popular jazz tune "Round Midnight" with pianist and composer Thelonious Monk. (Photograph by William Gottlieb, courtesy of the Library of Congress.)

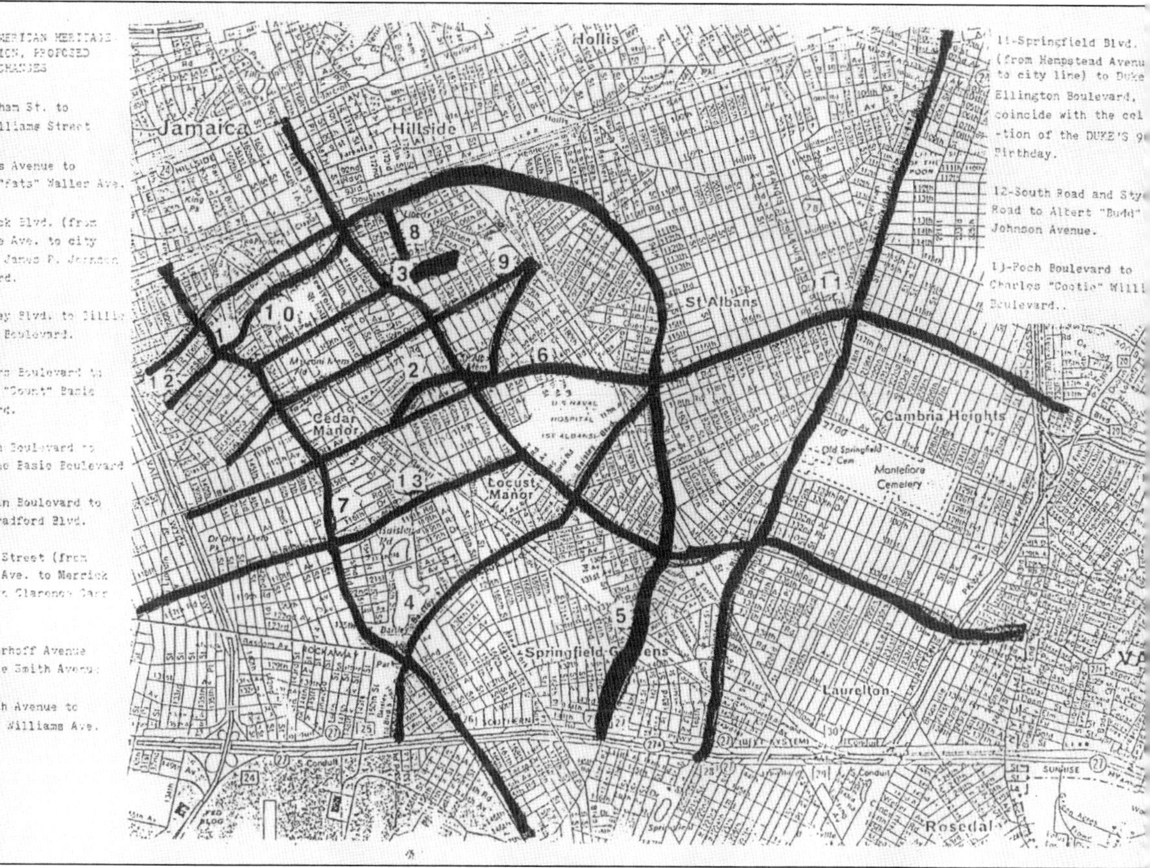

Historian Clarence L. Irving Sr. (1924–2014) established the Black American Heritage Foundation. He also created a map for a Jazz Heritage Trail to highlight the Queens neighborhoods where entertainers lived. Irving wanted his Black American Music Project to obtain federal funding for a research center. In 1987, Irving also proposed street name changes to Community Board 12 in Queens that did not come to fruition. He suggested that Waltham Street be changed to Fess Williams Street, Sayres Avenue to Thomas "Fats" Waller Avenue, Baisley Boulevard to Billie Holiday Boulevard, Farmers Boulevard to Willliam "Count" Basie Boulevard, Linden Boulevard to Catherine Basie Boulevard, Sutphin Boulevard to Perry Bradford Boulevard, 171st Street (from Liberty Avenue to Merrick Boulevard) to Clarence Carr Street, Brinkerhoff Avenue to Bessie Smith Avenue, 108th Avenue (from Merrick Boulevard to 175th Street) to Clarence Williams Avenue, and Foch Boulevard to Charles "Cootie" Williams Boulevard. Irving, however, successfully convinced US Post Office officials to honor highly successful African Americans with celebratory postage stamps. Over the years, stamps in the Black Heritage series have honored former St. Albans residents Count Basie, W.E.B. Du Bois, Ella Fitzgerald, Lena Horne, Jackie Robinson, and Roy Wilkins. (Courtesy of Lillie B. Crowder.)

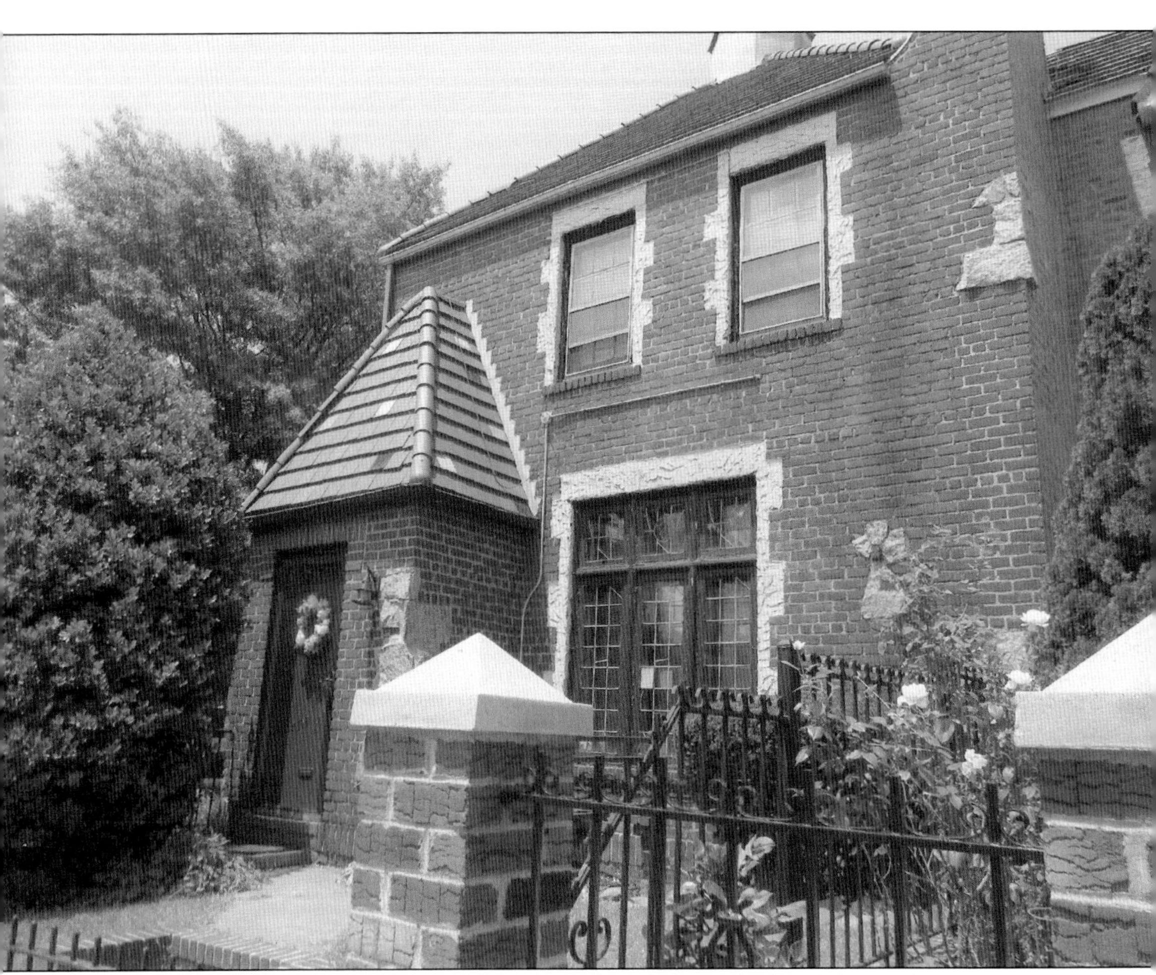

Seen here is the former home of Westervelt Taylor, who was the first African American assistant district attorney in Queens County, in the late 1940s. Taylor lived on the opposite end of Sayres Avenue from musician Fats Waller. (Photograph by Blair Garrett.)

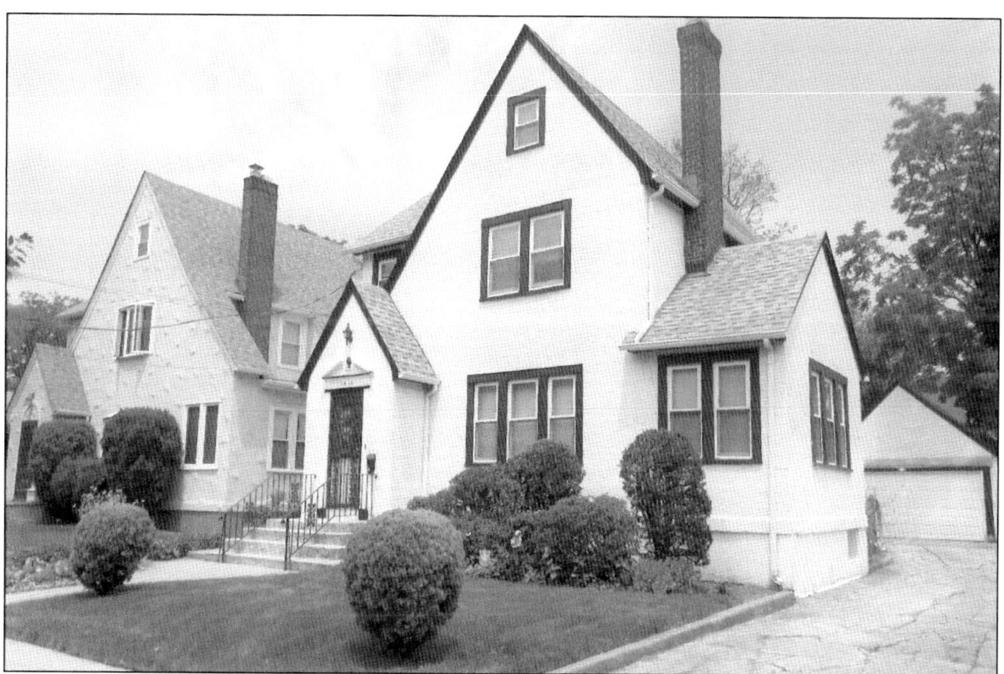

Business leader, civil rights attorney, and politician Percy Ellis Sutton (1920–2009) and his wife, Leatrice (1925–2017), raised their family in this Addisleigh Park home in the 1950s. The Suttons later moved to Manhattan when Percy became Manhattan borough president from 1966 to 1977. He and former St. Albans resident and veteran broadcaster Harold "Hal" Jackson co-founded the Inner City Broadcasting Corporation. The company acquired radio stations in several markets, including WLIB-AM, New York's first African American owned and operated radio station, and WBLS-FM. (Photograph by Blair Garrett.)

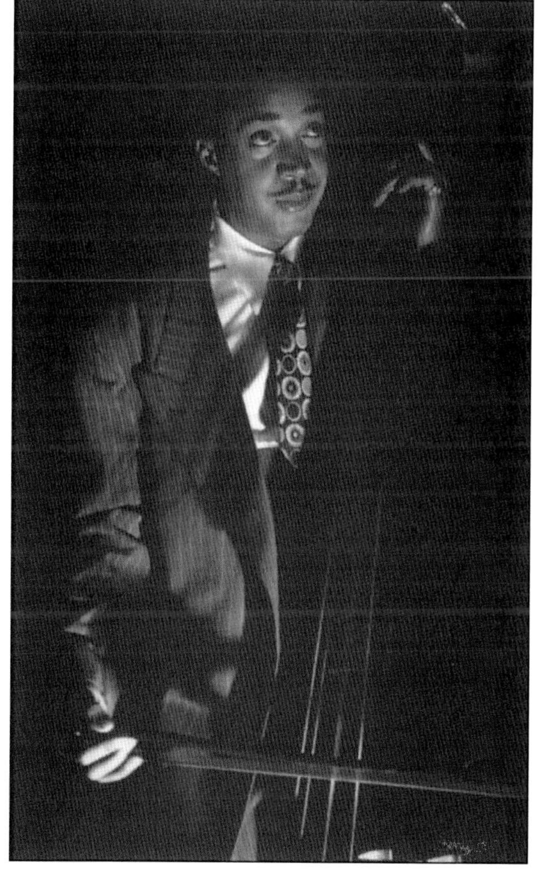

Jazz and classical double bassist Leroy Eliot "Slam" Stewart (1914–1987) lived in Addisleigh Park at 114-28 180th St. His nickname came from the way he slapped his instrument when he played. Stewart was known for singing with his solos. He co-wrote the 1938 hit song "Flat Foot Floogie." Stewart attended the Boston Conservatory and later taught at SUNY Binghamton and Yale University. (Photograph by William Gottlieb, courtesy of the Library of Congress.)

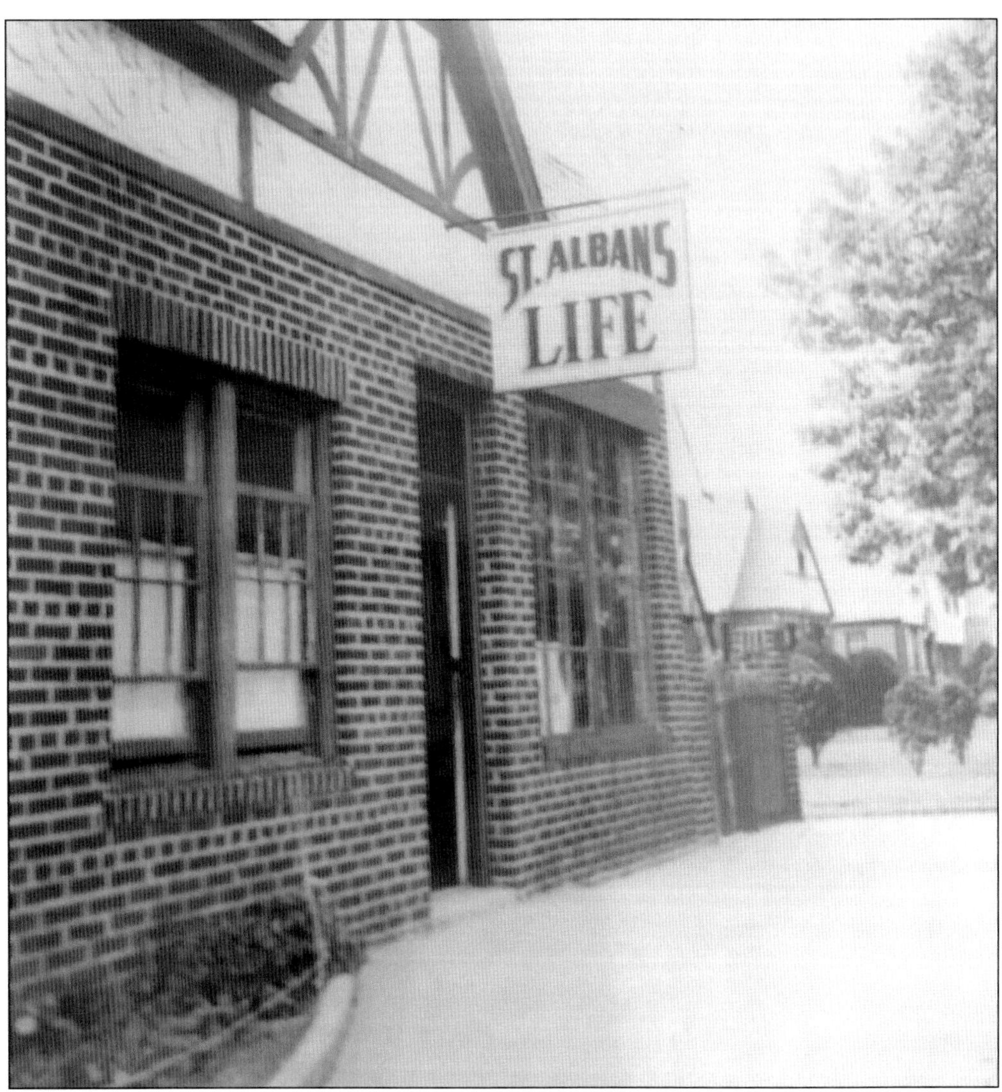

When St. Albans residents wanted to know the latest news around town, many turned to their local newspaper, *St. Albans Life*. From 1946 to 1952, the weekly periodical published by Roger Roddy Sr. featured news about crime, courts, and civic and social activities. The paper was published first out of Roddy's St. Albans home and later in a storefront on Linden Boulevard. It appealed to local business owners who wanted patrons from the targeted communities of St. Albans, Cambria Heights, and Hollis. At the time, shoppers knew spending their dollars within their immediate community would benefit everyone. Prior to becoming a publisher, Roddy worked as a reporter for the *Greenpoint Weekly Star* in Brooklyn and was a crime reporter for the *Journal American* in Manhattan. (Courtesy of Linda Roddy Leavy.)

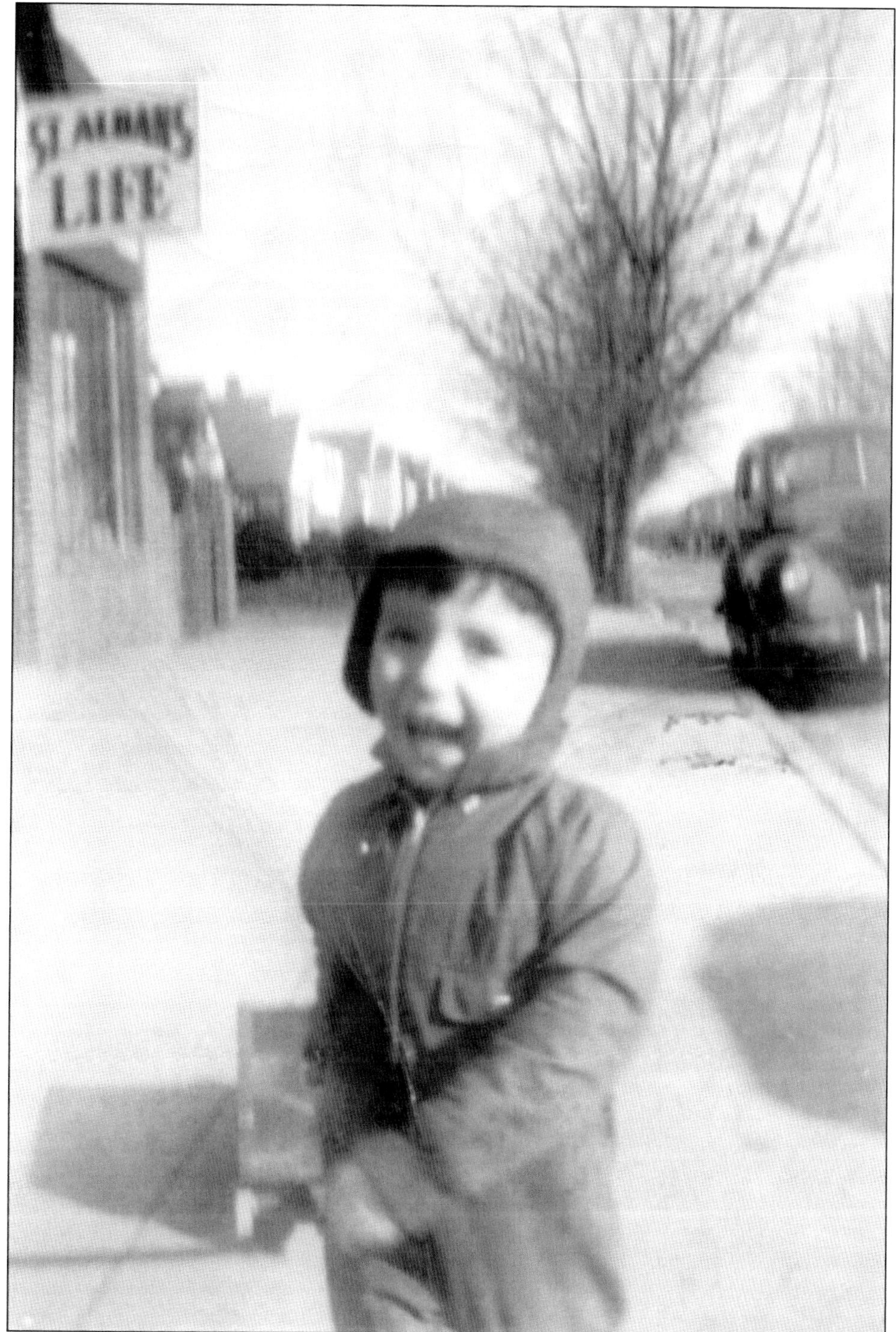

Roger Roddy Jr. plays newsboy in a 1946 photograph taken outside of the newspaper's office. Roddy often put his children to work, his daughter Linda Roddy Leavy recalled. *St. Albans Life* appeared as the area's demographics were changing. Roddy fought to put out a local newspaper that interested all readers. (Courtesy of Linda Roddy Leavy.)

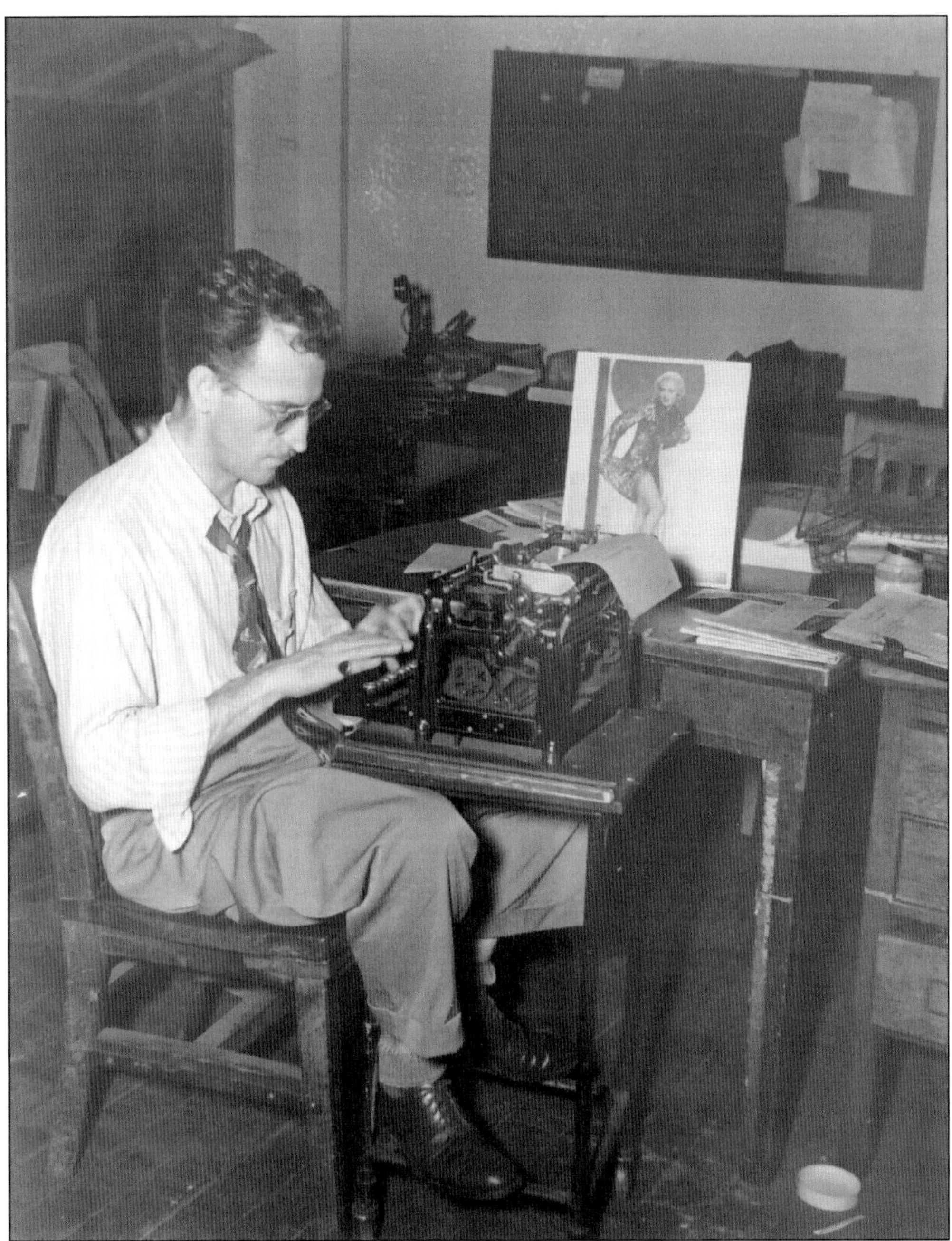

Roger Roddy Sr. is pictured inside *St. Alban's Life's* Linden Boulevard office. The periodical cost 5¢ a week and was full of advertisements from local restaurants, clothing stores, meat shops, and insurance companies—all seeking to tap into veterans returning home from the war and first-time homebuyers. Subscribers picked up the paper to see what double features were playing in the neighborhood's two cinemas: St. Albans Theatre on Linden Boulevard and the Linden Theatre on Merrick Boulevard. (Courtesy of Linda Roddy Leavy.)

Roger Roddy Sr. and his wife, Virginia, hold their first daughter, Linda, in front of their St. Albans home. Roddy published *St. Alban's Life* from 1946 until 1952, when it was sold to a new owner who ceased publication nearly a year later. The Roddys lived in Addisleigh Park from 1939 until 1942. The couple, who later had three more children, moved to 115-35 224th St., an address that was considered to be in St. Albans at that time. (Courtesy of Linda Roddy Leavy.)

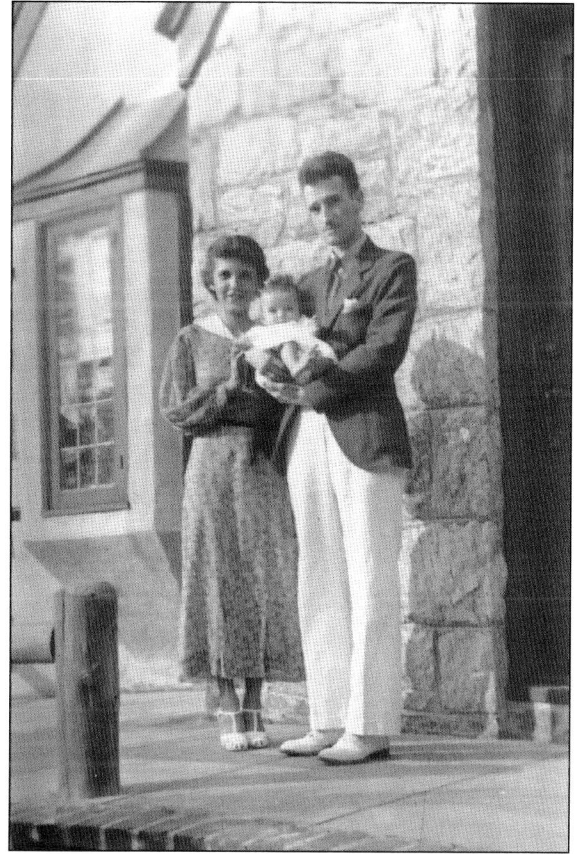

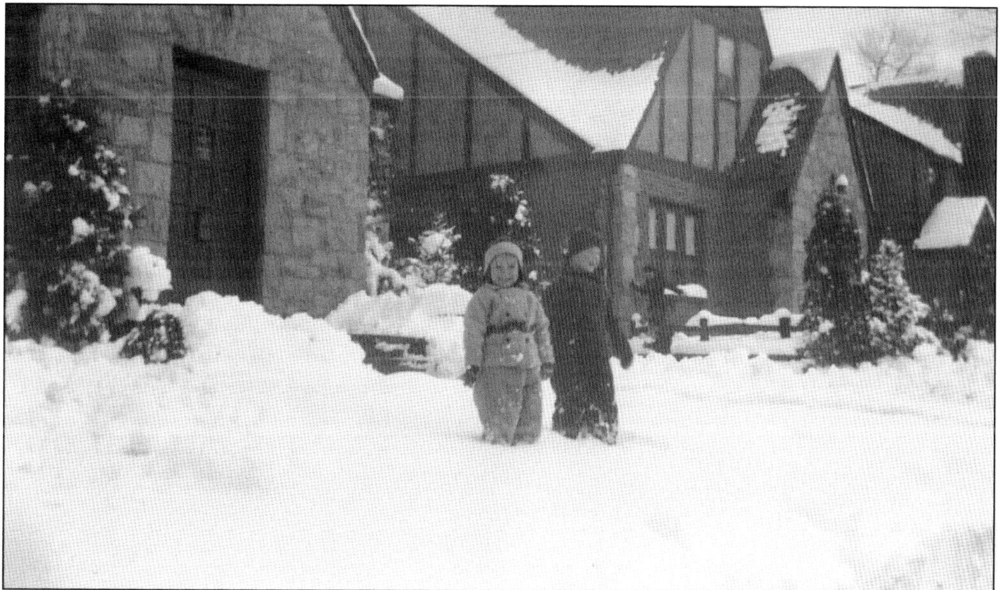

Linda Roddy examines the snow that accumulated in front of her home with her cousin Steve DeBrock. The children were delighted to make snowballs and play with friends after the snowstorm. (Courtesy of Linda Roddy Leavy.)

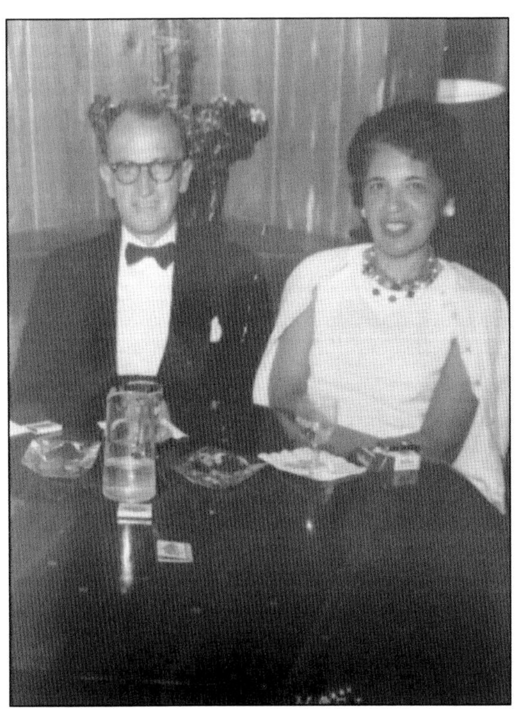

Roger and Virginia Roddy are pictured at a 1950s society event. When *St. Albans Life* ceased publication in 1952, Roddy worked as vice president for the Grolier Society in Manhattan. In 1963, the Roddys became co-publishers of the *Nassau Pennysaver*, a publication that advertised businesses and events on Long Island. Roger Roddy died in 1972 and Virginia Roddy died in 2005. (Courtesy of Linda Roddy Leavy.)

This is a 1932 confirmation class at Trinity Lutheran Church on Baisley Boulevard. The church was among several houses of worship that served St. Albans. (Photograph by Eugene Weber.)

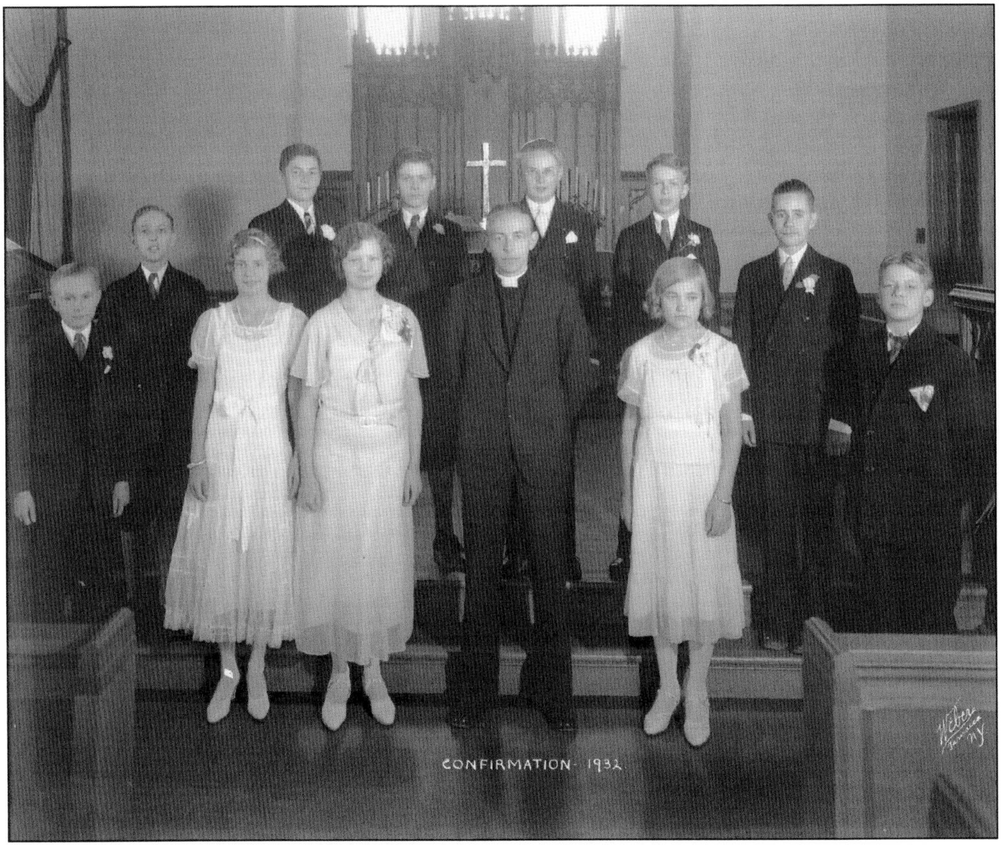

The Rev. Francis D. Wallace, pictured in 1937, led the Presbyterian Church of St. Albans as the neighborhood became more integrated with African Americans. Many credit Wallace with creating religious and social programs that welcomed newcomers to the church and neighborhood. (Courtesy of the Presbyterian Church of St. Albans.)

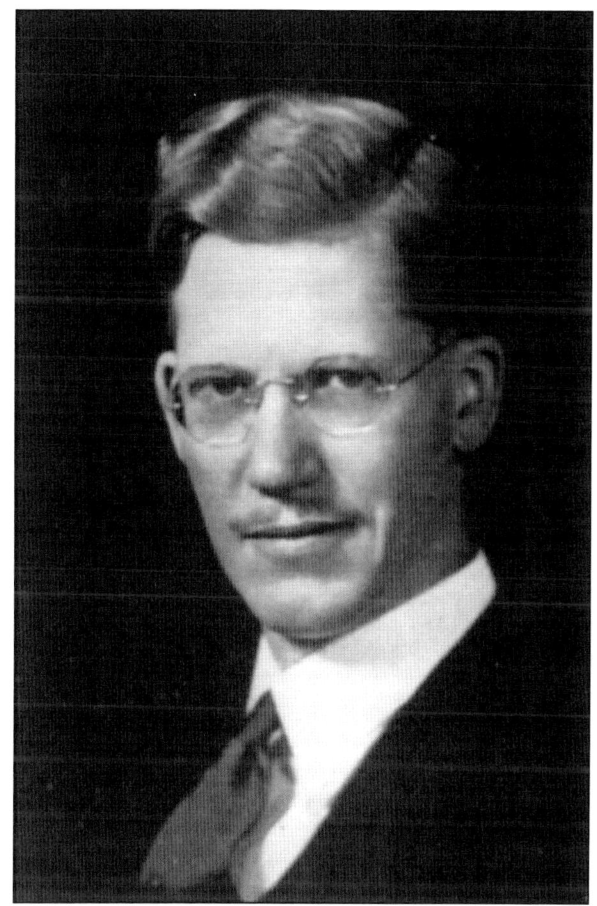

This postcard shows Irving Avenue. Note that no cars are visible on the street, and there are no fences in front of the attached English Tudors. (Courtesy of Bob Stonehill.)

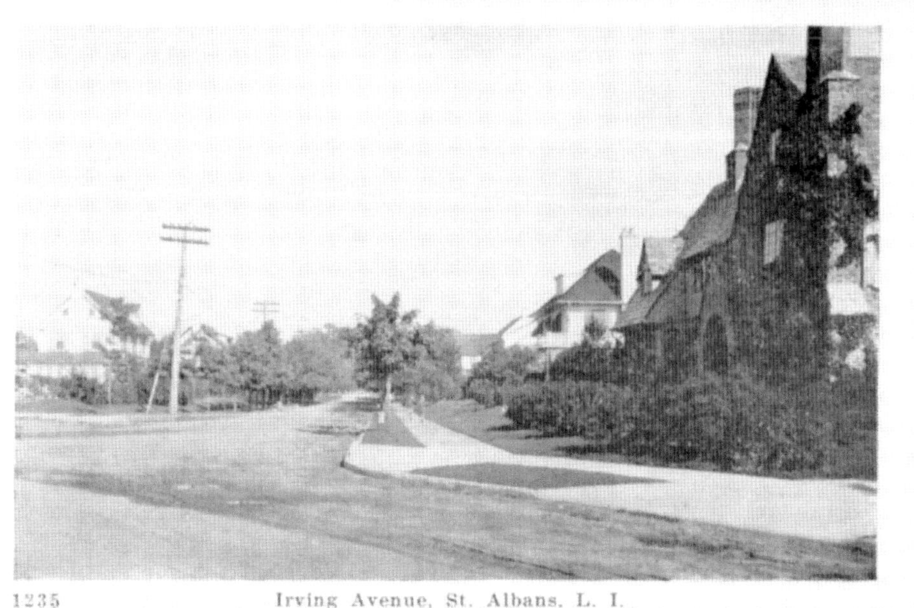

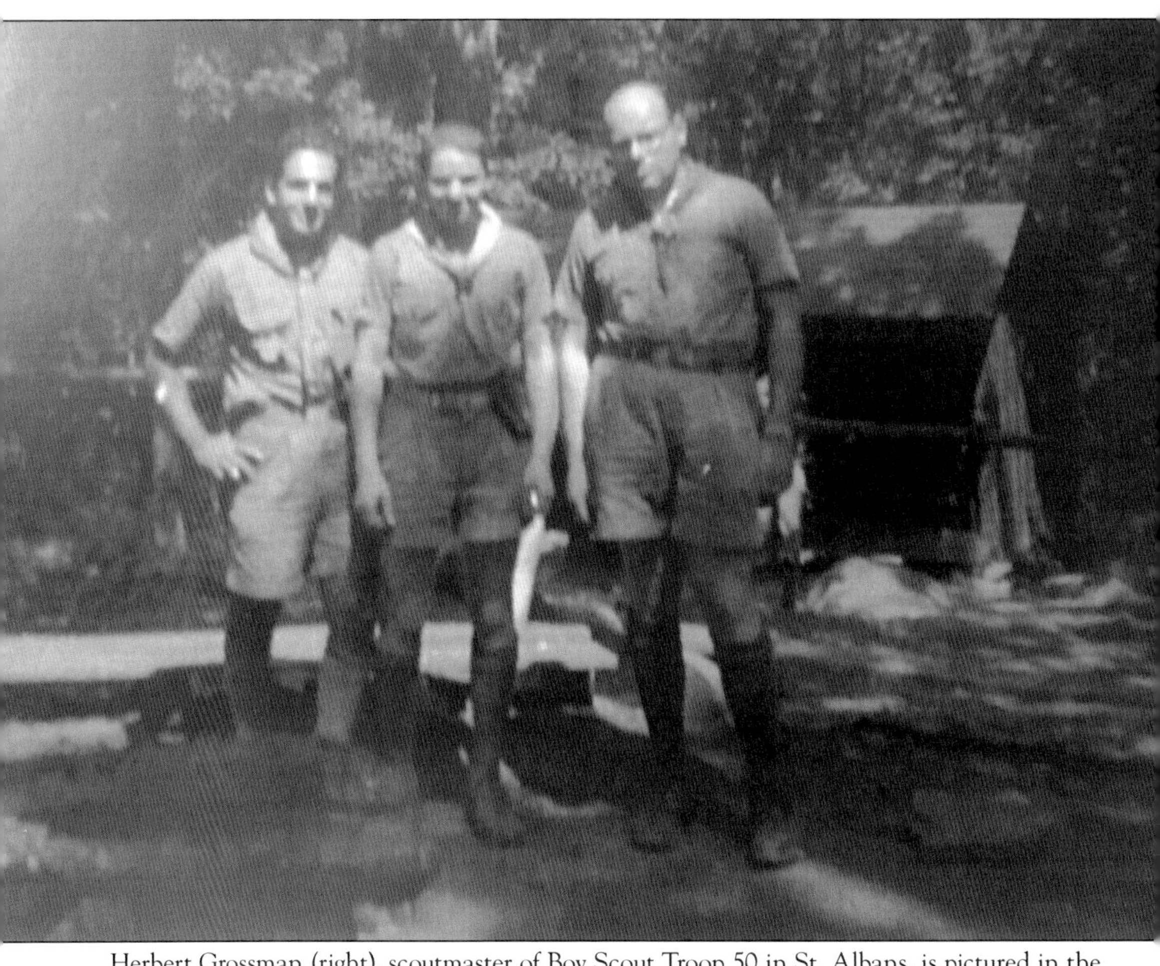

Herbert Grossman (right), scoutmaster of Boy Scout Troop 50 in St. Albans, is pictured in the 1950s with two scouts at Ten Mile River Boy Scout Camp in upstate New York. The group met at the Beth Israel Jewish Center on Farmers Boulevard. Pictured with Grossman are scouts George Wolfoff (left), senior patrol leader, and Ronald Katz. (Courtesy of Karl Grossman.)

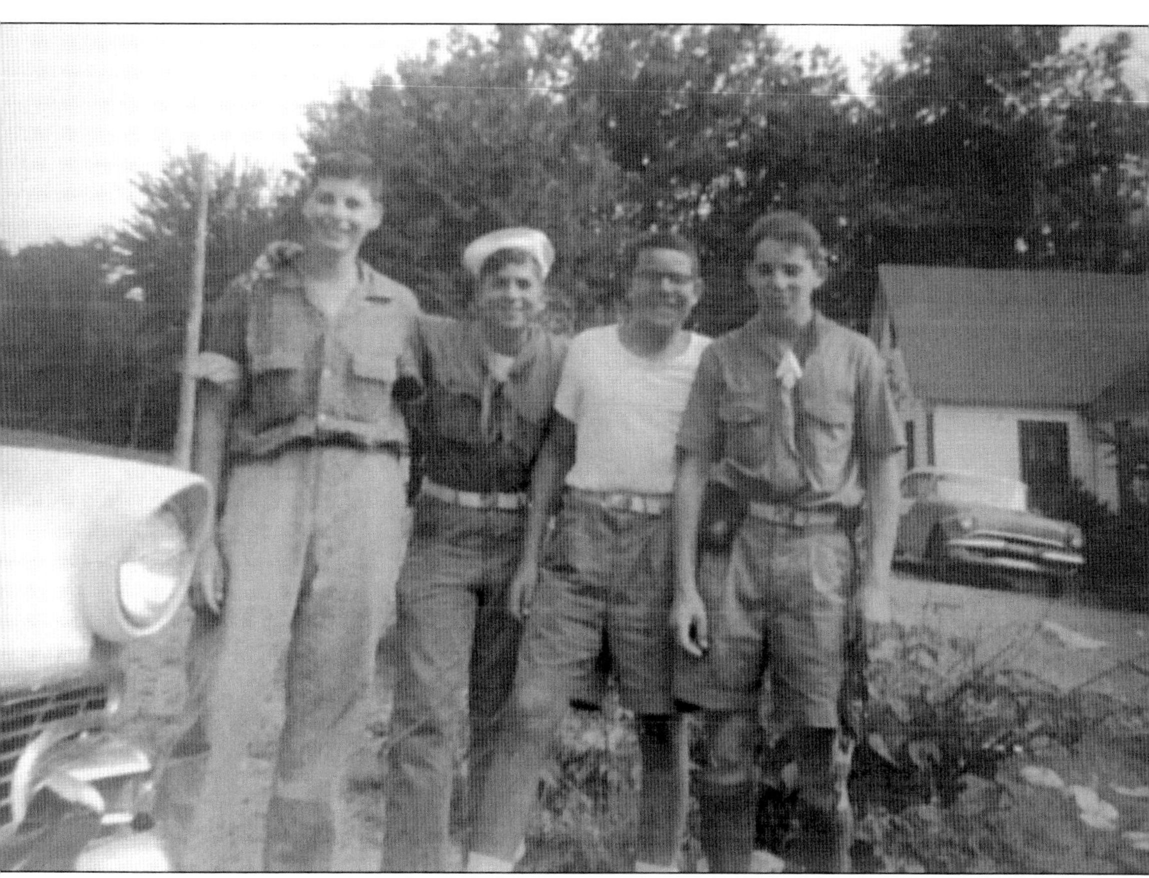

Boy Scouts with Troop 50 are seen at an upstate fishing retreat in 1955. From left to right are Sander Kirsch, "Flip" Diamond, Karl Grossman (Herbert Grossman's son), and Ronald Katz. Karl Grossman is a journalist who teaches undergraduate media classes at SUNY College at Old Westbury. He fondly recalls his old St. Albans neighborhood and reunites with his troop pals at least once a year. (Courtesy of Karl Grossman.)

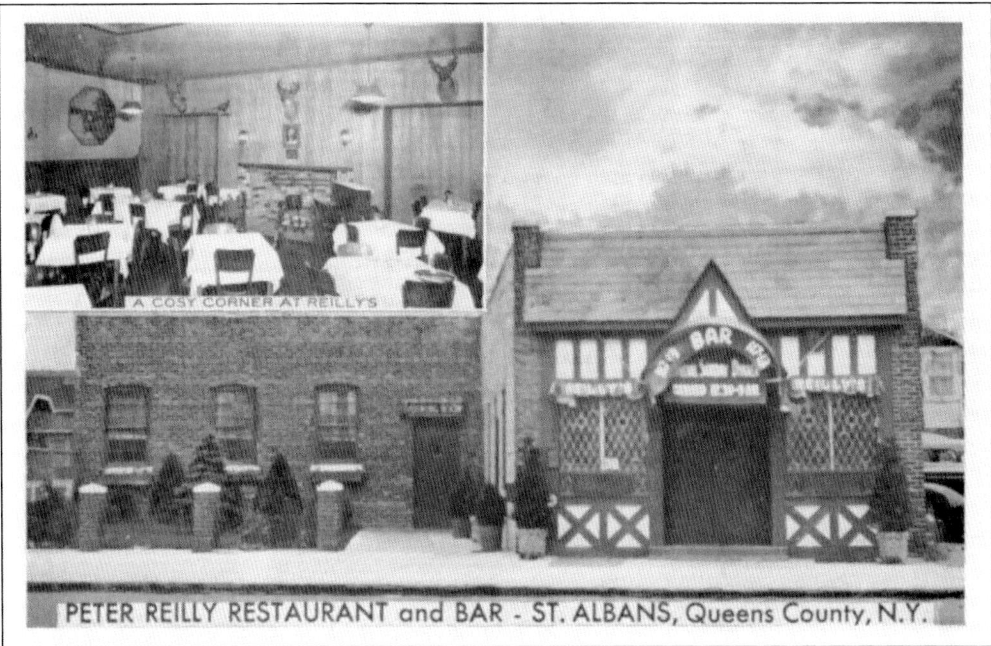

This postcard shows the fine dining enjoyed by patrons of Peter Reilly's Restaurant and Bar at 117-13 Farmers Boulevard in St. Albans. Without saying a word, the white tablecloths tell diners that a great experience awaits. A three-course daily luncheon cost 35¢, a seven-course regular dinner cost 65¢, and a seven-course Sunday dinner cost 75¢. (Courtesy of Bob Stonehill.)

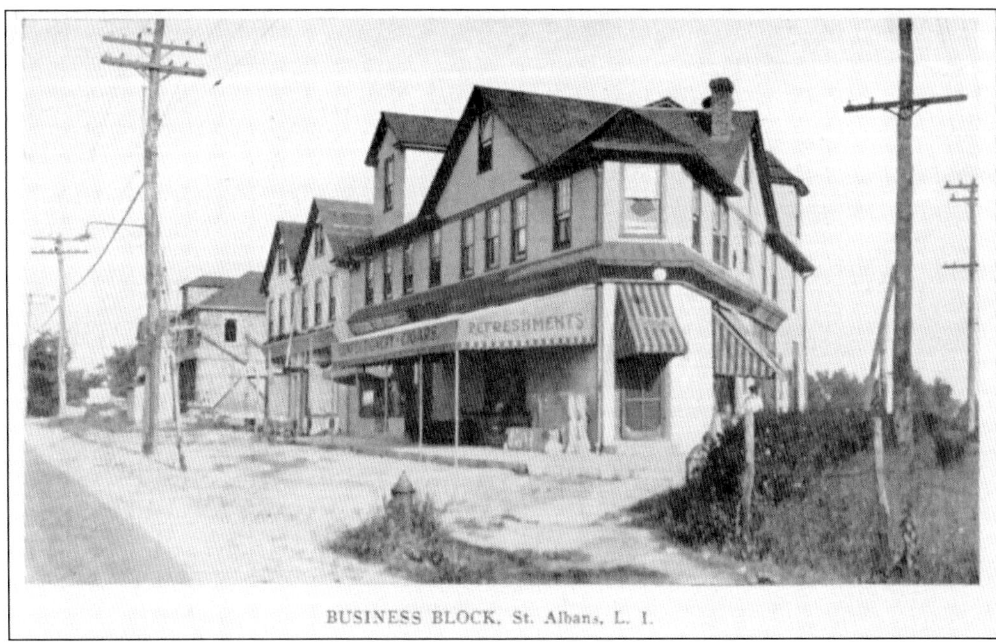

A Federal Food Stores location in St. Albans is pictured on this postcard. The awning advertises "confectionery," "cigars," "refreshments," and "soda." There is not much foot traffic in the area but during the housing boom that hit Queens in the 1920s and 1930s, shopkeepers saw an uptick in business. (Courtesy of Bob Stonehill.)

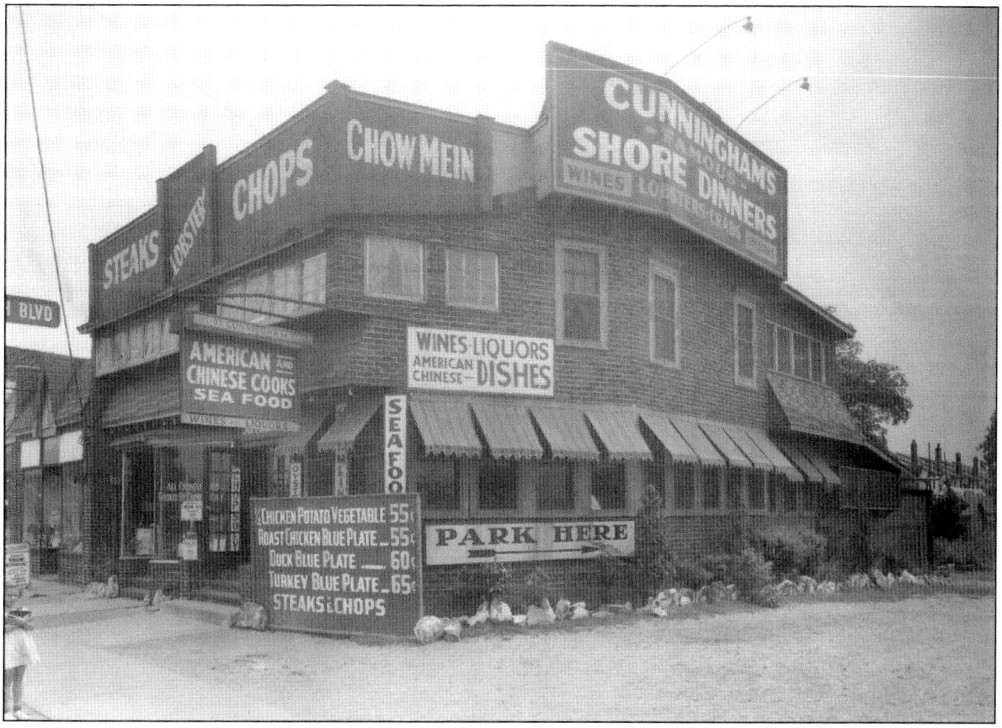

Cunningham's Famous Shore Dinners on Foch Boulevard offered American and Chinese food along with steaks and pork chops. One sign brags that the restaurant employed American and Chinese cooks, in case patrons wondered. (Courtesy of Queens Public Library archives.)

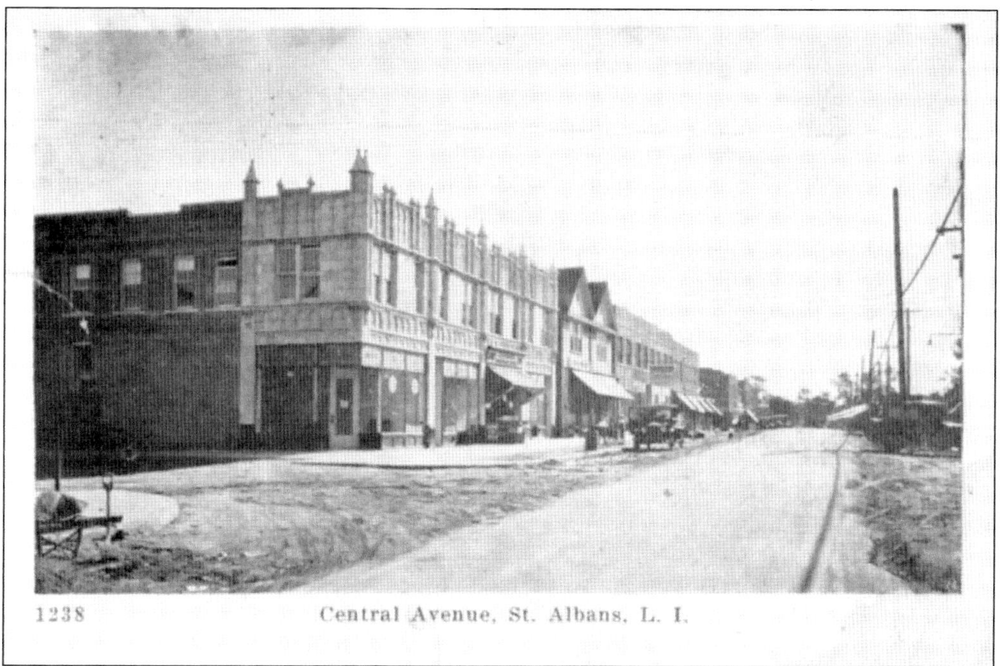

Central Avenue (now Linden Boulevard) is pictured on this postcard. The roadway looks unfinished on the opposite side of the street. (Courtesy of Bob Stonehill.)

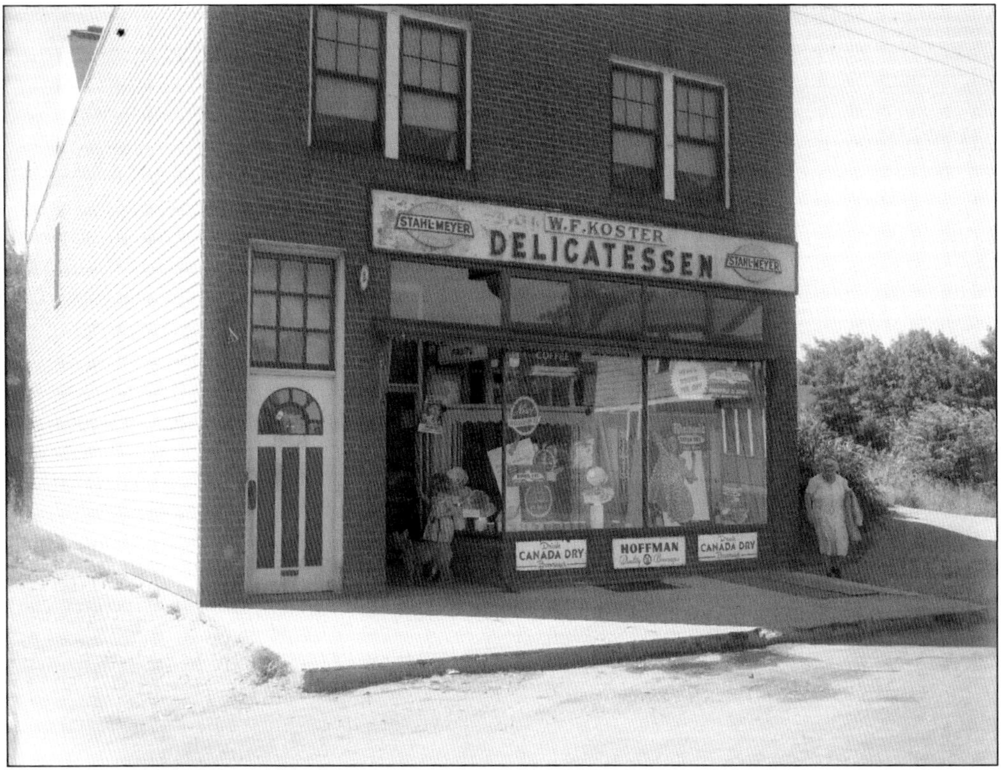

Many St. Albans residents depended on the small grocery stores in their neighborhood. Pictured here is the W.F. Koster Delicatessen. The window advertised Birds Eye vegetables, Rheingold beer, coffee, fruits, and other items. A little girl is attempting to bring her dog into the store. (Courtesy of Queens Public Library archives.)

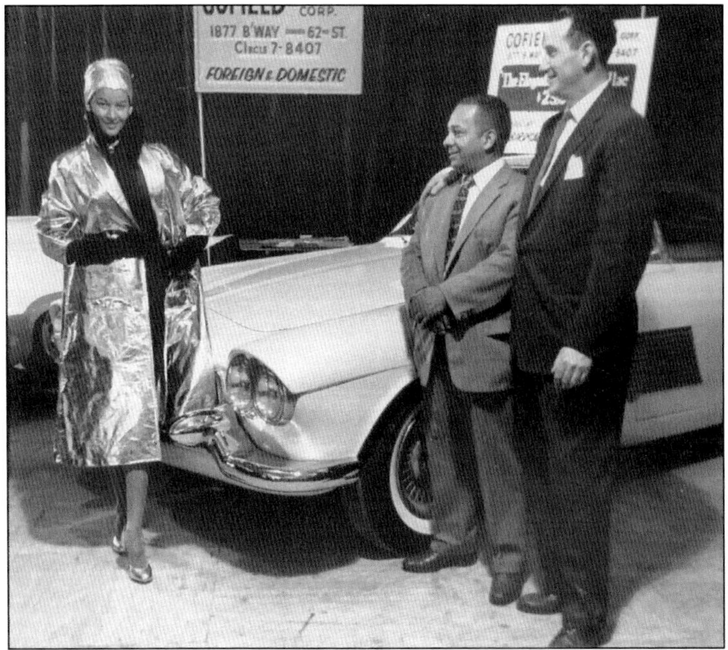

Addisleigh Park resident Thomas Cofield (center) is seen with an unidentified man and model at the Manhattan luxury car business he operated from the 1940s, Cofield Motor Corporation. This promotional photograph was used in an advertisement. (Courtesy of Brian McRae.)

Jacob "Jinx" Kaplan was co-owner of the famed Club Ruby nightclub on the corner of Baisley Boulevard and 120th Avenue. The popular jazz nightspot attracted integrated audiences and major artists such as Charles Mingus, Mercer Ellington, and John Coltrane. Catherine Basie and Mona Hinton visited frequently. The club opened in the early 1950s and closed in the mid-1960s after Kaplan was injured in a scuffle with an underage patron who struck him in the head with a bottle. Kaplan was a plasterer, and his other brothers were also in the construction trade. A younger brother, Ruebin "Ruby" Kaplan, was a co-owner. Club Ruby was originally an Irish bar named Club Fury. (Courtesy of Charles Kaplan.)

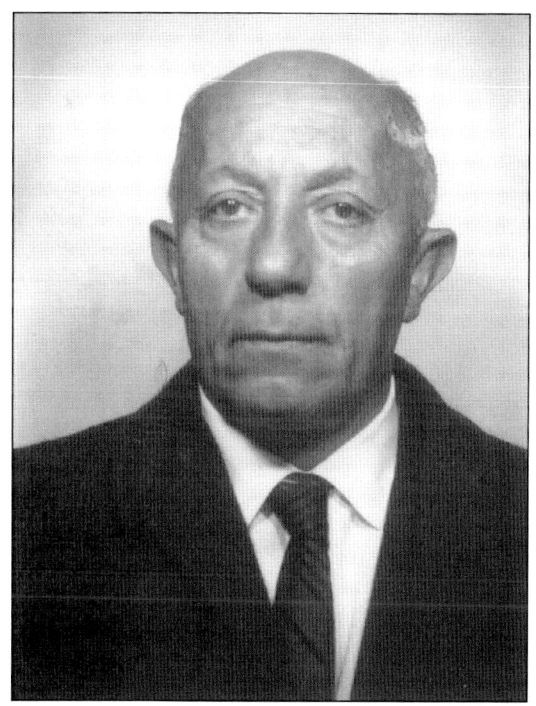

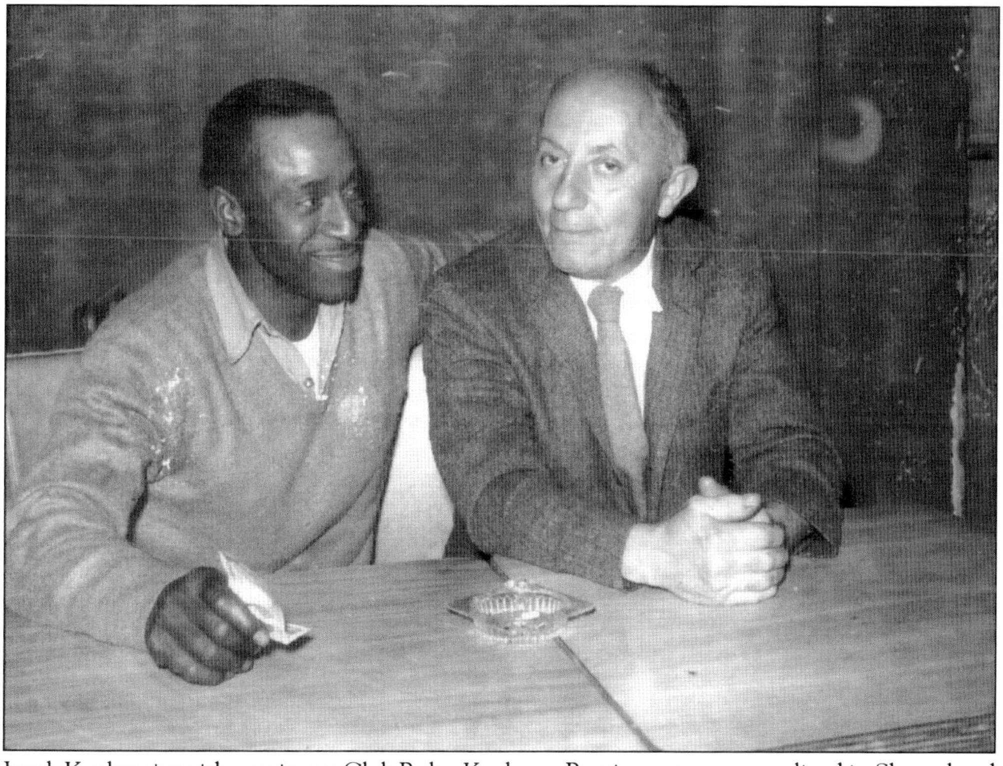

Jacob Kaplan sits with a waiter at Club Ruby. Kaplan, a Russian entrepreneur, lived in Sheepshead Bay, Brooklyn, and did not mind the commute because he liked to please his customers, according to his son Charles Kaplan. (Courtesy of Charles Kaplan.)

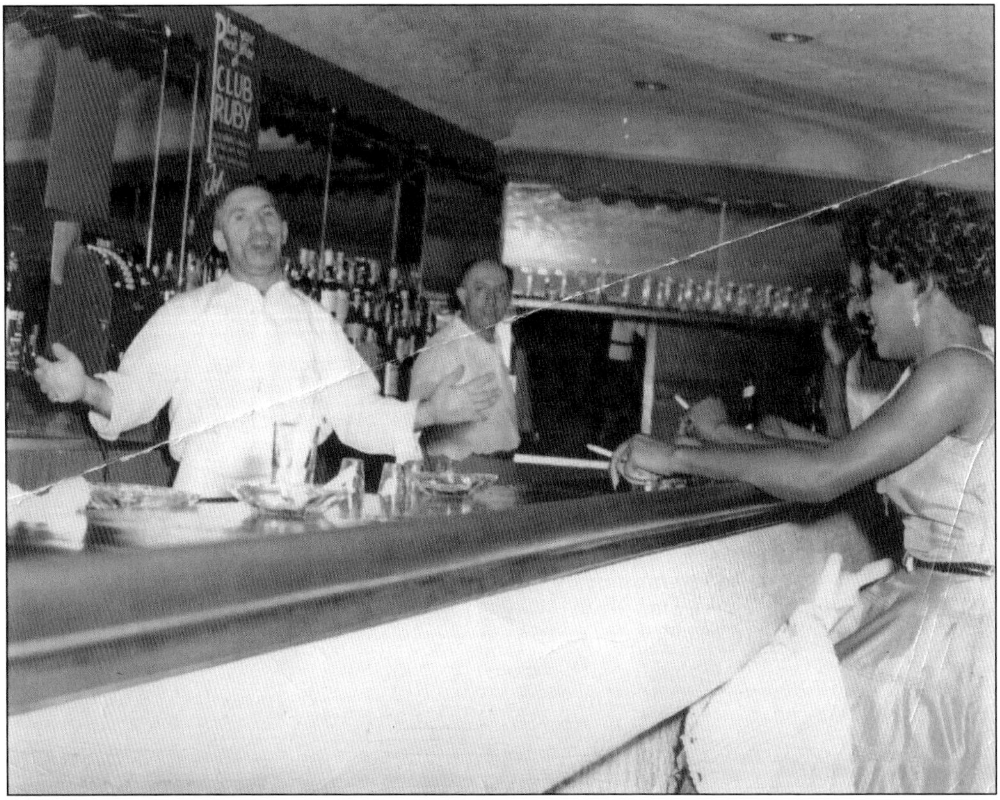

The Kaplan brothers are at work behind the bar at Club Ruby. Ruby Kaplan loved to sing and entertain customers, recalled his nephew Charles Kaplan. The club held at least 200 patrons. (Courtesy of Charles Kaplan.)

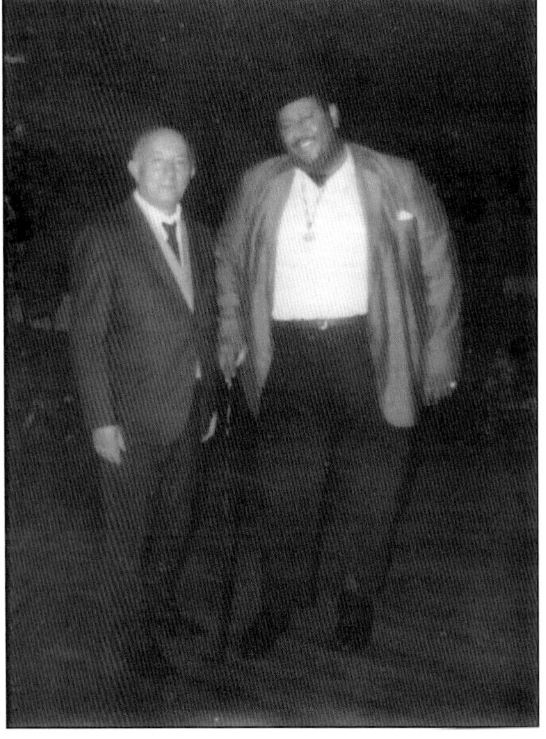

Jinx Kaplan is seen here with "Tiny," one of the security guards hired at Club Ruby over the years to keep order. (Courtesy of Charles Kaplan.)

Pictured is a May 1966 flyer for a Club Ruby performance that featured jazz trumpeter Freddie Hubbard and several other musicians. The club, located at 175-02 Baisley Boulevard, attracted major artists along with up-and-coming talent. (Author's collection.)

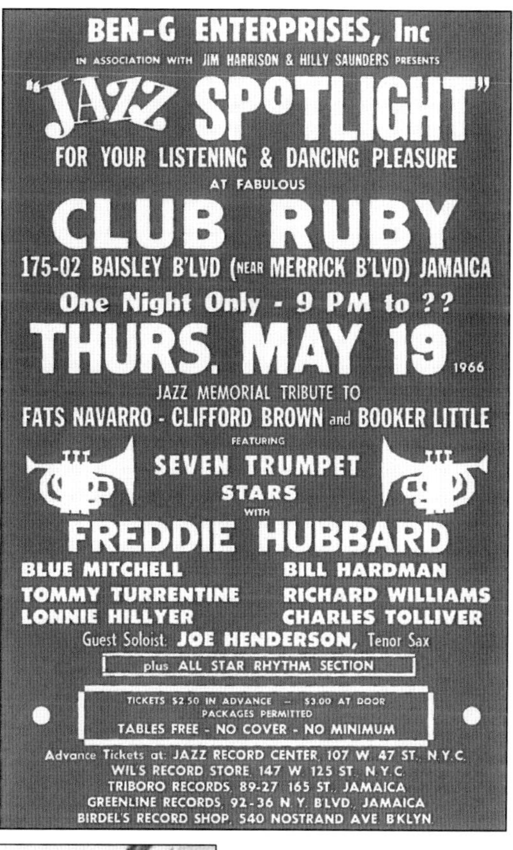

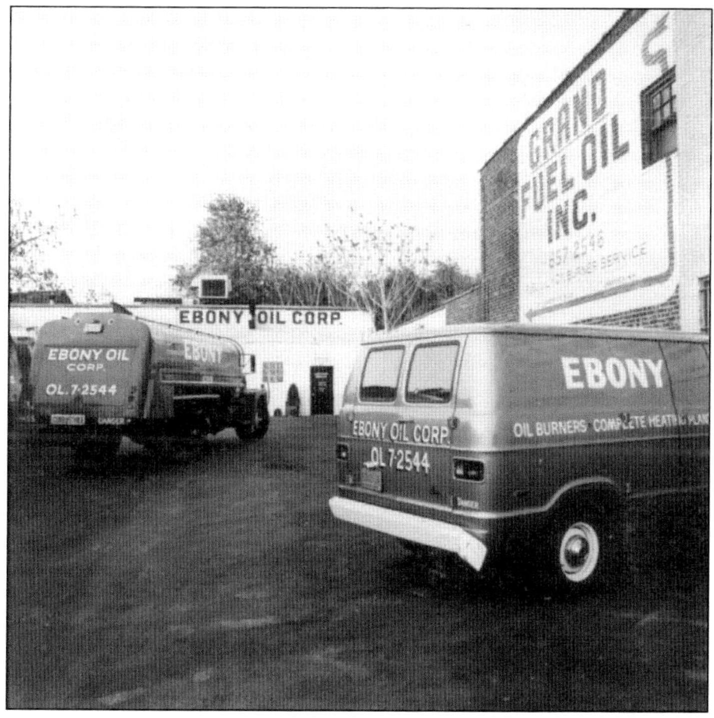

Ebony Oil Corporation was a Jamaica business in the 1950s and 1960s that was owned by long-time St. Albans resident Lawrence Cormier. The African American–operated energy enterprise served customers throughout Queens who needed oil to heat their homes. Singer Ella Fitzgerald was a client, along with other Addisleigh Park and St. Albans residents. (Courtesy of Lawrence Cormier.)

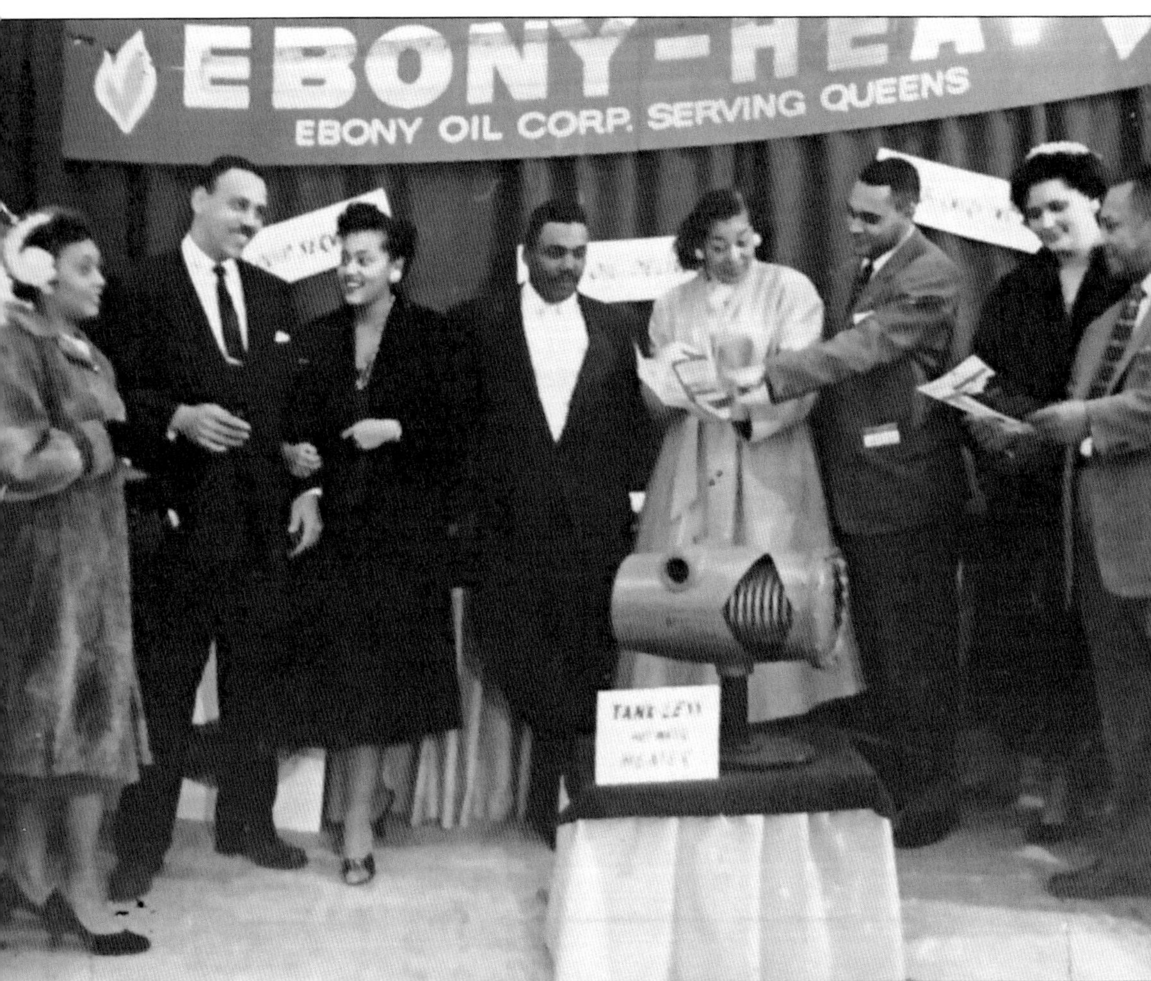

This photograph was taken during a celebratory event for the principals of Ebony Oil. Lawrence Cormier stands at left wearing a black suit. He went on to buy out his partners and continued the business on his own for several years. (Courtesy of Lawrence Cormier.)

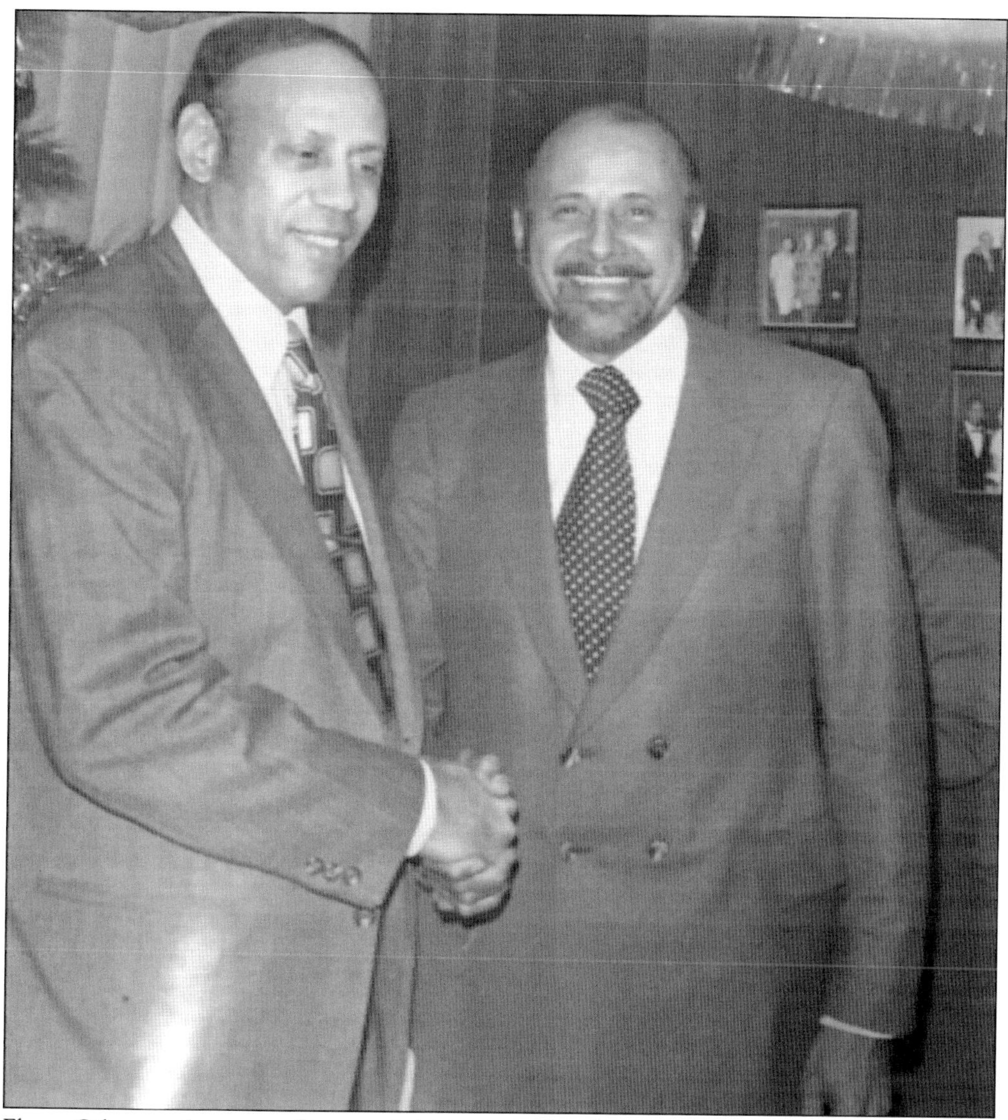

Ebony Oil owner Lawrence Cormier (left) is pictured with attorney and politician Percy Sutton. An Addisleigh Park resident, Sutton was among many southeast Queens residents who supported the black-owned heating oil company. (Courtesy of Lawrence Cormier.)

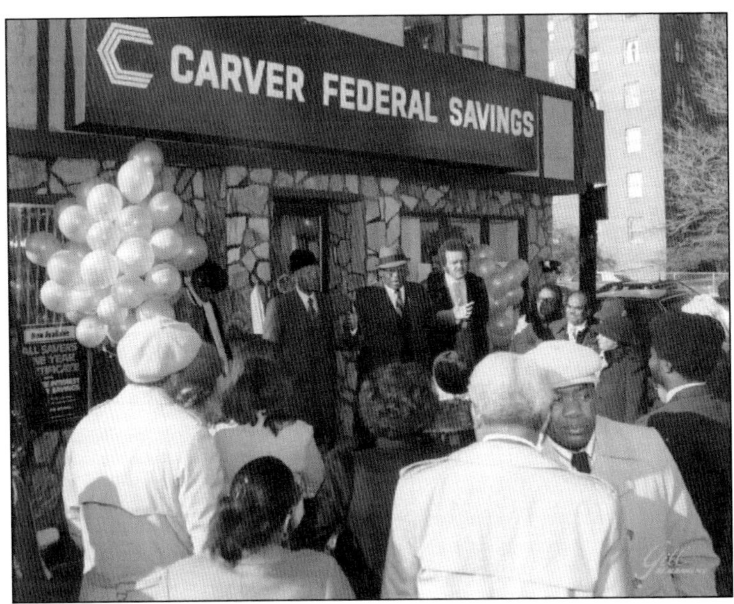

In December 1981, southeast Queens residents rejoiced at the grand opening of the Carver Federal Savings St. Albans branch on Merrick Boulevard. Facing the crowd from left to right are Carver president Richard Greene, unidentified, and civil rights activist and minister Rev. Timothy Mitchell. (Courtesy of Carver Federal Savings.)

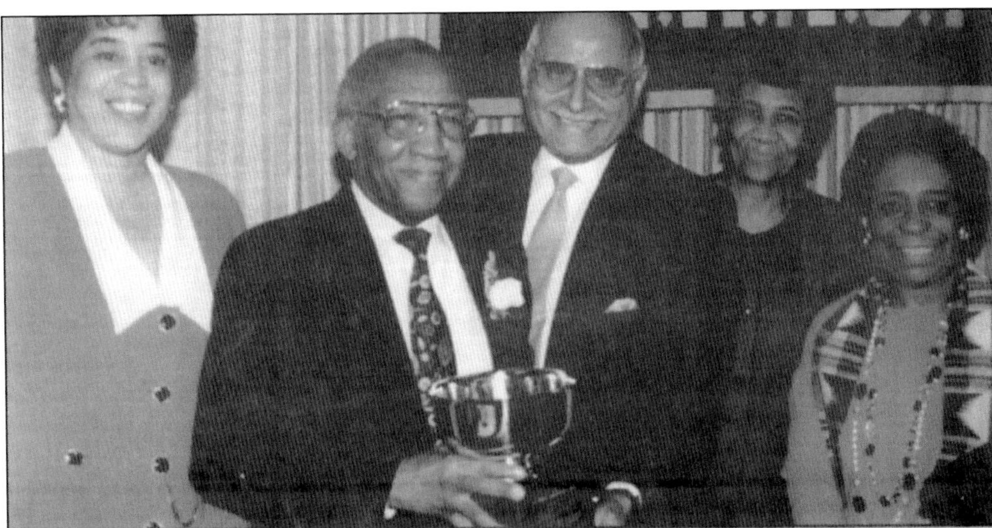

HUMANITARIAN AWARD: Richard T. Greene, president and director of Carver Federal Savings & Loan Association, (2nd l) is presented the Roy Wilkins Humanitarian Award by Percy Sutton, chairman emeritus of Inner City Broadcasting Co. , during the NAACP 14th Annual Awards program Wednesday at the Sheraton New York Hotel in New York City. Flanking them are Laura D. Blackburne, Esq., N.Y. State NAACP counsel (l) and Hazel N. Dukes, president of the N.Y. State Conference of NAACP Branches. See Related Photos, Pages 12-13 (Photo: LEM PETERKIN)

In March 1994, Carver Federal Savings president Richard Greene receives a humanitarian award from Inner City Broadcasting chairman emeritus Percy Sutton. Also pictured, from left to right, are Judge Laura Blackburne, a longtime St. Albans resident; Hazel Dukes, president of the New York State Conference of NAACP Branches; and unidentified. (Photograph by Lem Peterkin, courtesy of Carver Federal Savings.)

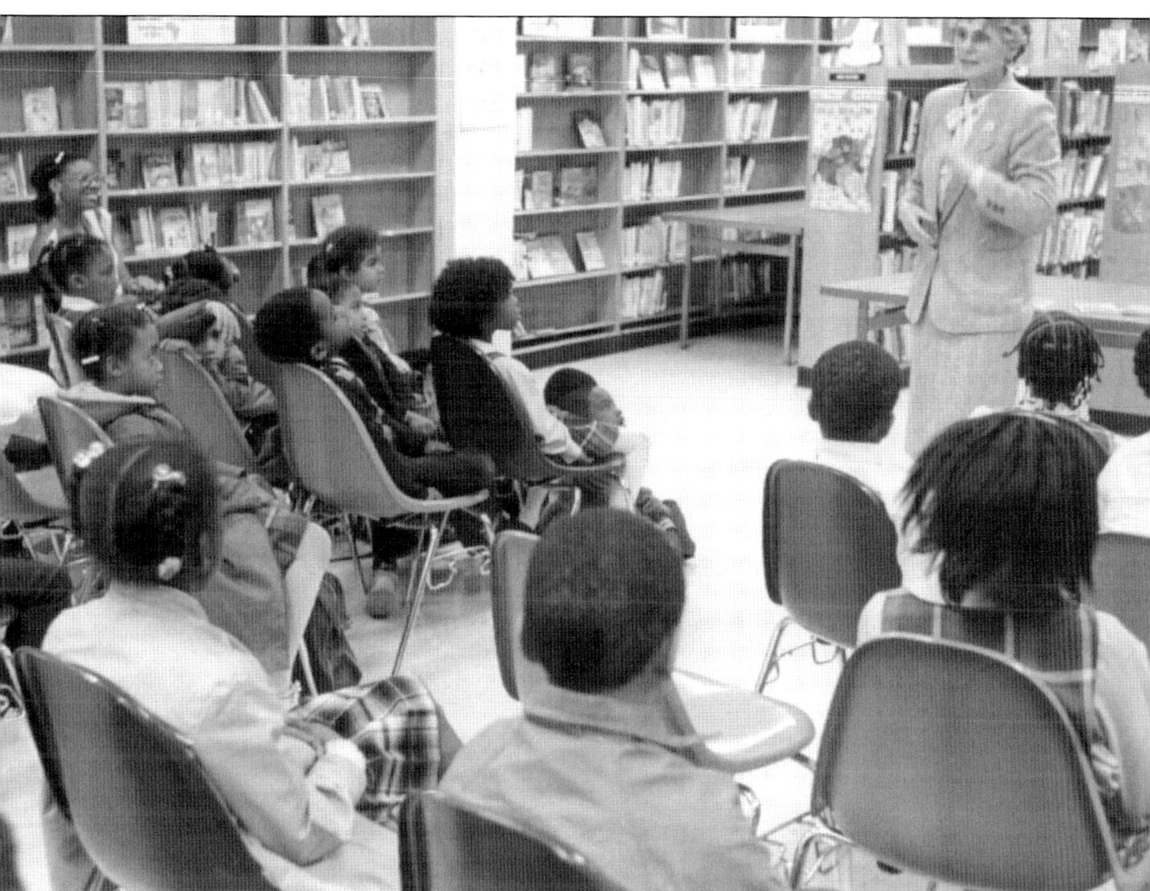

Students listen intently to a talk being by a librarian at the St. Albans branch of the Queens Public Library. The St. Albans branch opened in 1910 and became a full-service operation by 1932. The library's location along Linden Boulevard has changed over the years, but its customers' devotion to reading and learning has not dimmed. (Courtesy of Queens Public Library, St. Albans branch.)

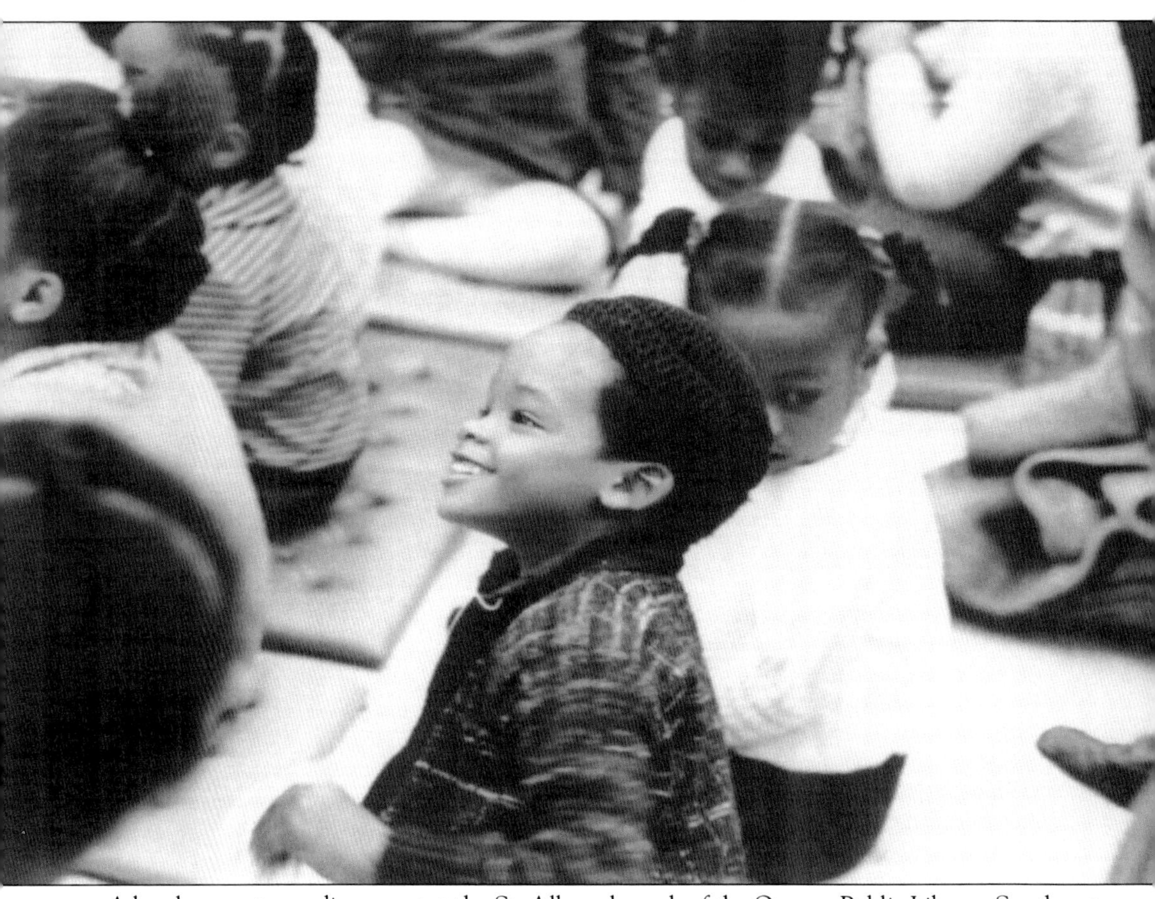

A boy beams at a reading event at the St. Albans branch of the Queens Public Library. Southeast Queens parents and their children depend on their local libraries to provide engaging education programs that encourage student success. (Courtesy of Queens Public Library, St. Albans branch.)

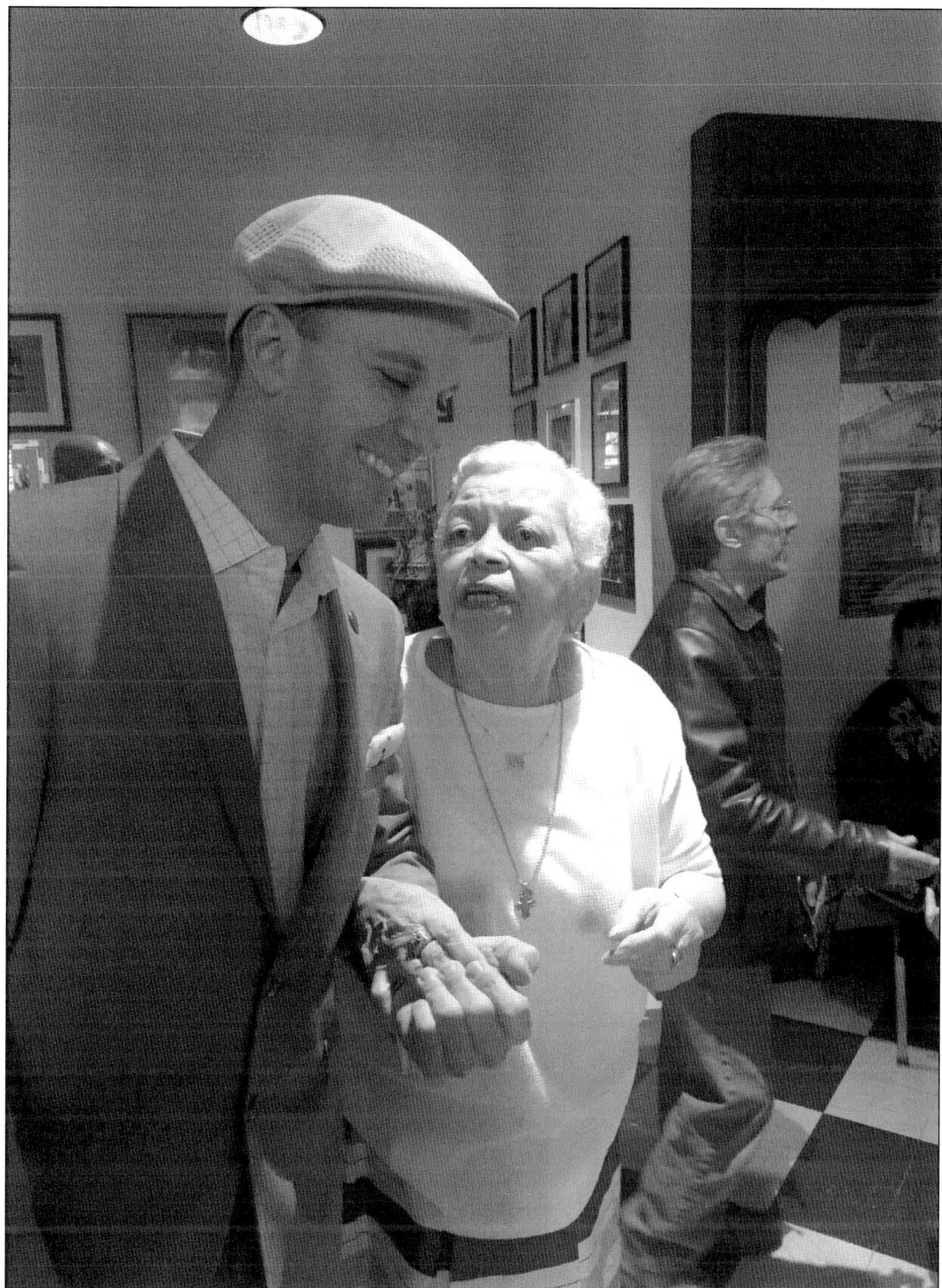

In June 2017, Jean Prysock and Dr. Thomas Manuel, curator and owner of the Jazz Loft in Stony Brook, celebrate her 90th birthday. Prysock is a supporter of the Long Island establishment that educates students and the public about jazz music and its historical significance. (Photograph by Blair Garrett.)

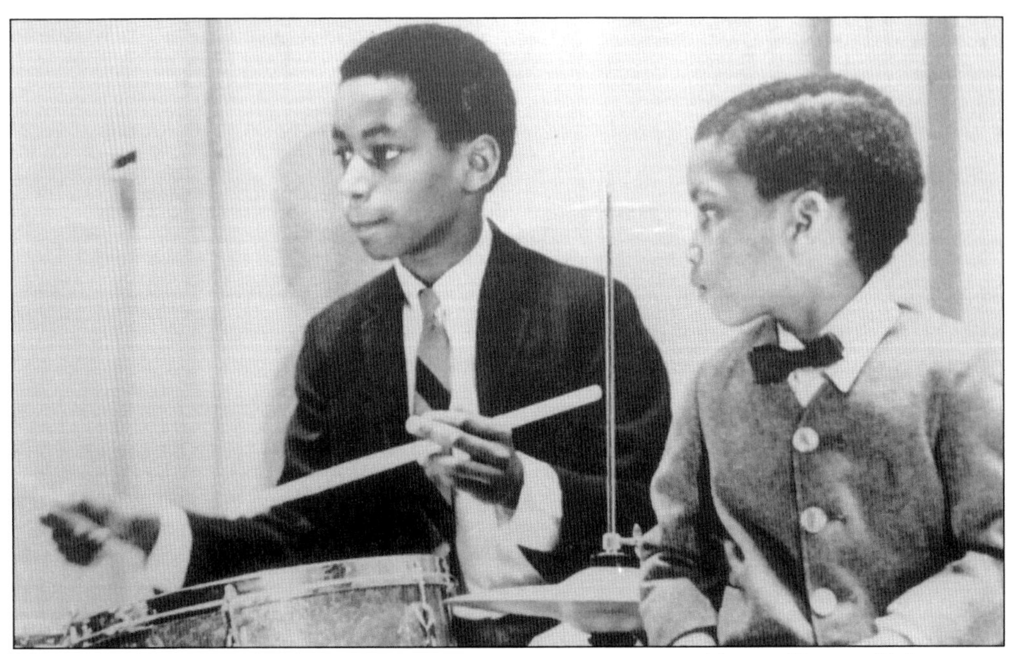

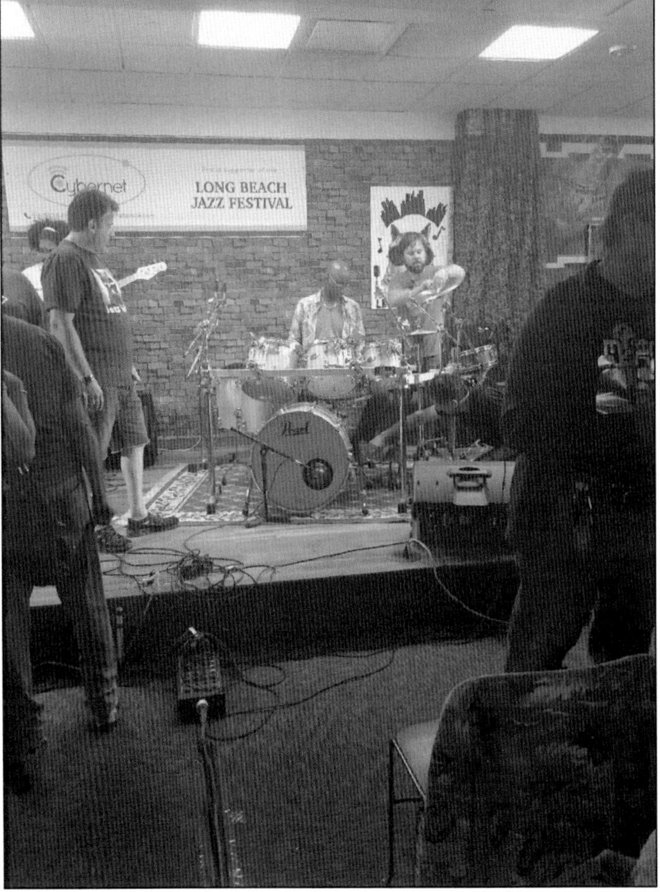

Above, 10-year-old drummer Omar Hakim performs his first gig at a talent show at Junior High School 8 in Jamaica in 1969. Hakim grew up in St. Albans and continued his music career playing with David Bowie, Mariah Carey, Miles Davis, Celine Dion, Dire Straits, George Benson, Journey, and many more. At left, Hakim warms up to thrill jazz and fusion fans at the September 2017 Long Beach Jazz Festival in New York. The group, the World of Oz, featured Hakim and his talented wife, pianist Rachel Z. Hakim. Omar's father, Hasan Hakim, was a trombonist with Count Basie and Duke Ellington's bands. (Both, courtesy of Omar Hakim and Claire Serant.)

Four

Black Spectrum Theatre Company

For 50 years, Black Spectrum Theatre Company has captured artistic imagination and tapped into the social consciousness of art enthusiasts in St. Albans and beyond. Numerous budding thespians, musicians, and dancers, along with playwright and production crew aspirants, started their careers under the direction of Black Spectrum's founder and executive producer Carl Clay. The theater is housed in a 50,000-square-foot complex in Roy Wilkins Park near Baisley Boulevard at 177th Street.

Black Spectrum produces professional theater performances and brings jazz concerts, comedy shows, and independent filmmaking to New Yorkers of all ages. The entertainment company has won 10 Audience Development Committee awards for excellence in African American theater. Community support for Clay's venture has been unwavering.

The theater company was a natural progression for Clay, who became interested in the arts in high school. Black Spectrum was established in 1970. The teenaged Clay managed to get his friends and other arts-loving peers to collaborate on shows. Black Spectrum's first home was a retail space on Linden Boulevard and 200th Street. The well-traveled commercial strip and Black Spectrum's curtain-free storefront meant curious would-be patrons and performers could view rehearsals and see Clay's vision.

In his 2009 book *Poor-ducing Theatre*, Clay recalled Black Spectrum's humble beginnings. "Our window, through which passersby could watch our renovation and rehearsals, would be our advertisement, an education on what Black Spectrum was about. The acting process fascinated most people. I knew it would help folks see us in action," Clay said. "As a result, some of our best recruits came to us just by allowing people to watch us."

Over the years, Black Spectrum helped launch the careers of several Queens residents, including Tichina Arnold formerly of the television show *Martin*, Deborah Burrell Cleveland from the hit Broadway play *Dreamgirls*, Ella Joyce of the television show *Roc*, Desiree Coleman Jackson of the long-running off-Broadway show *Mama, I Want to Sing*, and Shari Headley, who landed a lead role opposite comedian Eddie Murphy in the 1988 movie *Coming to America*.

Black Spectrum also attracted support from veteran performers. Actors Ruby Dee and her husband Ossie Davis, Tony-nominated actress Theresa Merritt, comedian Dick Gregory, singer Roberta Flack, actress Tonya Pinkins, and actor/director Melvin Van Peebles are among the celebrities who have spent time at Black Spectrum. Meanwhile, St. Albans residents such as composer and pianist Onaje Allan Gumbs, percussionist Steven Kroon, and saxophonist Jerome "Najee" Rasheed and Carl Bartlett of the Bartlett Contemporaries have all performed at Black Spectrum.

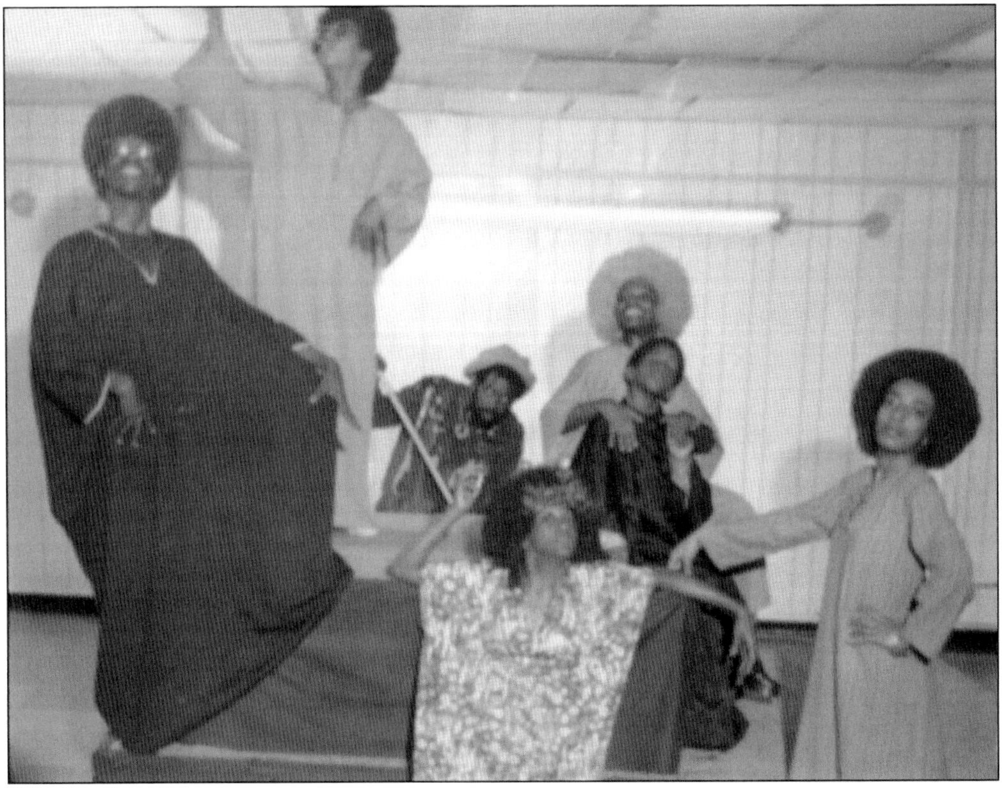

Seen here is the cast of *2000 Black*, one of Black Spectrum's early productions. The futuristic musical was a visionary tale of what life might be like in the year 2000. In the early 1970s, African Americans were never shown in movies depicting the future. Strangely, many of the play's predictions came to pass: a shortage of available men, fighting wars in Africa, and realizing that all African Americans are not required to think alike. While these notions today might seem quite simple, or even silly, in the early 1970s, they were quite real. The cast included, from left to right, Damani Henderson, Jeffrey Hood, Carl Clay, Pat Murphy, Romaine Martin, and Ty and Marjorie Lawrence. (Courtesy of Carl Clay.)

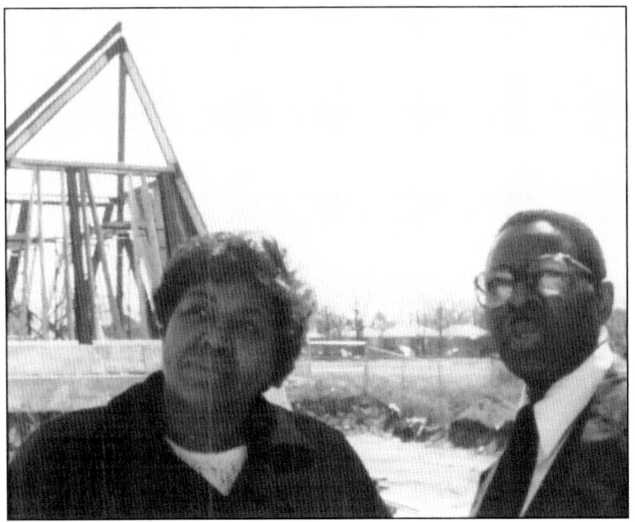

In 1985, Broadway star and Hollis resident Theresa Merritt Hines and her husband, Benjamin Hines, looked at the grounds of Roy Wilkins Park where Black Spectrum Theatre Company's new building was under construction. Black Spectrum was started in a Linden Boulevard storefront. The theatre gained a 425-seat auditorium and office space when it moved into the Roy Wilkins Park facility on the grounds of the former St. Albans Golf and Country Club. (Courtesy of Carl Clay.)

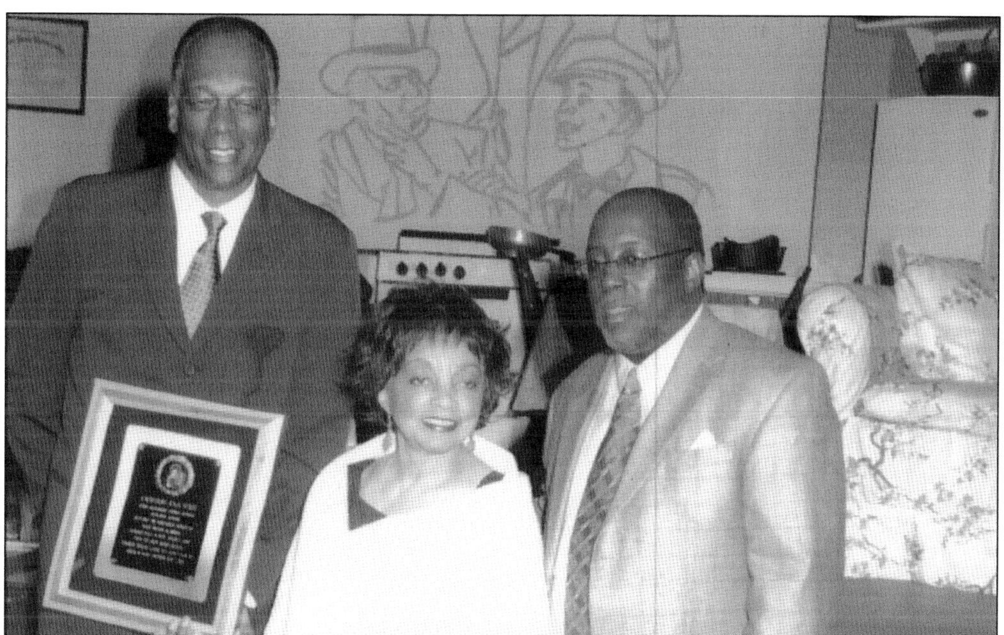

Actress Ruby Dee (1922–2014) is seen with Carl Clay and Black Spectrum board chairman and nationally syndicated radio host Bob Law. The Cleveland-born thespian was known for her civil rights activism and stage and film productions, such as the 1961 film adaptation of Lorraine Hansberry's play *A Raisin in the Sun* and Spike Lee's 1989 film *Do The Right Thing*, where she appeared with her husband, actor Ossie Davis (1917–2005). (Courtesy of Carl Clay.)

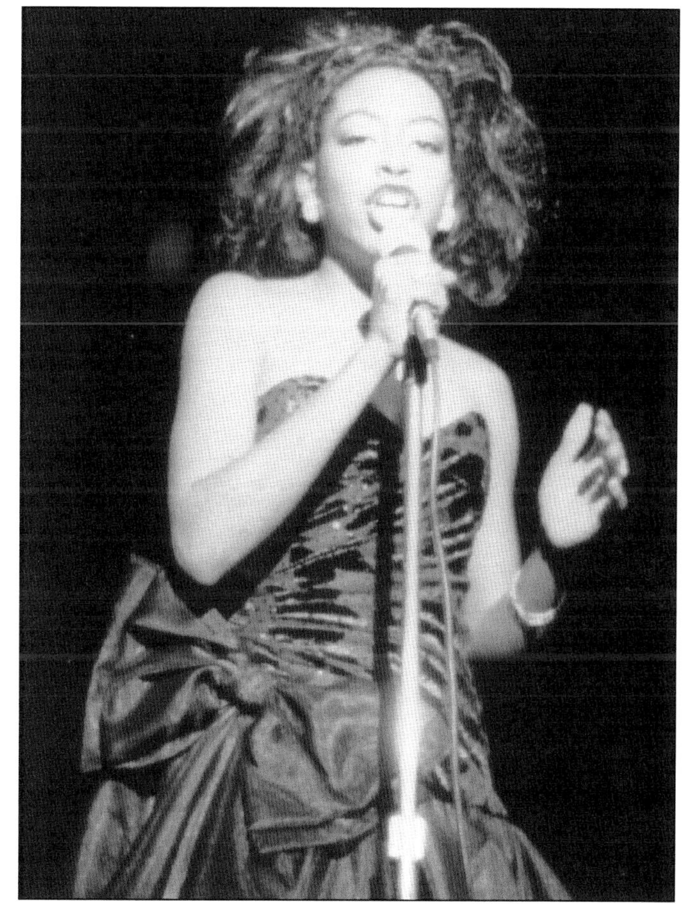

Television actress Tichina Arnold sings at a 1993 Black Spectrum Theatre Company event. The South Ozone Park native participated in community theatre productions around the city before she landed her role in the popular television show *Martin*. (Courtesy of Carl Clay.)

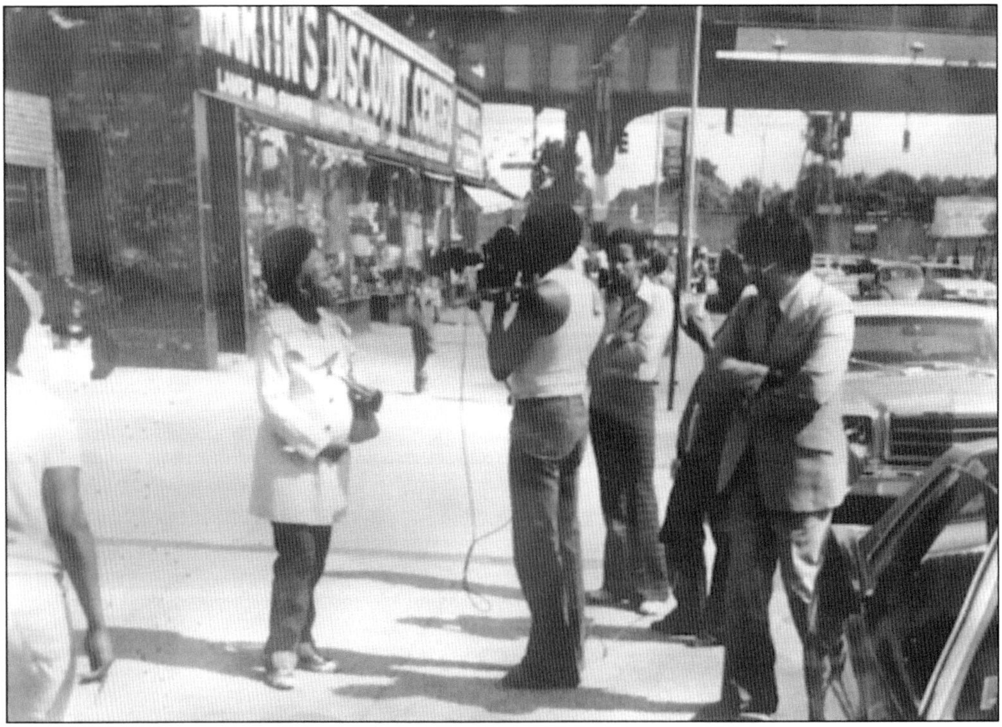

Taking social commentary and putting it on film was the inspiration for one of Black Spectrum's first documentary projects, *Babies Having Babies*. The 1978 film explored teenage pregnancy in New York City's African-American community and was shot in downtown Jamaica. Since then, Black Spectrum has produced over 20 films.

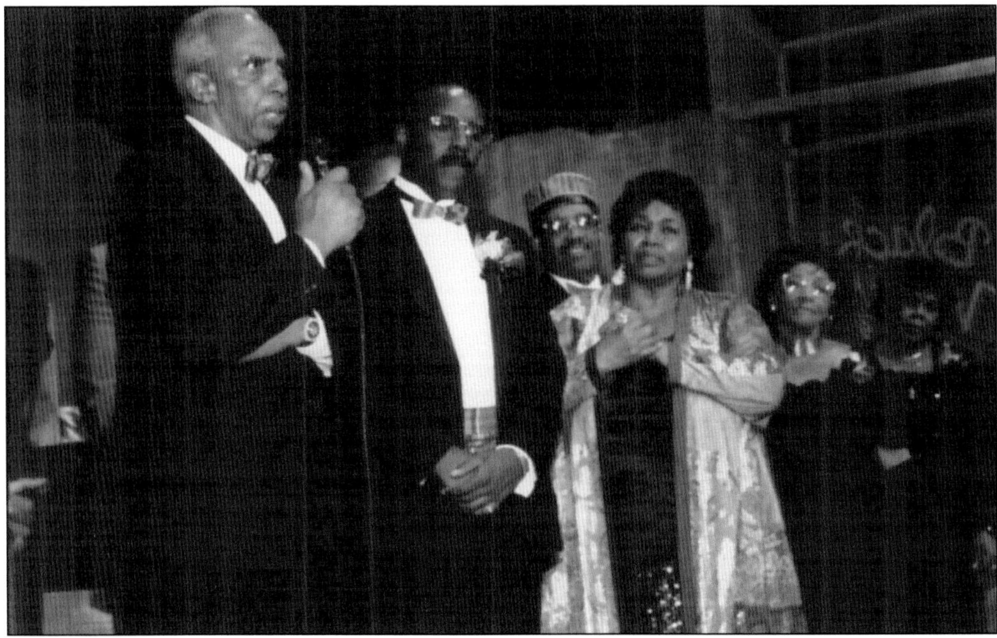

Beloved Queens physician Dr. Gerald Deas, Carl Clay, and the late Broadway stage and screen actress Theresa Merritt celebrate Black Spectrum's 30th anniversary in 2000. (Courtesy of Carl Clay.)

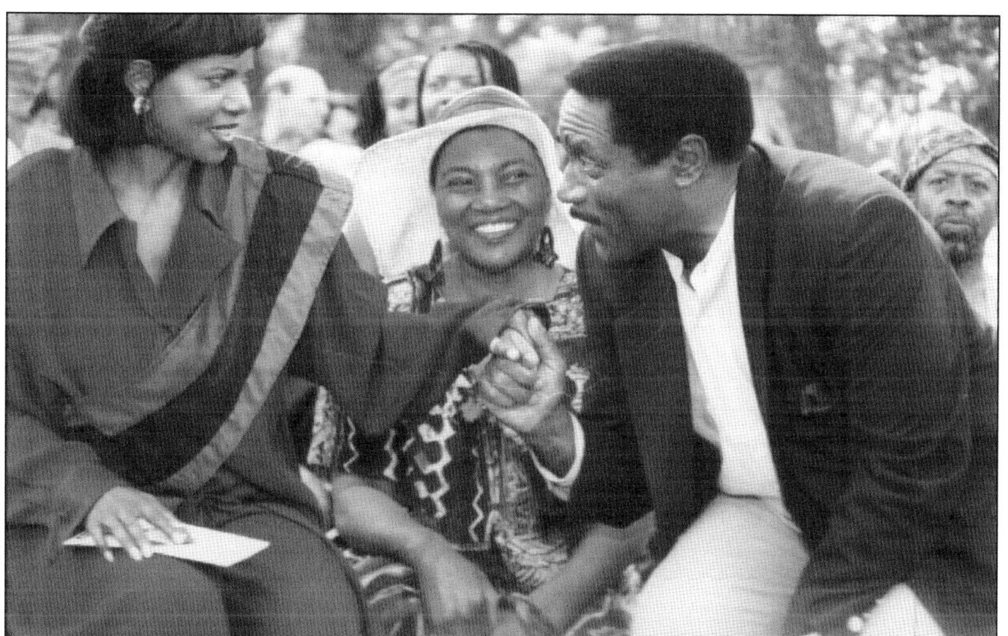

Singer-actress Melba Moore and former Fox News anchor and executive producer Bill McCreary shake hands at an outdoor event at Black Spectrum. (Courtesy of Carl Clay.)

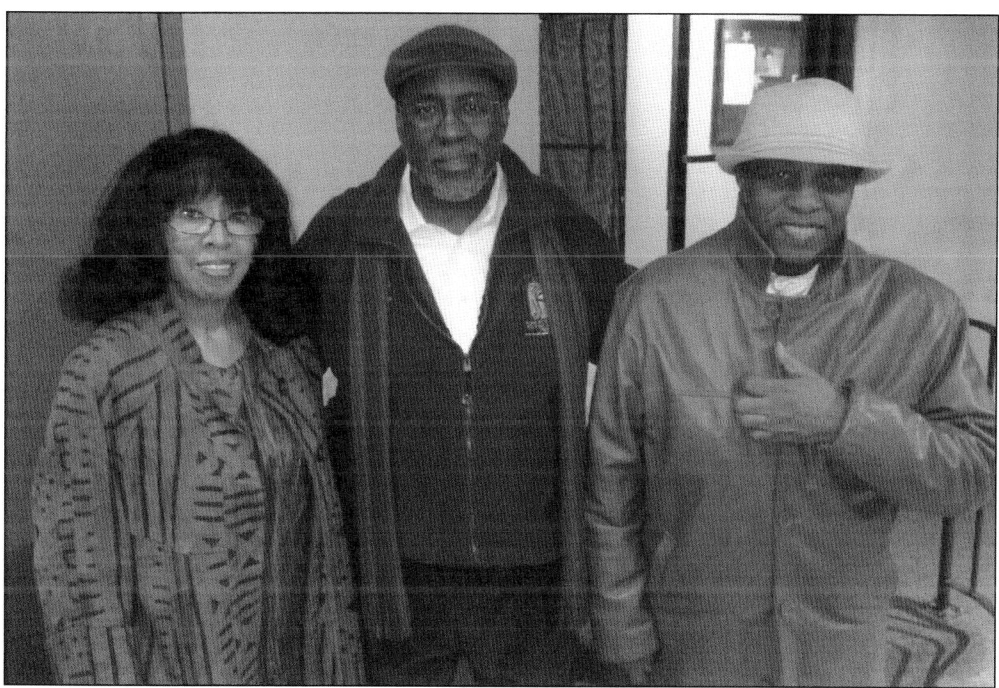

Jazz singer Jeane Carne (left) is pictured with Carl Clay and composer and producer Norman Connors at Black Spectrum. Carne is also known for popular songs such as "Don't Let it Go to Your Head," and "Was That All it Was." Connors is a jazz drummer who penned hit songs such as "You are My Starship" and "Invitation." Connors also arranged singer Phyllis Hyman's popular rendition of the song "Betcha By Golly Wow." (Courtesy of Carl Clay.)

Daymond John (left) and Carl Clay are seen at a city hall event in Manhattan where they both received awards for their contributions to the Big Apple. John, a co-founder of the popular FUBU clothing company, went on to become an author and motivational speaker. FUBU, which stands for "For Us By Us" was launched in the 1990s in Hollis, Queens. Daymond John also serves as a judge on the hit *Shark Tank* television show. (Courtesy of Carl Clay.)

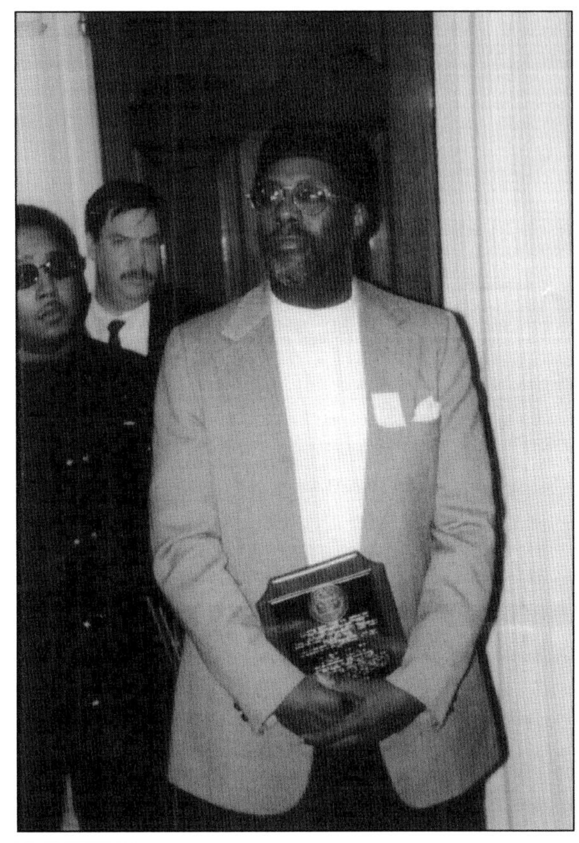

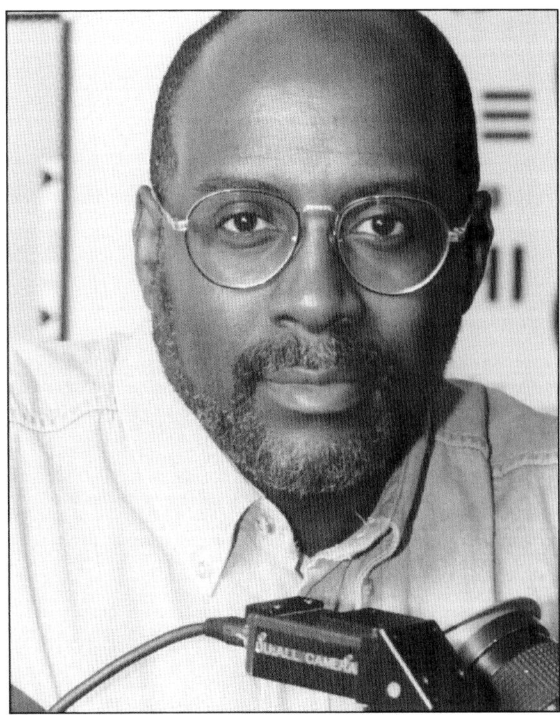

St. Albans native Carl Clay would like to create an independent charter school for middle-school students interested in pursuing theater and film careers. The proposed school would have a studio where teen films could be edited and produced. (Courtesy of Carl Clay.)

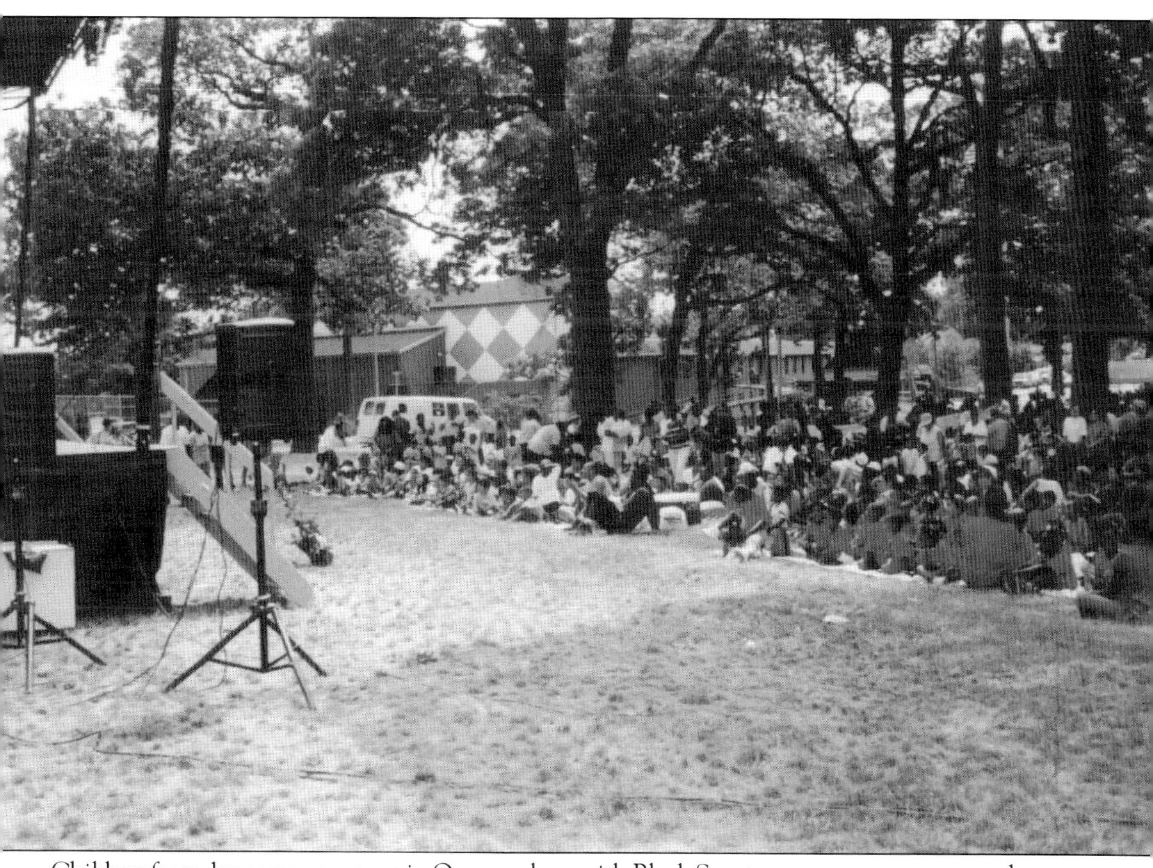

Children from day camp programs in Queens along with Black Spectrum summer camp attendees enjoy a theatrical production held outdoors. (Courtesy of Carl Clay.)

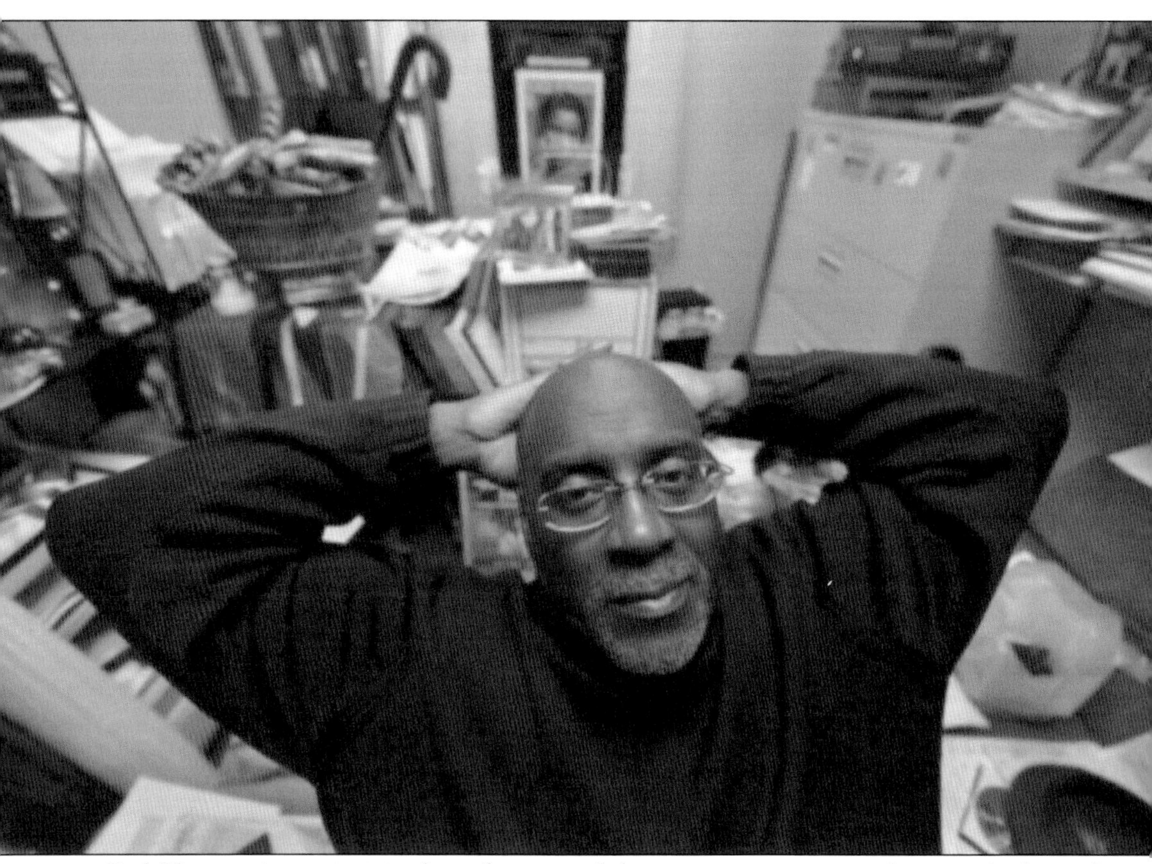

Carl Clay remains optimistic about the arts and the positive impact it can have on the lives of young people. He wants Black Spectrum to sponsor an international film festival in the future. This photograph was taken in Clay's office at Black Spectrum. (Courtesy of Carl Clay.)

Five

FIGHTING FOR CHANGE

There were numerous times in the course of St. Albans history that local residents formed committees and utilized civic, social, and religious groups to voice their opinions about changes that would affect the quality of their lives. Former Fox News anchor Julian Phillips, who grew up on Ursina Road, recalled a time when his parents and other neighbors fought against an unsavory business that had set up shop on Merrick Boulevard in the 1960s.

Quality of life concerns were raised decades earlier when fears emerged over boisterous military men who frequented the quiet neighborhood's bars. Neighbors claimed rowdy soldiers left debris on sidewalks as they traveled to and from the St. Albans Naval Hospital in the 1940s and 1950s. Other area residents, ever mindful of New York City's tense racial climate, joined organizations like the Jamaica branch of the NAACP, which now has its headquarters on Linden Boulevard in St. Albans. Jamaica NAACP officials worked with community leaders to open a daycare center for southeast Queens families on Linden Boulevard in September 1970.

Concern about racial equality for African Americans in St. Albans and beyond drove area residents and political leaders such as Roy Wilkins, Guy R. Brewer, J. Foster Phillips, Judge W. Eugene Sharpe, Judge William H. Booth, Dr. Charles Reid, Judge Richard Rutledge, Percy Sutton, Lawrence Cormier, Purcell Bailey, Elmer and Judge Laura Blackburne, Dr. Canute Bernard, Archie Spigner, Rafael Batine, Judge Alton R. Waldon, Viola Plummer, Dora Young, and Reverends Floyd Flake, Charles Norris, Edward Davis, Lucile Chambers Hill, and Robert Ross Johnson, to name a few, to make their voices heard.

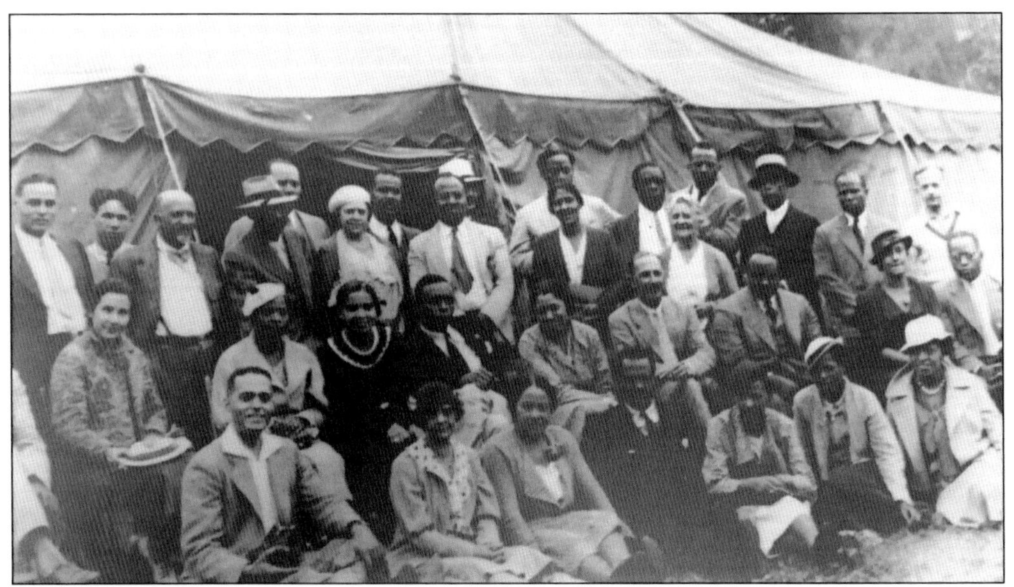

Jamaica NAACP members are pictured at a campground outing. While many of the members are unidentified, a closer look will show, in the back row at far left, American diplomat Ralph Bunche (1903–1971). Standing third from left wearing a bow tie is NAACP *Crisis* magazine editor and sociologist W.E.B. Du Bois (1868–1963), who later lived in Addisleigh Park. (Courtesy of Monica Pringle and Jamaica NAACP.)

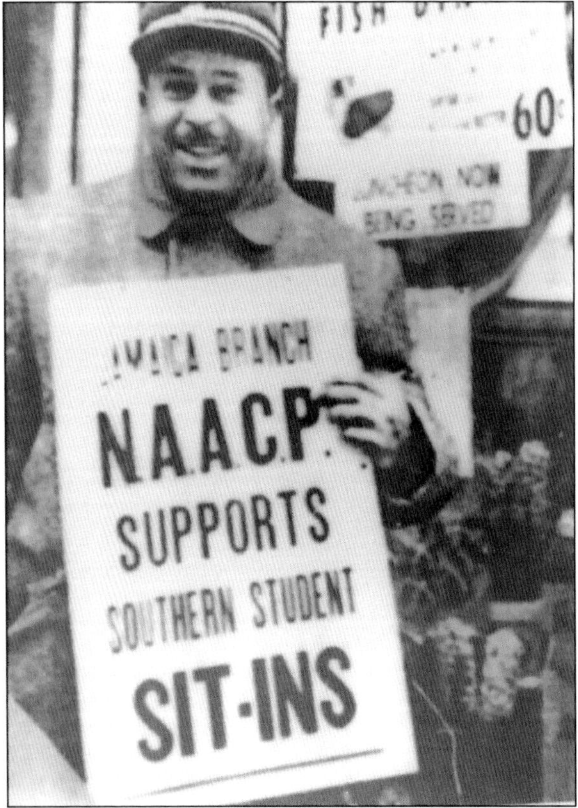

Guy R. Brewer (1904–1978) was a St. Albans resident and president of the Jamaica NAACP branch in 1952. Brewer supported the sit-ins that took place in southern cities during the civil rights era. He went on to become a New York state assemblyman, the first African American from Queens elected to that position, from 1969 through 1978. After his death, New York Boulevard in Jamaica was renamed Guy R. Brewer Boulevard. The Guy R. Brewer Democratic Club in St. Albans also honors the memory of the late politician. His wife, Marie Brown Brewer (1906–1984), was an accountant and insurance broker who became involved in politics. She moved to Queens in 1939 and became the first African-American woman to become district leader in that borough. (Courtesy of Monica Pringle and the Jamaica NAACP.)

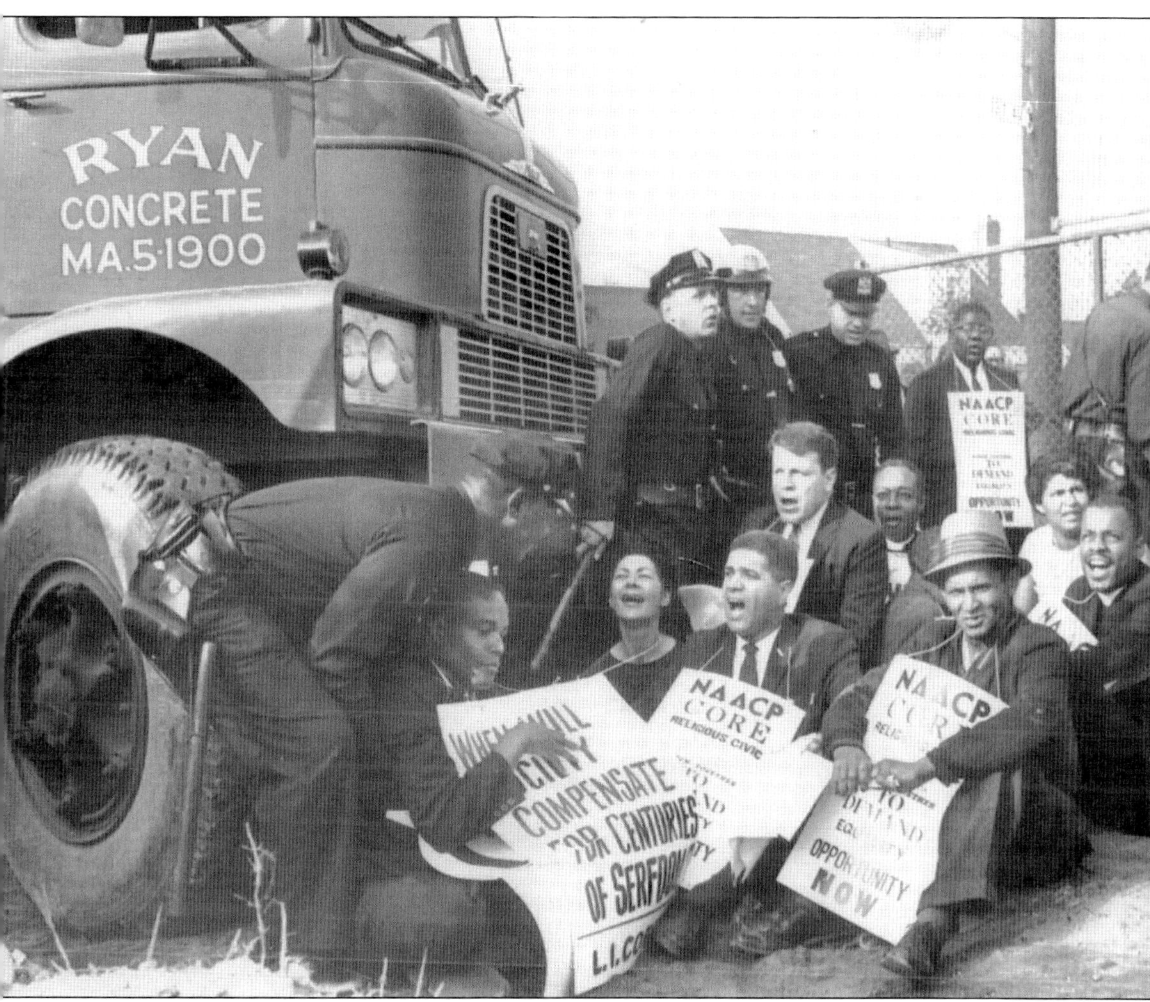

Upset that African Americans were not employed as laborers during the construction of Rochdale Village Cooperative Housing Complex in southeast Queens, Addisleigh Park's William H. Booth (seated in first row, center) sat down in front of delivery trucks with other NAACP members in 1963. The protests lasted 16 weeks. The demonstrations upheld strong beliefs that the publicly funded Mitchell-Lama housing development should not discriminate in its hiring practices. Booth, a civil rights attorney, was the NAACP's New York state president. From 1966 to 1969, he chaired the city's Human Rights Commission. He later became a New York State Supreme Court judge. (Courtesy of Gini Booth.)

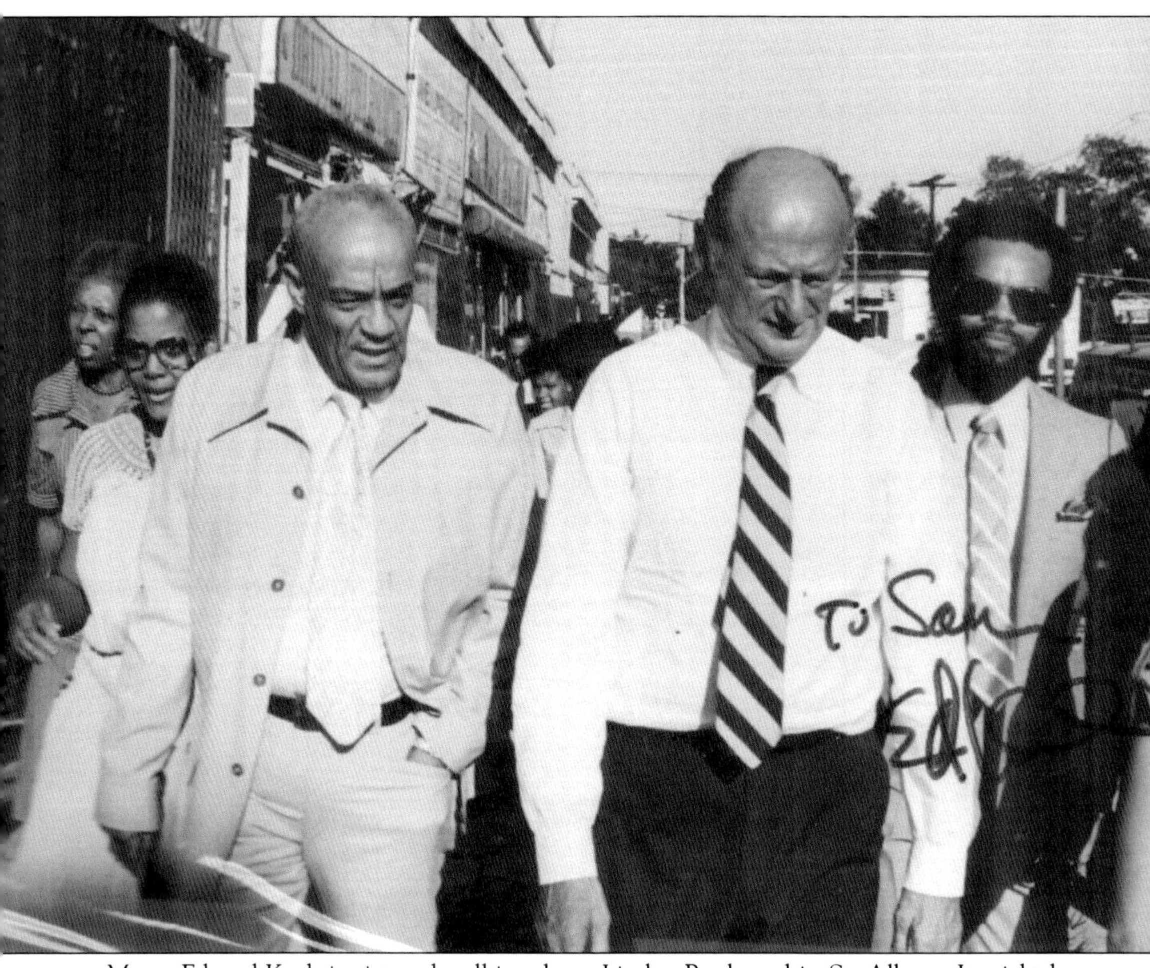

Mayor Edward Koch is pictured walking down Linden Boulevard in St. Albans. It might have been an election year, and the mayor wanted votes from his Democratic constituents in the area who routinely show up at the polls. (Courtesy of the *Press of Southeast Queens*.)

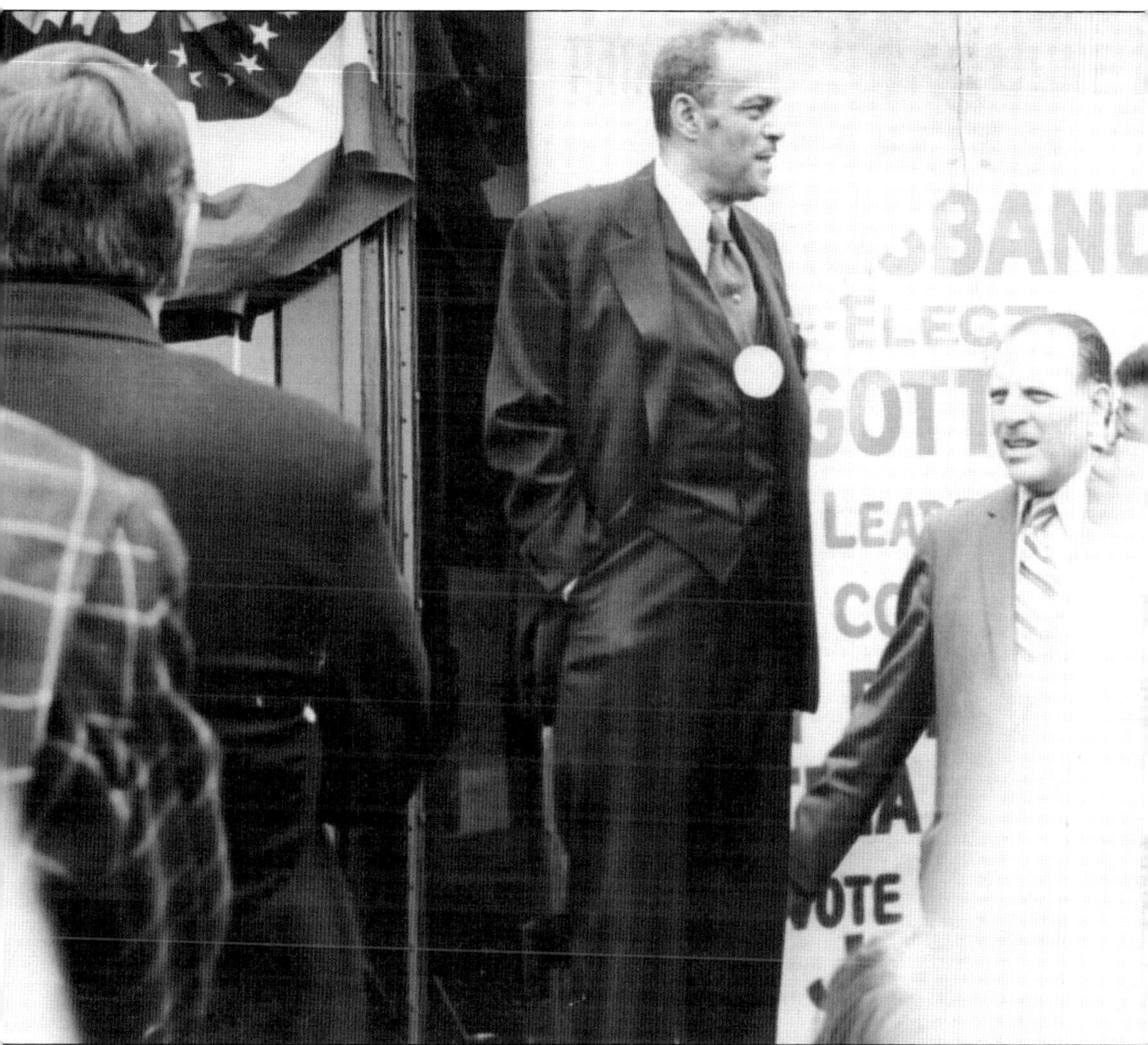

Samuel Husbands (1917–1982) is pictured at a political rally. Husbands was a southeast Queens business owner and longtime St. Albans resident. He operated two Linden Boulevard establishments: Rib Shack in Jamaica and St. Albans Wine and Liquors. The Harlem-born entrepreneur ran unsuccessfully for a Queens district leader position in the 1970s. After his 1982 death, the St. Albans Chamber of Commerce memorialized his service with a bronze plaque and a small park on Linden Boulevard. (Courtesy of Junie Saunders.)

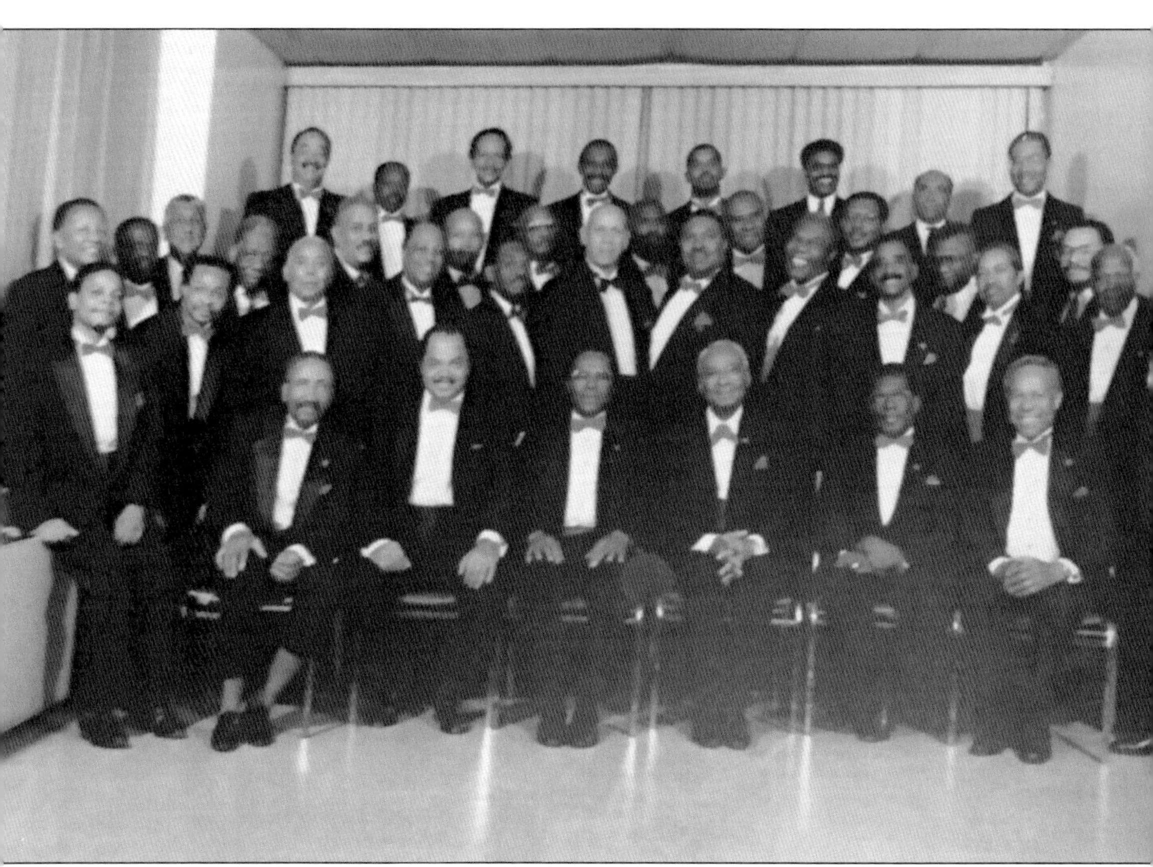

Dedicated members of United Black Men of Queens are pictured at a 1995 event. The group, established in the mid-1970s, has several participants from the greater St. Albans community. They are focused on the education and support of at-risk youths in Queens County through mentorship programs. (Courtesy of Lawrence Cormier.)

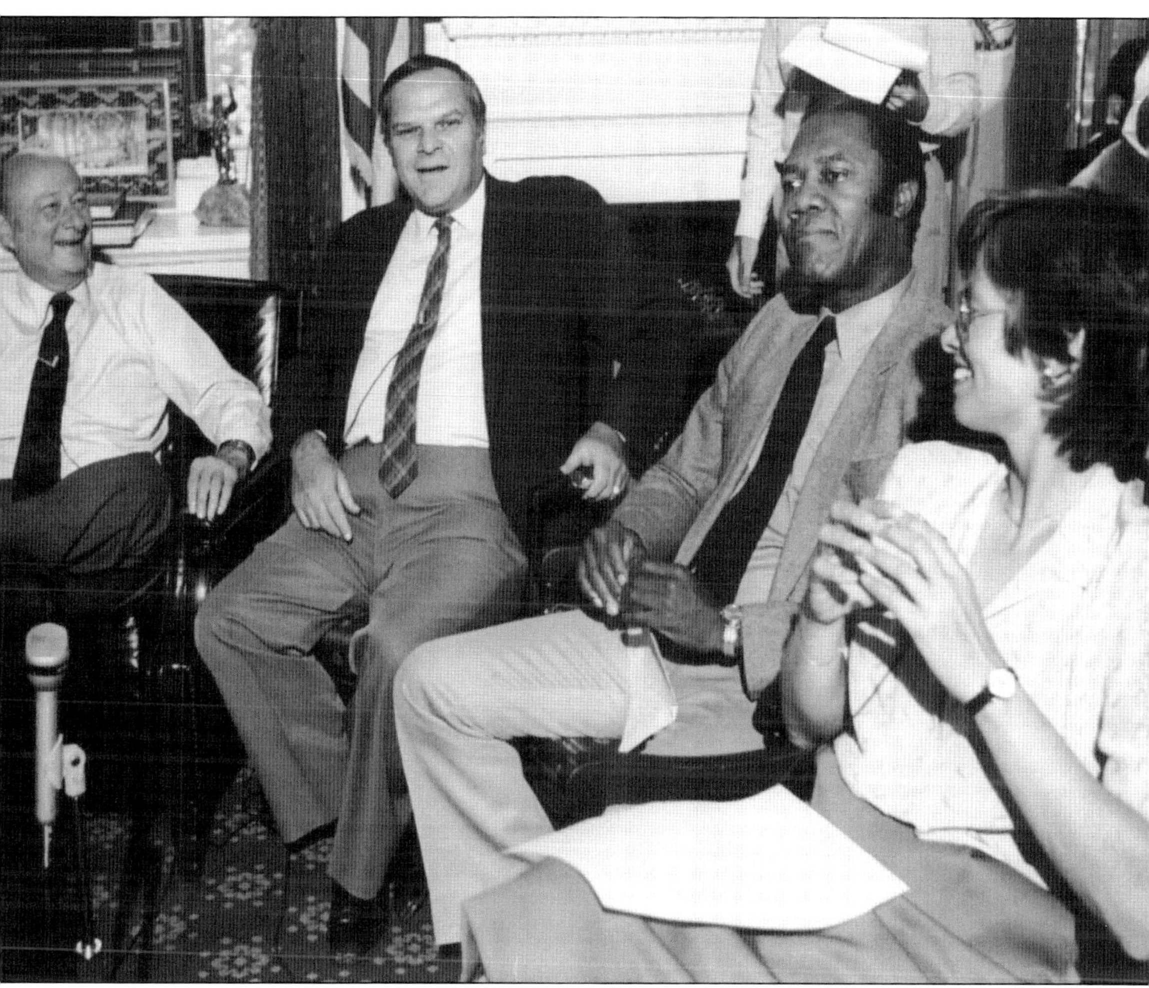

Former Queens city councilman Archie Spigner is seated with Mayor Ed Koch, former Queens borough president Donald Manes, and New York City Council president Carol Bellamy at a city hall meeting. Spigner, an Addisleigh Park resident, is often called the "Dean of Southeast Queens." He served nearly 30 years in the city council. Spigner was not always a politician. He was a bus driver who was promoted to bus dispatcher with the New York City Transit Authority. He left that position to pursue his political interests after his 1968 election as a Queens district leader. Spigner was the first African American to represent southeast Queens on the city council, in the mid-1970s. In 2004, the St. Albans Post Office on Linden Boulevard was renamed the Archie Spigner Post Office in his honor. (Courtesy of the *Press of Southeast Queens*.)

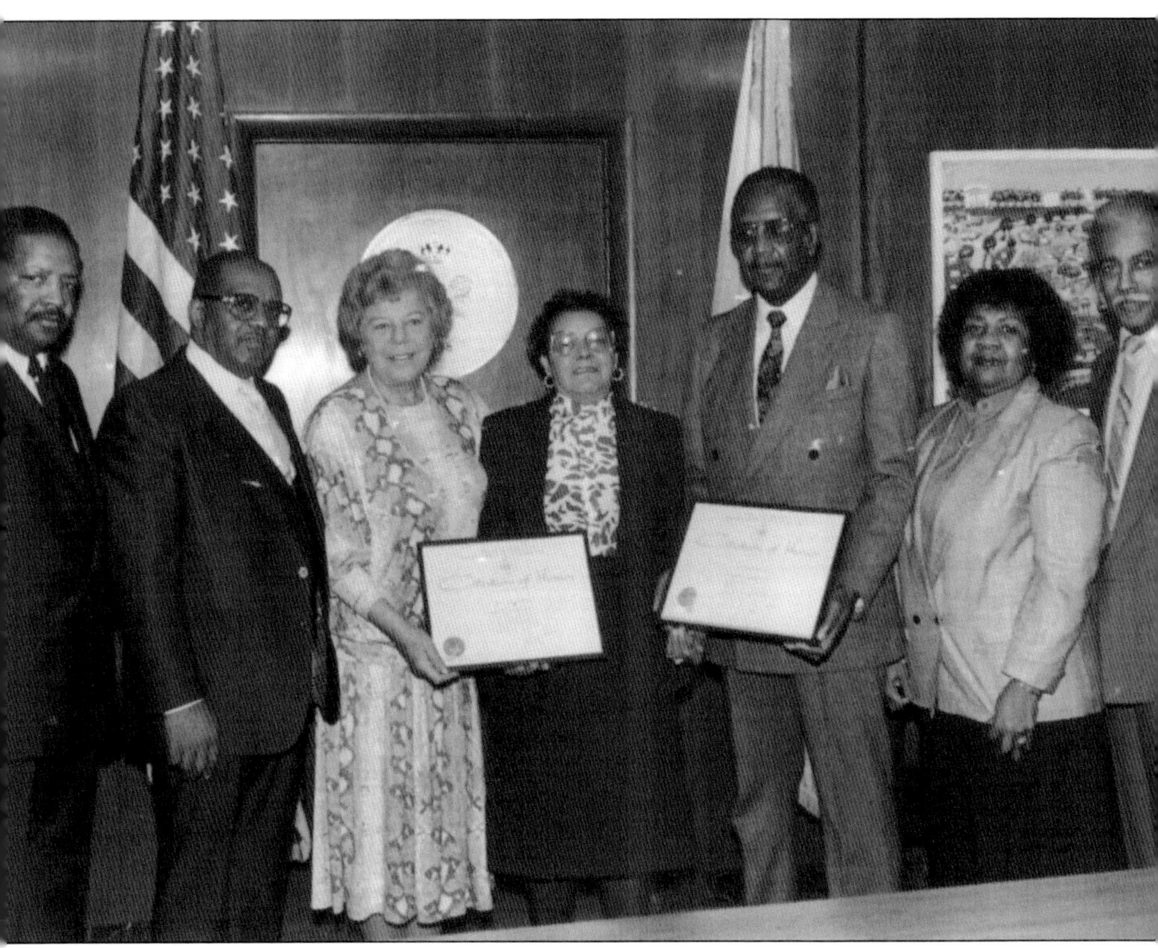

Rev. Robert Ross Johnson, first pastor and founder of the St. Albans Congregational Church, receives a citation of honor for his civic work in southeast Queens from Queens borough president Claire Shulman. The Rev. Charles Norris, standing at far right, also attended the event. (Courtesy of the *Press of Southeast Queens.*)

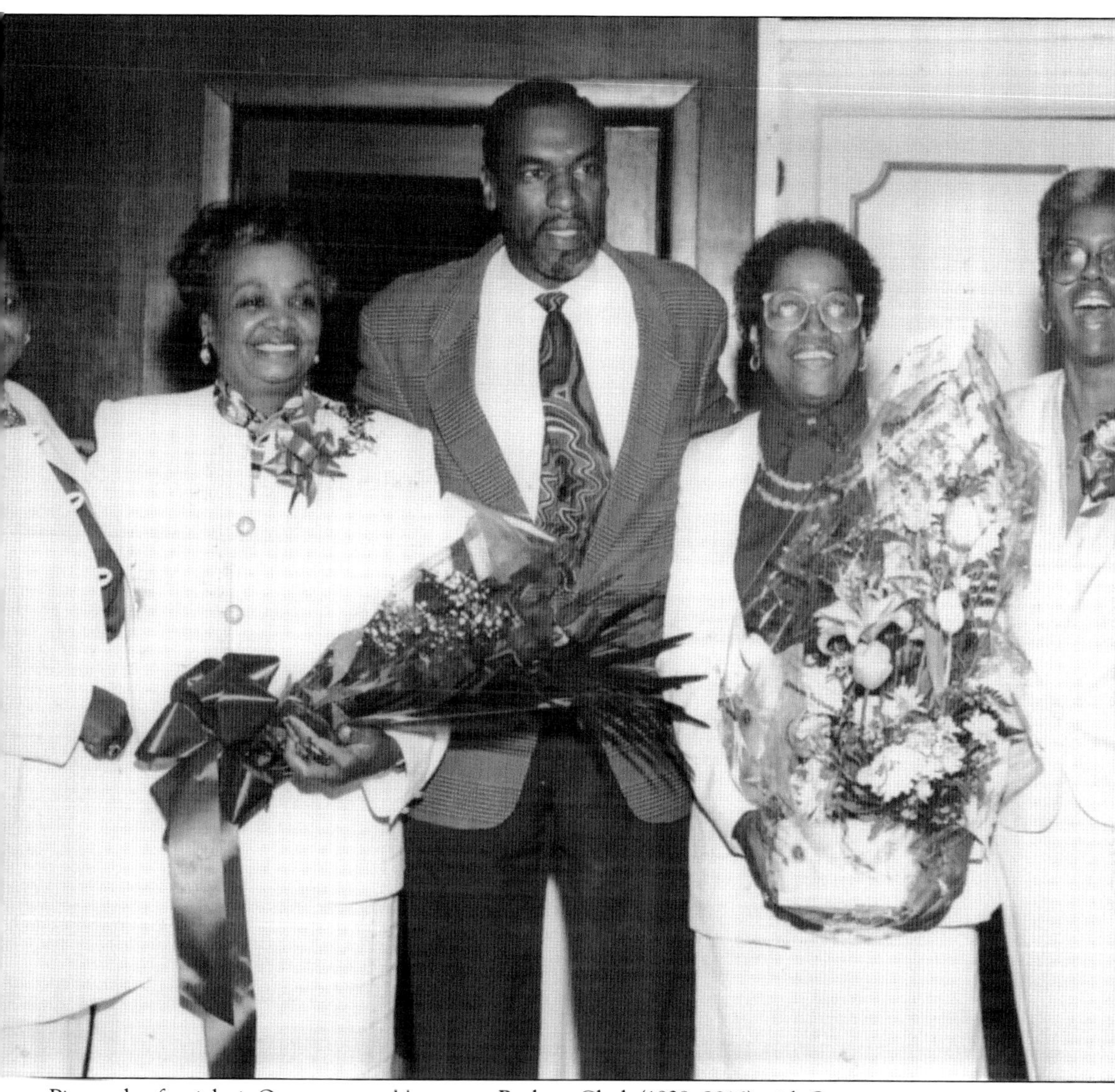

Pictured at far right is Queens assemblywoman Barbara Clark (1939–2016) with Queens congressman Rev. Floyd Flake of St. Albans and three unidentified women. Clark represented the 33rd district, which includes St. Albans. Flake represented the congressional district that was once held by Congressman Joseph P. Addabbo, who died in May 1986. (Courtesy of the *Press of Southeast Queens*.)

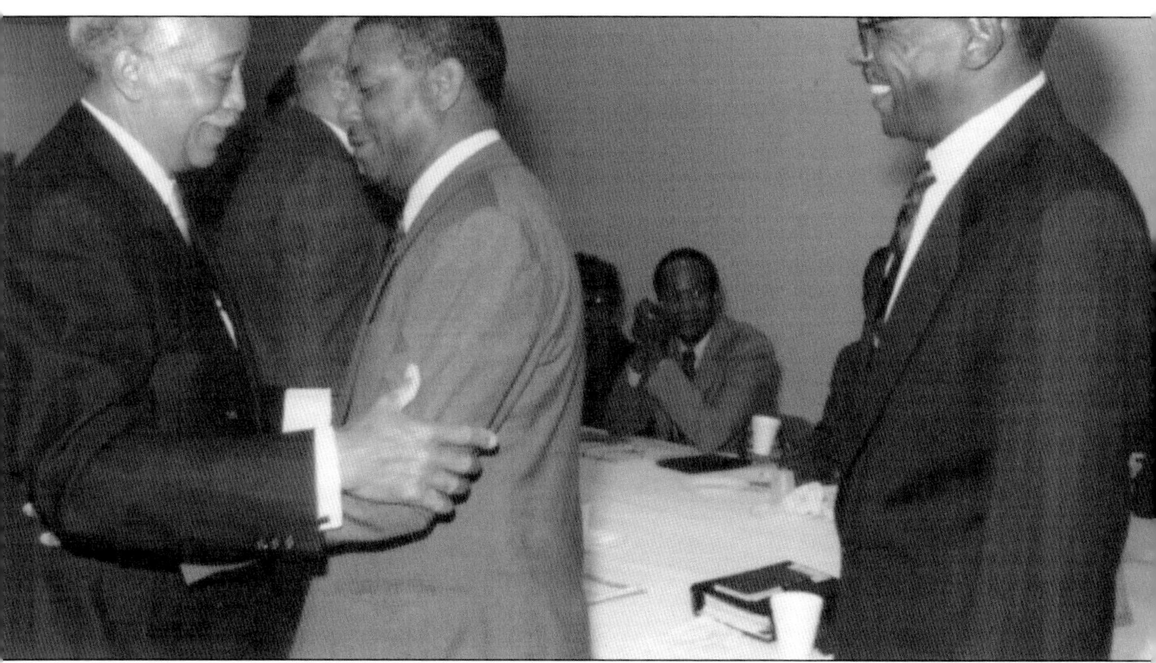

David Dinkins (far left), New York City's first African American mayor, speaks with an unidentified man and the Rev. Henry Simmons (far right), pastor of St. Albans Congregational Church. (Courtesy of the *Press of Southeast Queens*.)

Six

Notable Residents

Most locals know that singers James Brown, Billie Holiday, Rose Murphy, Wynonie Harris, Bill Kenny of Ink Spots fame, and Harry Douglas with the Deep River Boys once called St. Albans home. Jazz musicians John Coltrane, "Wild" Bill Davis, Eddie "Lockjaw" Davis, Oliver Nelson Sr., and Lester Young were also attracted to the neighborhood. Some people joke that the reason St. Albans produced so many musicians is that the area's one- and two-family homes have many places for fledgling performers to practice, like basements and garages. Whatever the reason, St. Albans has contributed musicians, educators, writers, and other professionals to the world.

Not everyone knows that the family behind the regional home improvement chain Pergament Home Centers got its start behind the counter of a Linden Boulevard storefront. Louis Pergament and his three sons turned a neighborhood hardware store into a major northeast retail chain.

St. Albans has its share of writers, including James McBride, author of *The Color of Water*; children's book authors Patricia Reilly Giff and Irene Haas; and poetess Lindamichelle Baron. The neighborhood has also produced its share of journalists, including Louis Lomax, Karl Grossman, Natalie Byfield, Julian Phillips, Olivera Perkins, Nancy Giles, and Rob Parker. Veteran radio broadcaster Harold "Hal" Jackson raised his children in St. Albans as he played his *Sunday Classics* on the airwaves. Another former St. Albans resident, the Rev. Al Sharpton, hosts *Politics Nation*, a weekend political talk show on MSNBC. And everyone has seen St. Albans's own meteorologist Al Roker on *The Today Show*.

Alto saxophonist Ed Jackson's musical family has operated Jackson Tax Service in the area for 50 years. Jackson also oversees the Jackson Room, a jazz hall venue on Linden Boulevard. His brother Dave Jackson, who died in 2013, played with many of the neighborhood jazz greats. Tenor saxophonist Jerome "Najee" Rasheed and percussionist Steve Kroon also hail from St. Albans. Rapper-actor James Todd Smith, better known as LL Cool J, faithfully returns to Daniel M. O'Connell Playground on 113th Avenue every summer for Jump & Ball, the basketball clinic for youths aged 8 to 18 that he sponsors.

One former St. Albans resident has traveled to outer space: Anna Lee Tingle Fisher. Many sports fans know that former Boston Celtics star Bob Cousy and former New York Knick turned sports commentator Mark Jackson are from St. Albans. Boxers Tommy "Hurricane" Jackson and Floyd Patterson at one time lived in the area. This chapter is dedicated to former St. Albans residents who made contributions to New York City and beyond.

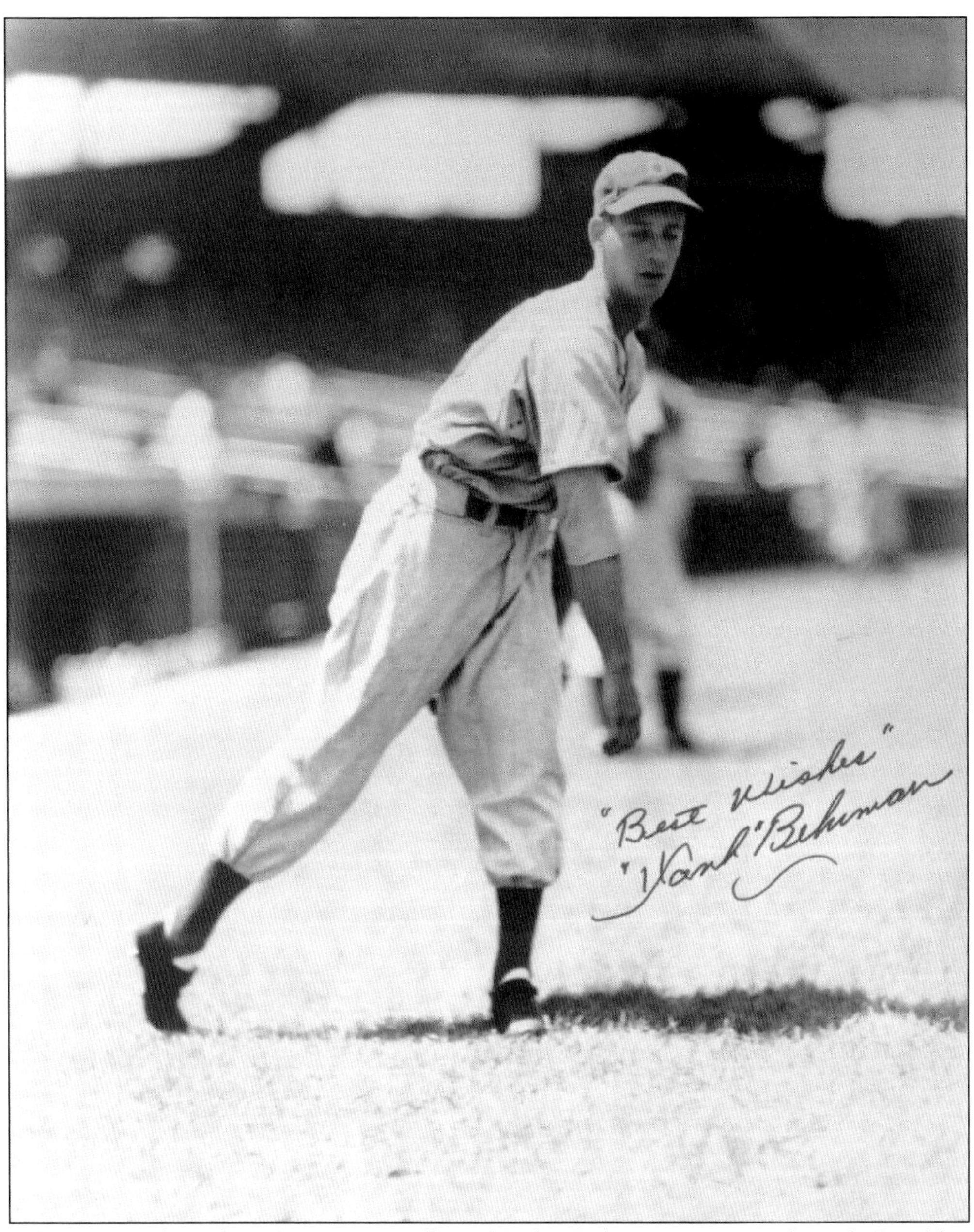

Addisleigh Park residents Roy Campanella and Jackie Robinson were not the only Brooklyn Dodgers to call St. Albans home. Henry "Hank" Bernard Behrman, a Brooklyn Dodgers pitcher, purchased a home in St. Albans in 1947, the same year that Robinson broke the color barrier in Major League Baseball. Behrman made his mark from 1946 to 1949 when he pitched for the Brooklyn Dodgers, Pittsburgh Pirates, and New York Giants. He often clashed with Dodgers general manager Branch Rickey over curfew rules and pregame reporting times. Behrman played five games for the Dodgers in the 1954 World Series. However, off-field troubles hounded him and curtailed his promising career. He was traded to several minor league teams and then returned to the Dodgers when Rickey assigned him to Ebbets Field as a groundskeeper. Behrman eventually left the sport. He died in 1987. (Courtesy of John Griffith.)

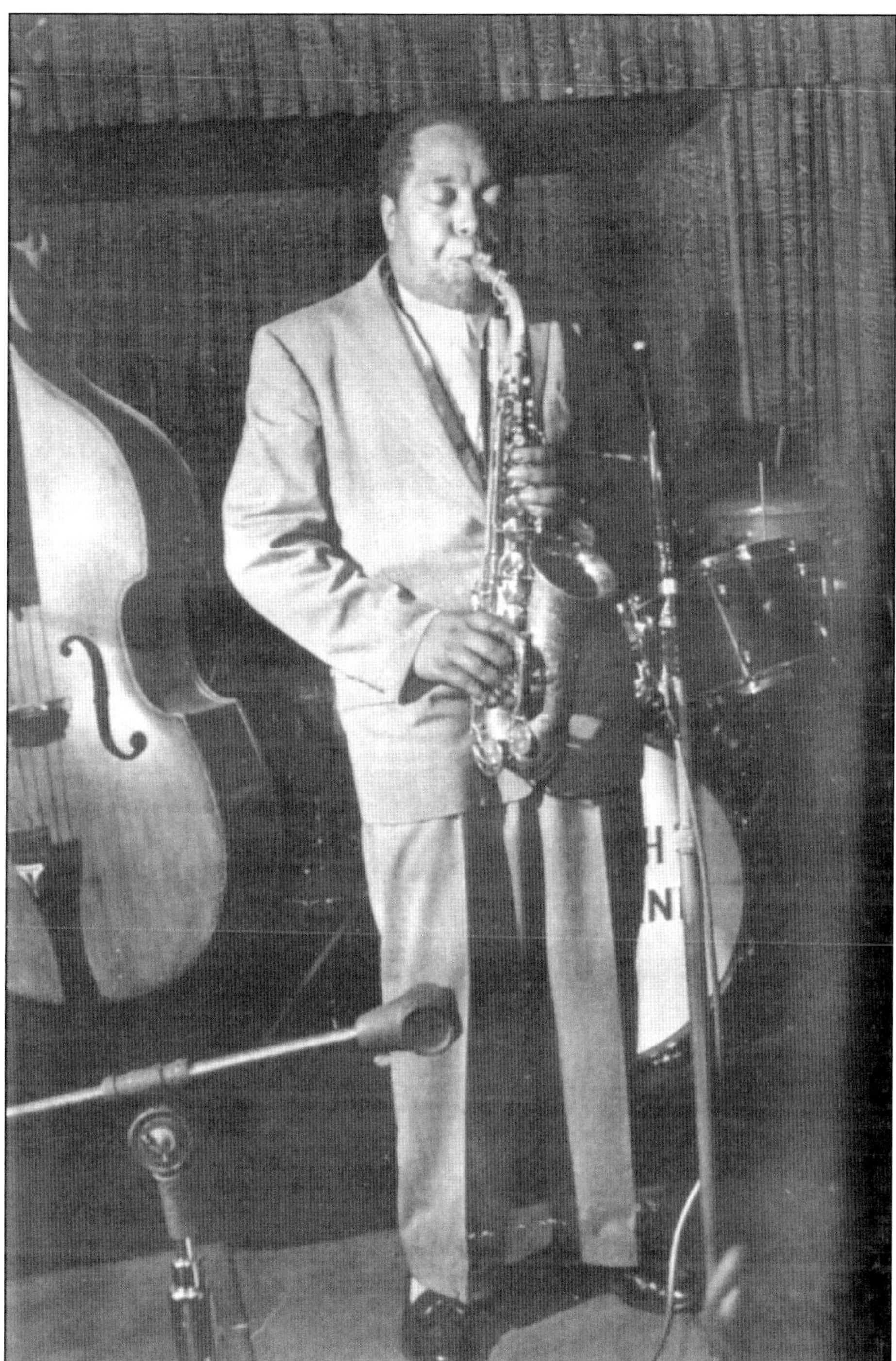

Eugene Earl Bostic was a gifted jazz and swing alto saxophonist who recorded hundreds of songs for King Records. The Tulsa, Oklahoma, native came to New York City to pursue his music career. He lived at 178-16 Murdock Ave. in Addisleigh Park. His music was praised by his peers, including John Coltrane. Bostic's sax work can be heard on popular tunes such as "Harlem Nocturne" and "Flamingo." (Courtesy of Lillie B. Crowder.)

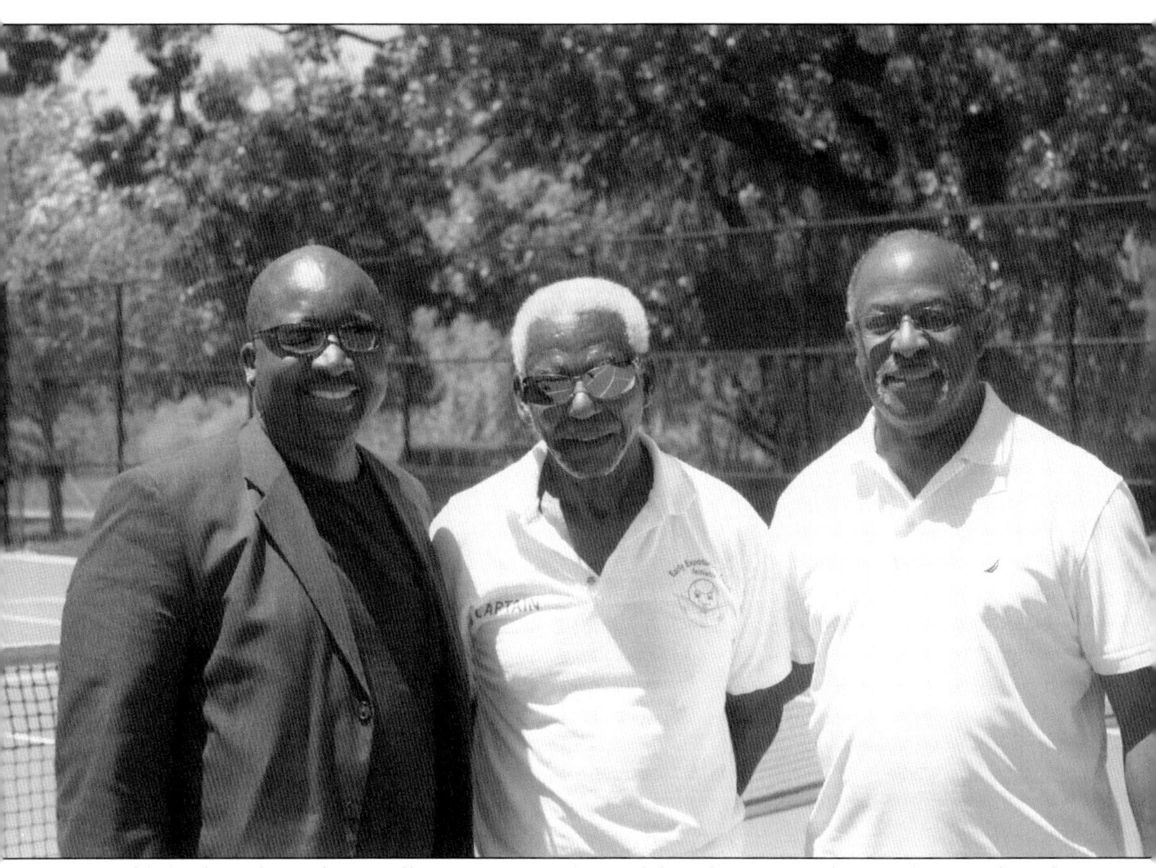

Addisleigh Park resident William G. Briggs (center) loved tennis and never hesitated to share his appreciation with New York City youths. The sports enthusiast was inspired by his idol, the late tennis great Arthur Ashe. Briggs wanted young people to pick up tennis rackets to broaden their experiences. By trade, Briggs was a cytologist; he diagnosed diseases and conditions by examining tissue samples. In 1972, he launched the National Academy of Junior Tennis and Youth, starting with five kids and growing his organization to include several students aged 4 to 19 who took classes at various sites around the city. Briggs found a permanent home for his Youth and Tennis Academy at Roy Wilkins Park. He also developed the School for Academic and Social Development, a program that held numerous workshops for youths on job readiness, fire safety, and other topics that encouraged participants to "strive for greatness," which was his favorite motto. Over the years, Briggs received numerous community service awards. He was inducted into the New England Tennis Association Hall of Fame for his 30 years in the sport. In 2017, Queens borough president Melinda Katz honored Briggs with an award. (Courtesy of Dr. Belinda Johnston Briggs.)

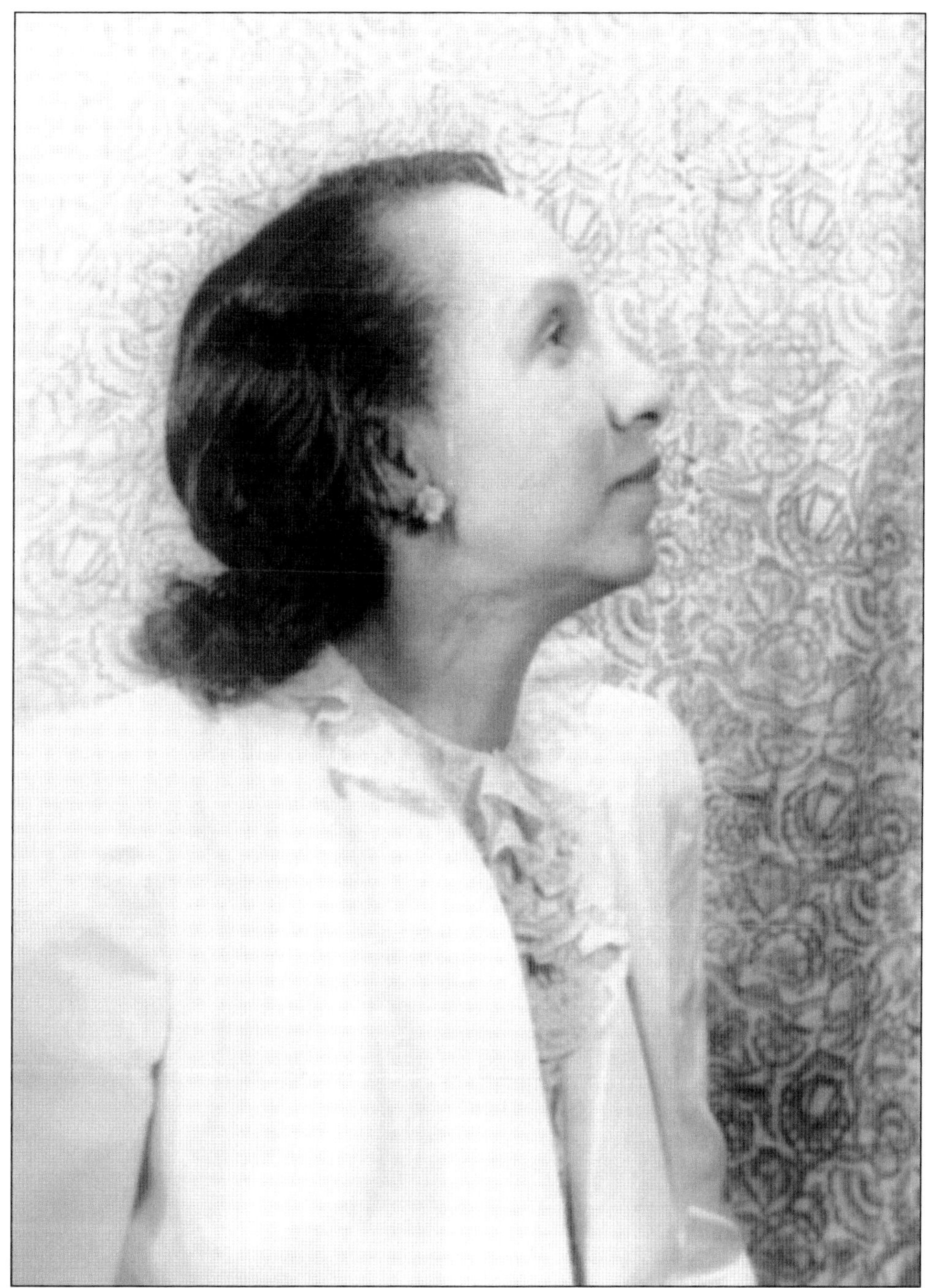

Activist, author, playwright, and composer Lola Shirley Graham Du Bois lived at 173-19 113th Rd. in Addisleigh Park in 1948. She became the second wife of W.E.B Du Bois, co-founder of the NAACP, when she married him in 1951 at her home. Graham was the first African American to write and direct a play with an all-black cast—*Tom-Toms: An Epic of Music and the Negro*—in 1932. She also wrote biographies of the scientist George Washington Carver, actor/singer/attorney Paul Robeson, and activist Frederick Douglass. She worked as a field director for the NAACP and opened branches of the organization throughout the nation.

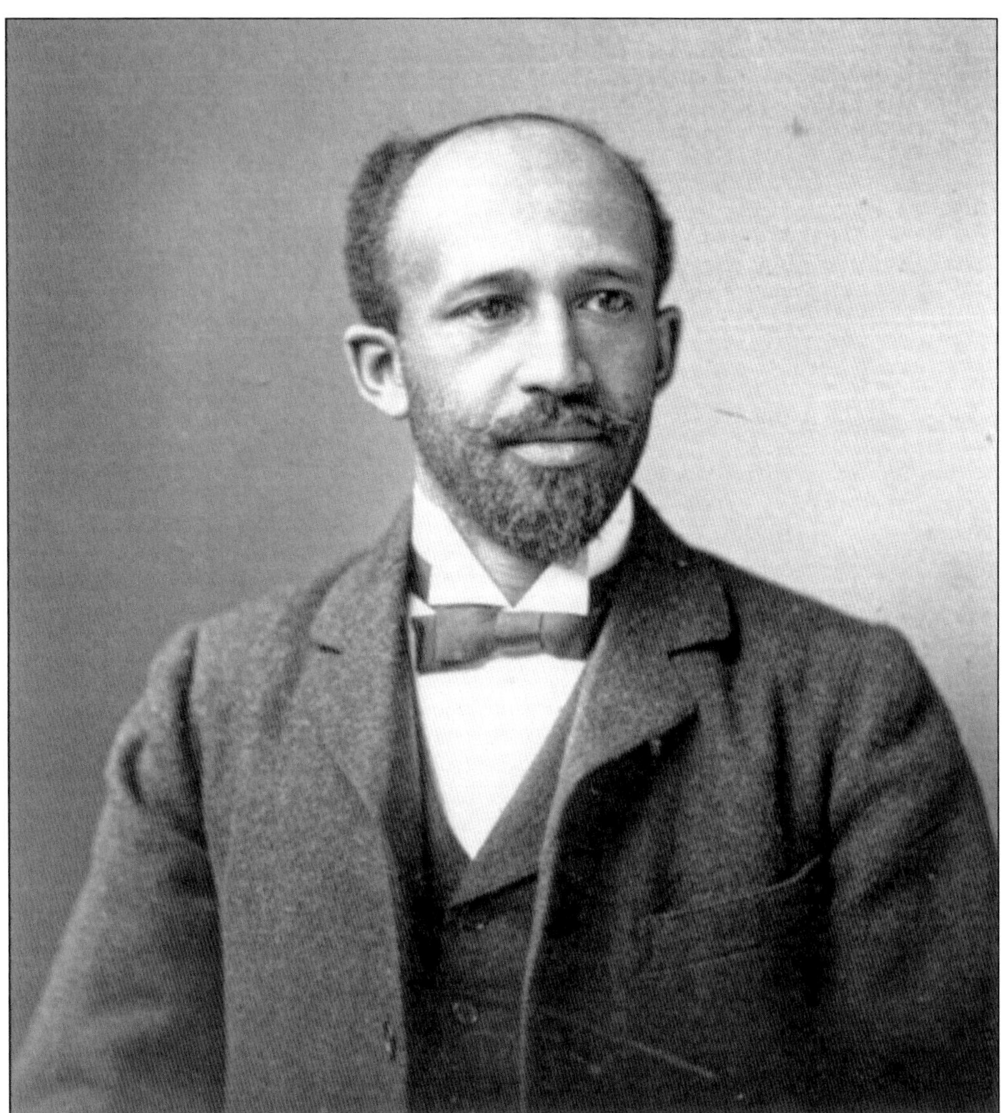

William Edward Burghardt "W.E.B." Du Bois was a co-founder of the NAACP and an author, civil rights activist, educator, sociologist, and historian. In 1888, Du Bois graduated from Fisk University in Tennessee and earned a second degree from Harvard University in 1890. After teaching at Wilberforce University in Ohio, he decided to return to Harvard to pursue a doctorate degree. In 1895, Du Bois became the first African American with a PhD from Harvard. His teaching career continued at the University of Pennsylvania and Atlanta University. In 1903, he wrote what became a classic book, *The Souls of Black Folks*. In 1905, Du Bois started the Niagara Movement, a group that wanted to eliminate racial prejudice throughout the nation. One of Du Bois's most groundbreaking scholarly works was *The Philadelphia Negro*. It examined factors behind the lack of employment and job opportunities for northern blacks. Du Bois was the editor of the NAACP's quarterly magazine, the *Crisis*, from 1909 until 1934. He also wrote *Black Reconstruction* in 1935 about his Pan-Africanist sentiments, which made the work popular in the 1960s and 1970s. Du Bois married his second wife, Addisleigh Park resident Shirley Graham, an accomplished writer and composer, in 1951. The couple later moved to Brooklyn and then left the United States for Ghana, where he died in 1963.

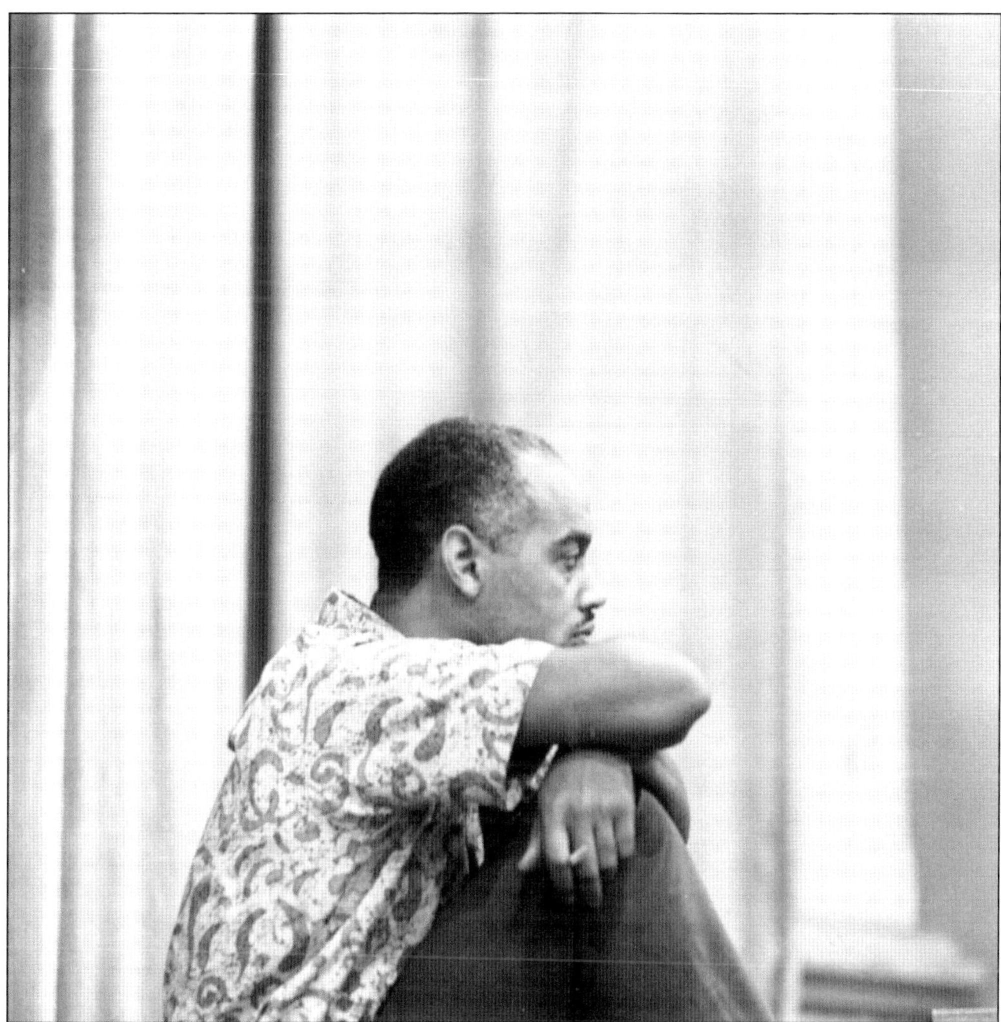

Music was in Mercer Ellington's blood. The son of orchestra leader and composer Duke Ellington, the younger Ellington was a bandleader and composer who lived at 113-02 175th St. in Addisleigh Park. After studies at Columbia University, New York University, and the Juilliard School, Ellington formed his own band in the 1930s. He wrote jazz standards "Things Ain't What They Used to Be" in 1942 with lyricist Ted Persons and "Blue Serge" with Billy Strayhorn in 1959. Ellington managed the career of jazz trumpeter and fellow St. Albans resident Charles Melvin "Cootie" Williams and other performers. When Duke Ellington died in 1974, Mercer assumed responsibility for the Duke Ellington Orchestra. By 1981, he was the musical director for *Sophisticated Ladies*, a Broadway musical revue of his father's songs. (Courtesy of Lillie B. Crowder.)

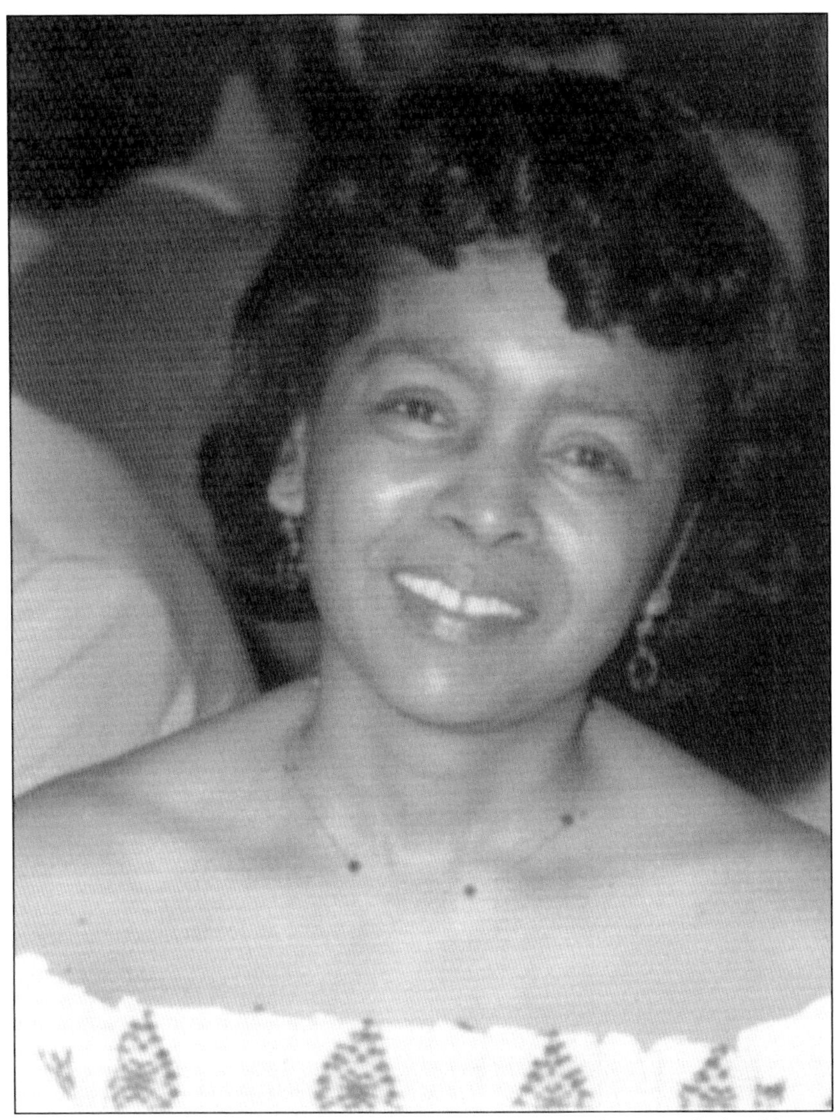

Bernadine Coles Gines was the first African American woman to be a certified public accountant in New York State in 1954 and the 34th African American CPA in the nation at that time. The Charlottesville, Virginia, native earned a bachelor's degree from Virginia State University and graduated first in her class. Because of the south's Jim Crow laws, she was unable to attend graduate school in Virginia, so she headed to New York in 1946 and enrolled in New York University. The following year, she received a master's degree in business administration with an accounting major. However, finding an accounting job in the Big Apple was difficult. She worked as a bookkeeper with the *New York Age*, a weekly African American newspaper. Through that position, she learned about Lucas & Tucker, an African American CPA firm, but unfortunately, they did not hire women. It took two years of searching for the right opportunity before Coles landed a job with a small Jewish-owned accounting firm. Later, she worked as an accountant in various positions with New York City's office of the comptroller for 40 years. In 2002, Gines, a Baisley Boulevard resident, was featured in Theresa Hammond's book *A White Collar Profession: African-American Certified Public Accountants Since 1921*, along with her sister Ruth Harris, the first female African American CPA in Virginia. (Courtesy of Richard E. Gines Jr.)

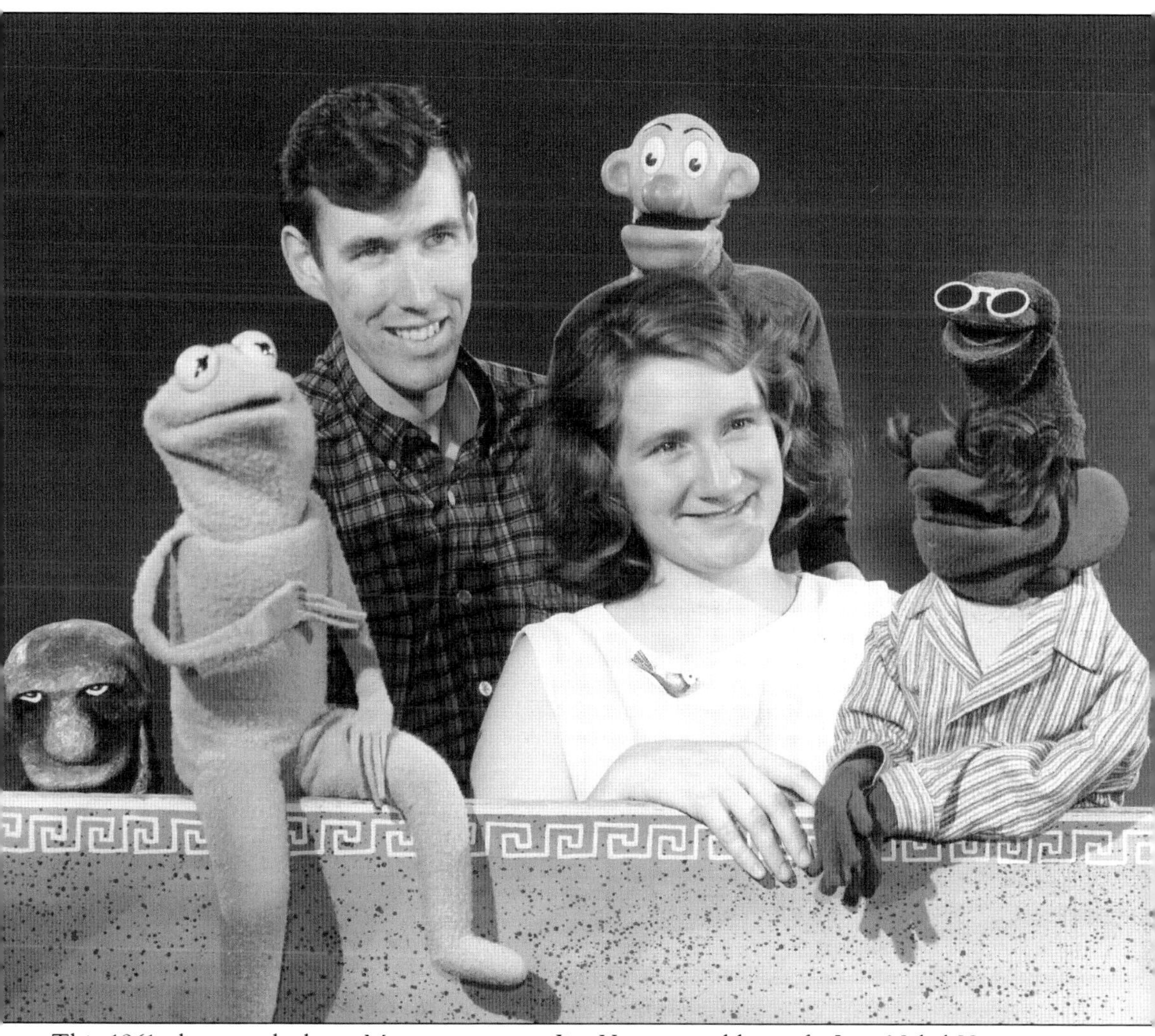

This 1961 photograph shows Muppets creators Jim Henson and his wife, Jane Nebel Henson, a puppeteer who grew up in St. Albans. The 1940 US Census lists the Nebel family including parents Adalbert and Winifred and their three children—son Brereton Edward and daughters Margareta Regina and Jane Ann—living at 205-07 118th Ave. Adalbert was an American astrologer who was also known as Dal Lee. He established *Astrology Guide Magazine* in 1938 and authored two books: *Dictionary of Astrology* in 1968 and *Understanding the Occult* in 1969. His youngest daughter, Jane, met her future husband at a puppetry class at the University of Maryland, College Park, in 1954. Jim Henson was still in college when he was asked to appear as a puppeteer on a local NBC affiliate show in Washington, DC. Jane was his co-performer. The couple created the world-famous Muppets in 1955 and married four years later. Besides being a performer, puppet designer, and her husband's longtime business partner, Jane Henson was an art teacher and mother of five children. Jim died in 1990, and Jane followed in 2013. (Photograph by Del Ankers, courtesy of Jim Henson Company.)

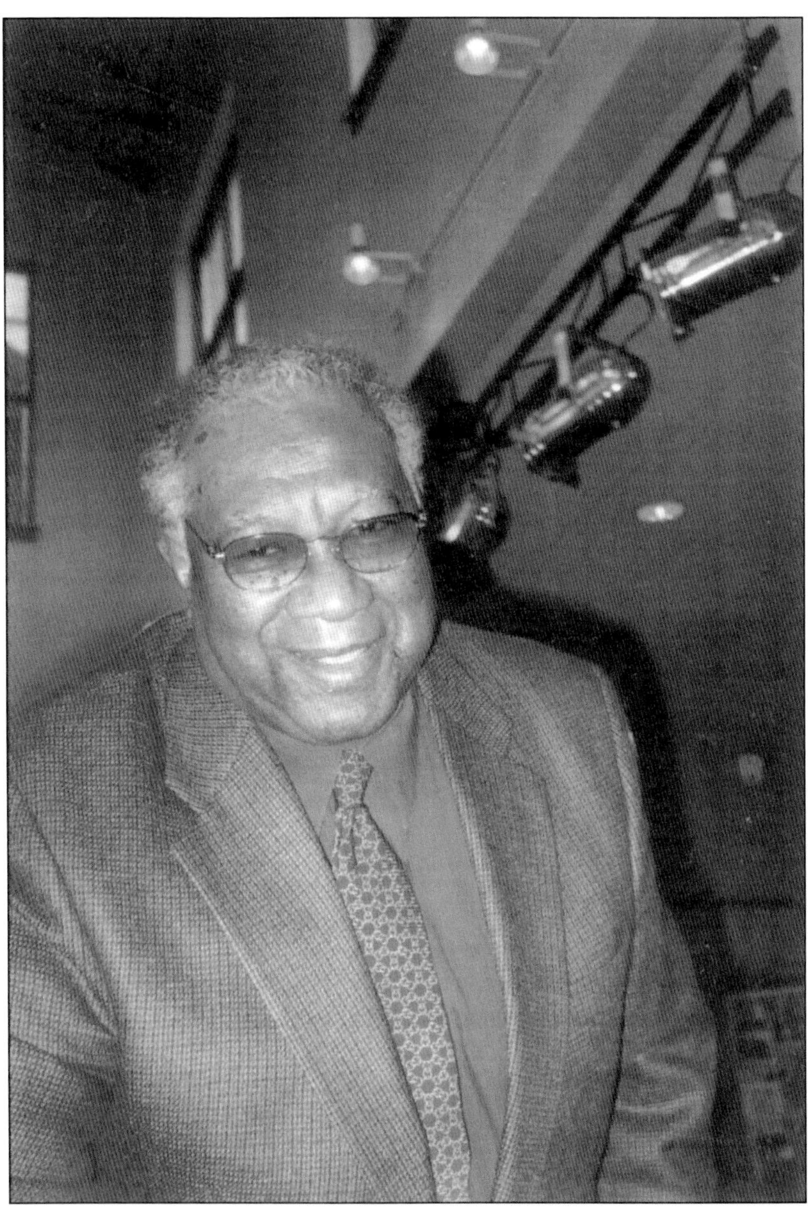

It was no secret that Clarence L. Irving Sr. loved music and history. The former Addisleigh Park resident was a widely respected historian and cultural activist who collected vast amounts of books, stamps, records, and literature about black history that included facts about southeast Queens. Irving established the Black Heritage Foundation to promote the image of African Americans in the United States. He lived on the same block as jazz bassist Milt Hinton and down the street from entertainer Count Basie. That must have been a treat for Irving, who researched where other Queens musicians and entertainers lived when he created the Queens Black Heritage Jazz Trail. Irving proposed a walking tour of places to learn more about black history in Queens. The tour stops included local businesses and the Allen African Methodist Episcopal Church, which was founded in 1834 in Jamaica. Irving's map also highlighted L.B. Griffin Landscaping Company, the first and largest black-owned industrial landscaping company in New York. (Courtesy of Lillie B. Crowder.)

Trombonist and composer Juan Tizol developed his musical talents while growing up in Puerto Rico. He met bandleader Duke Ellington in 1929 and wrote many songs, such as "Caravan" in 1936 and "Perdido" in 1941. Tizol worked with Ellington in the 1930s and 1940s and is widely credited with bringing Latin sounds to songs such as "Moonlight Fiesta" and "Conga Brava." Tizol later worked with orchestra leader Harry James. (Courtesy of Dr. Thomas Manuel.)

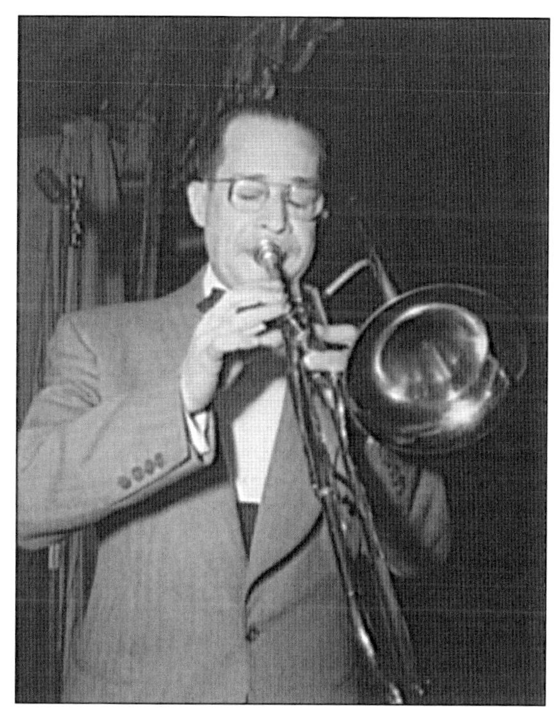

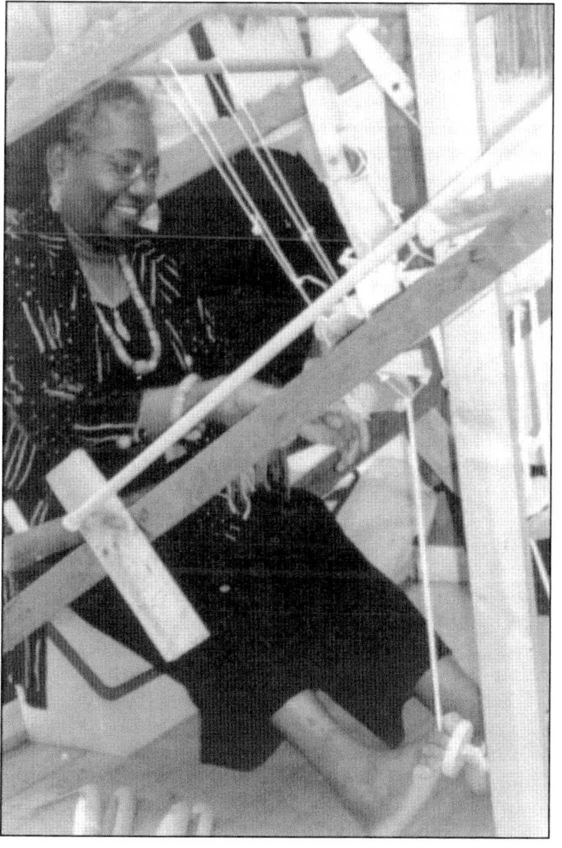

Addisleigh Park resident Dr. Luberta Fields Mays was a well-regarded elementary school and college educator who taught in New York City public schools. She started her teaching career in 1954 at PS 157 in Harlem. She later worked at PS 140 (Edward K. Ellington School) in Queens and PS 40 (Samuel Huntington School) in Queens. She also taught at the Bank Street School for Children in Manhattan. Dr. Mays met her husband of 59 years, Frederick D. Mays Jr.—another teacher—while working at an after-school program. In 1974, Dr. Mays became a teacher educator at Medgar Evers College (MEC) in Brooklyn. She later became MEC's provost and retired in 1992. Dr. Mays was active in several civic and social organizations. She became a master quilter and world traveler. (Courtesy of Frederick Mays.)

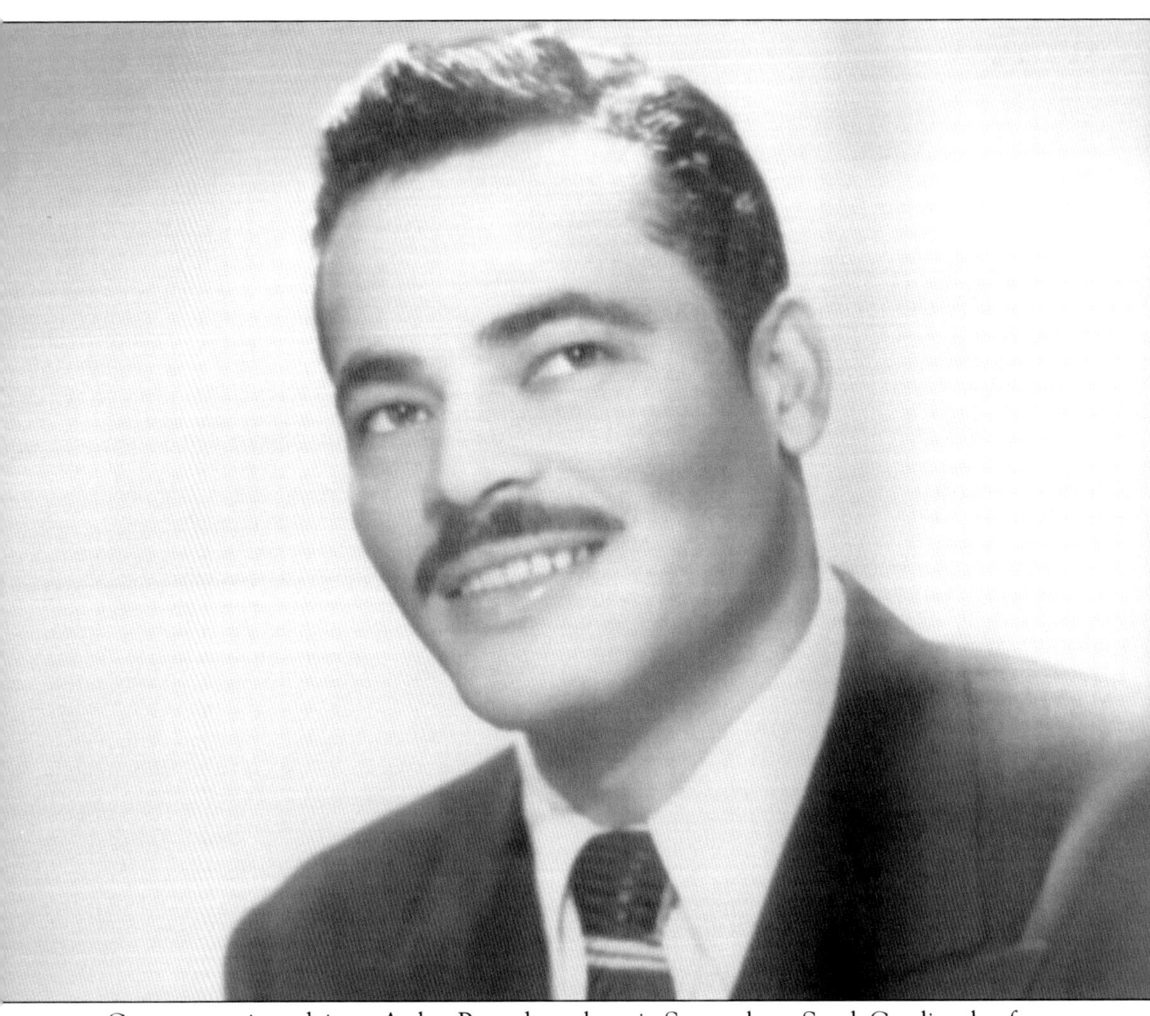

Grammy-nominated singer Arthur Prysock was born in Spartanburg, South Carolina, but for many years, the handsome jazz and rhythm and blues crooner called St. Albans home. Prysock lived near Foch Boulevard in a modest home he shared with his wife, Jean, and two young daughters Jeanatta and Jeanine. He got his start as a teen vocalist with blues pianist/bandleader Buddy Johnson's orchestra in 1944, and recorded "They Say I'm the Biggest Fool" in 1946. The smooth baritone went solo by 1952 with "I Didn't Sleep a Wink Last Night." Among other Prysock songs were "The Very Thought of You" (1960) and "When Love Was New" (1976). The 1980s brought more fame for Prysock. Lowenbrau Beer hired Prysock to sing on its commercials, which included the famous line, "Tonight, let it be Lowenbrau." Prysock was twice nominated for Grammy awards for "Teach Me Tonight" with singer Betty Joplin (1987) and "This Guy is in Love With You" in 1987. Always civic-minded, Prysock frequently performed for servicemen and women at St. Albans Naval Hospital. He also sponsored recreational activities for local youths, including bowling leagues and baseball teams for several years. Prysock socialized with other St. Albans musicians such as Count Basie and record producer Henry Glover. (Courtesy of Jean Prysock.)

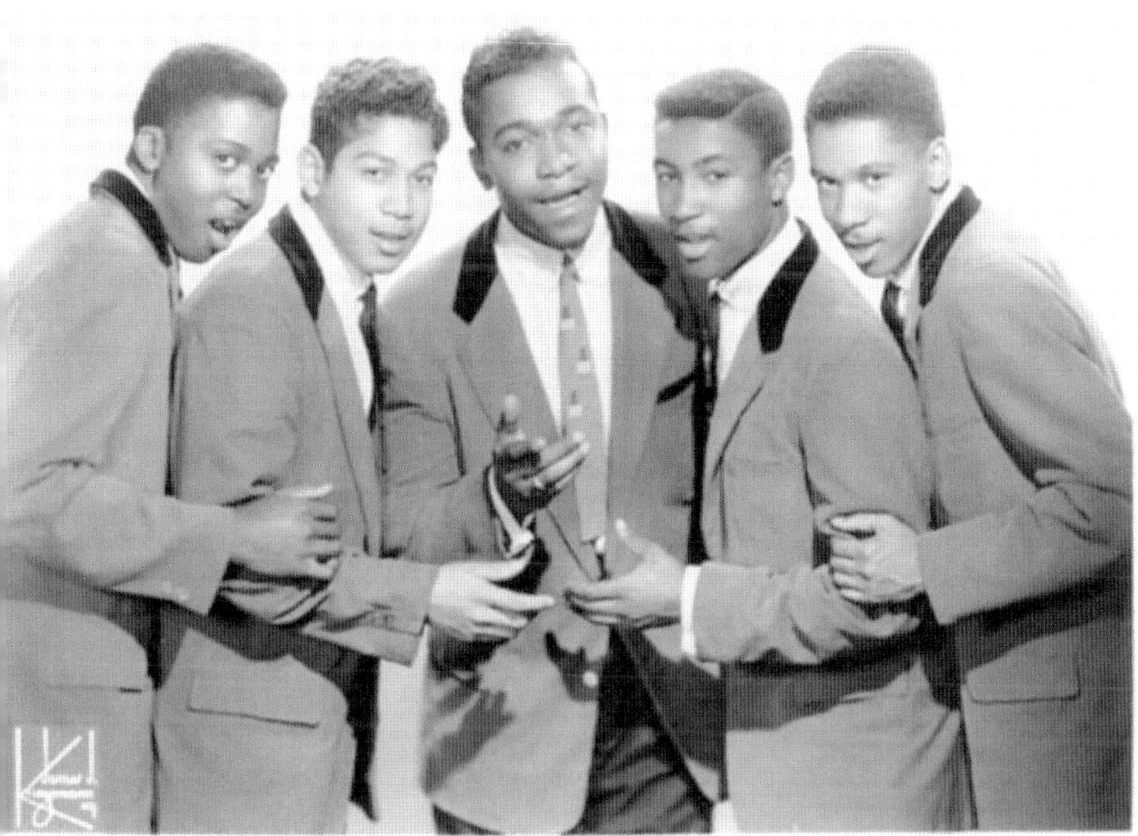

Singer and music executive Christian Walderman "Wally" Roker (second from left) was known as "the Godfather of Doo-Wop." The bass singer grew up in Addisleigh Park and attended Woodrow Wilson High School in Jamaica (now known as August Martin High School). He heard a schoolmate, Vernon Sievers, singing in the school's bathroom and decided to form a group in 1953. Roker and Crump were joined by neighborhood friends Albert Crump, Robbie Tatum, and later, James Sheppard. They practiced in nearby St. Albans Memorial Park. They had several popular hits, including "A Thousand Miles Away," "Your Way," and "Darling How Long." Roker credited the group's early success to his pestering Addisleigh Park residents and musicians Illinois Jacquet and his brother Russell Jacquet with getting the Heartbeats in a recording studio. After the Heartbeats broke up, Roker became a music promoter and had his own record label at one time. His cousin is *Today Show* meteorologist Al Roker. (Courtesy of Wally Roker and Marv Goldberg.)

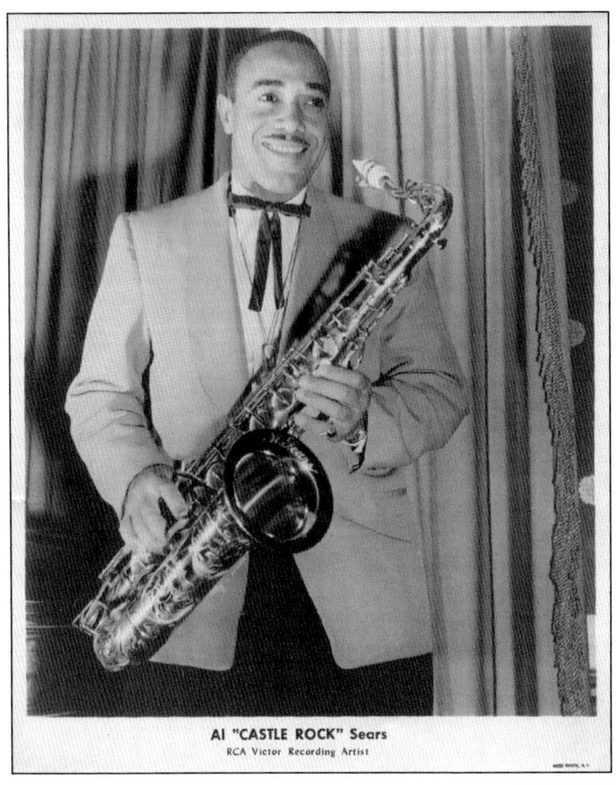

Tenor saxophonist Albert Omega Sears is best known for writing "Castle Rock," a song that was first recorded by saxophonist Johnny Hodges in 1951. The song was later covered by other artists, including Henry Mancini and Woody Herman. The Macomb, Illinois, native performed with jazz greats such as vibraphonist Lionel Hampton in 1943 and Duke Ellington's orchestra in 1944. He was a studio musician with several R&B bands in the 1950s. Sears also owned the Arock and Gator record labels. After Sears's death, his wife, Ruth, donated one of his instruments to York College in Jamaica. (Courtesy of Lillie B. Crowder.)

William Grant Still is considered the "dean" of American composers. He was a gifted music arranger and composer who played every instrument except the piano. He was the first African American to have a major orchestra—the Rochester Philharmonic—perform one of his compositions, *Afro-American Symphony*, in 1931. Still was also the first African American to conduct a major orchestra—the Los Angeles Philharmonic—in 1936, at the Hollywood Bowl. He also arranged music for W.C. Handy, Artie Shaw, and Paul Whiteman. Born in Mississippi, Still moved to Arkansas with his mother after his father was murdered in Mississippi shortly after he was born. He enrolled in the Oberlin Conservatory of Music and headed to New York City to work with W.C. Handy from 1921 to 1934. In 1928, he resided at 108-15 172nd St. in St. Albans. Among his works are "Darker America" (1924), "From the Black Belt" (1926), and "Troubled Island" (1949). His daughter has written a screenplay about his life that a major studio is considering making a film. (Courtesy of Judith Anne Still.)

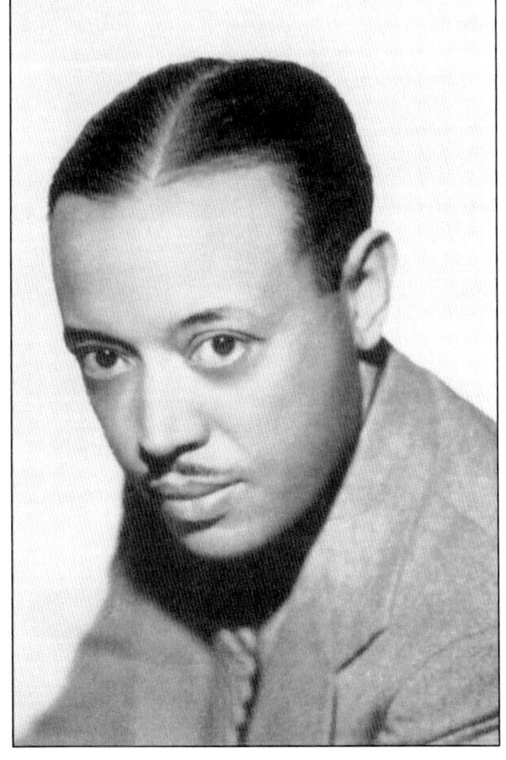

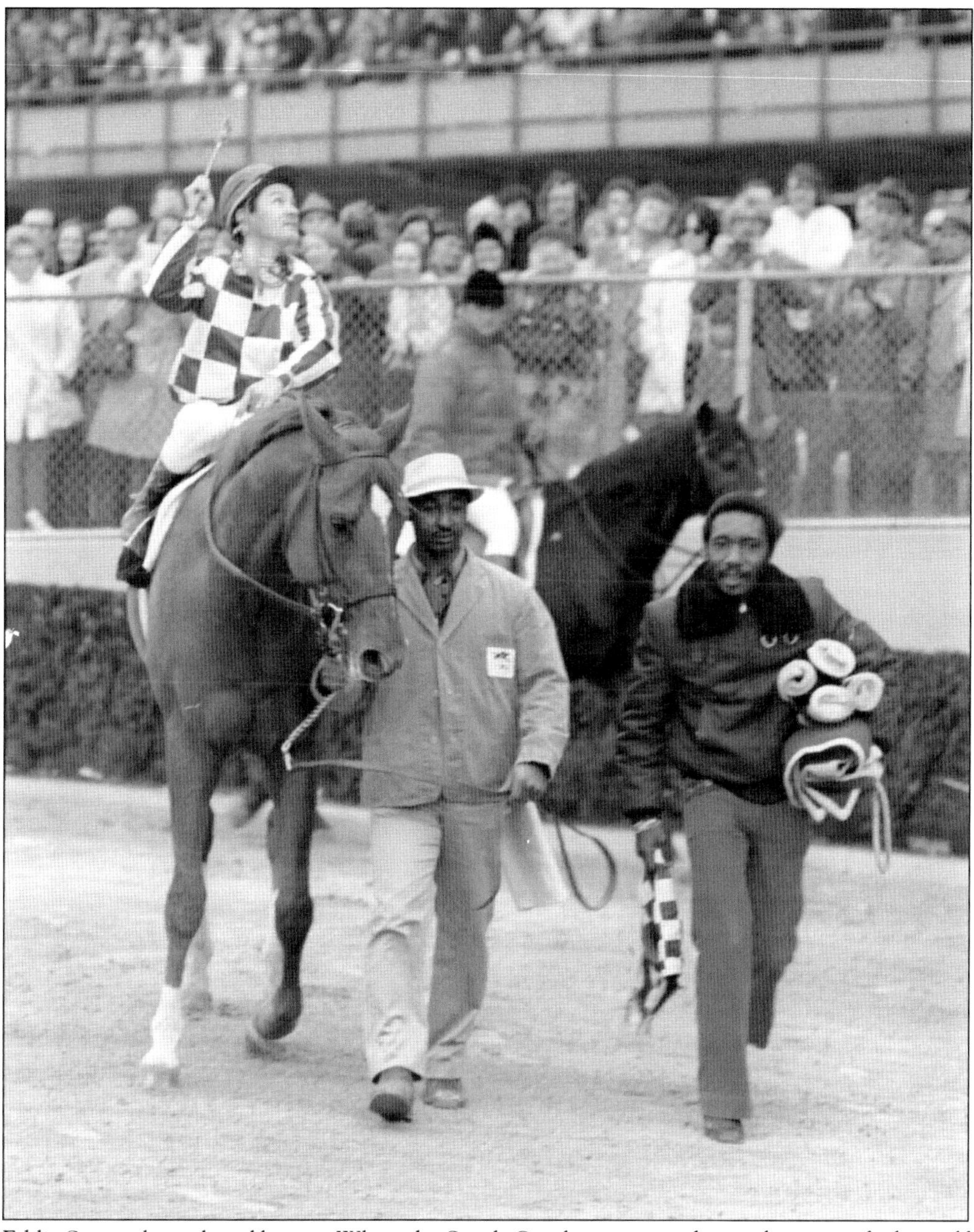

Eddie Sweat always loved horses. When the South Carolina native who made a name for himself as an exceptional horse handler relocated to New York, he settled in St. Albans to be closer to Belmont race track in nearby Elmont, Long Island. The 1970s brought Sweat a lot of work and attention as the groom for Kentucky Derby–winning horses Riva Ridge and Secretariat. In 1972, Secretariat was named American Horse of the Year. In 1973, Secretariat won the Triple Crown, and as a result, Sweat gained more notoriety, being frequently photographed with the famous horse. Author and horse enthusiast Lawrence Scanlan wrote a 2007 book that included a look at Sweat and his connection with Secretariat in *The Horse God Built*. Sweat's impressive list of horses he cared for include Filly Quill, Angie Light, and Chief Crown. (Courtesy of the New York Racing Authority.)

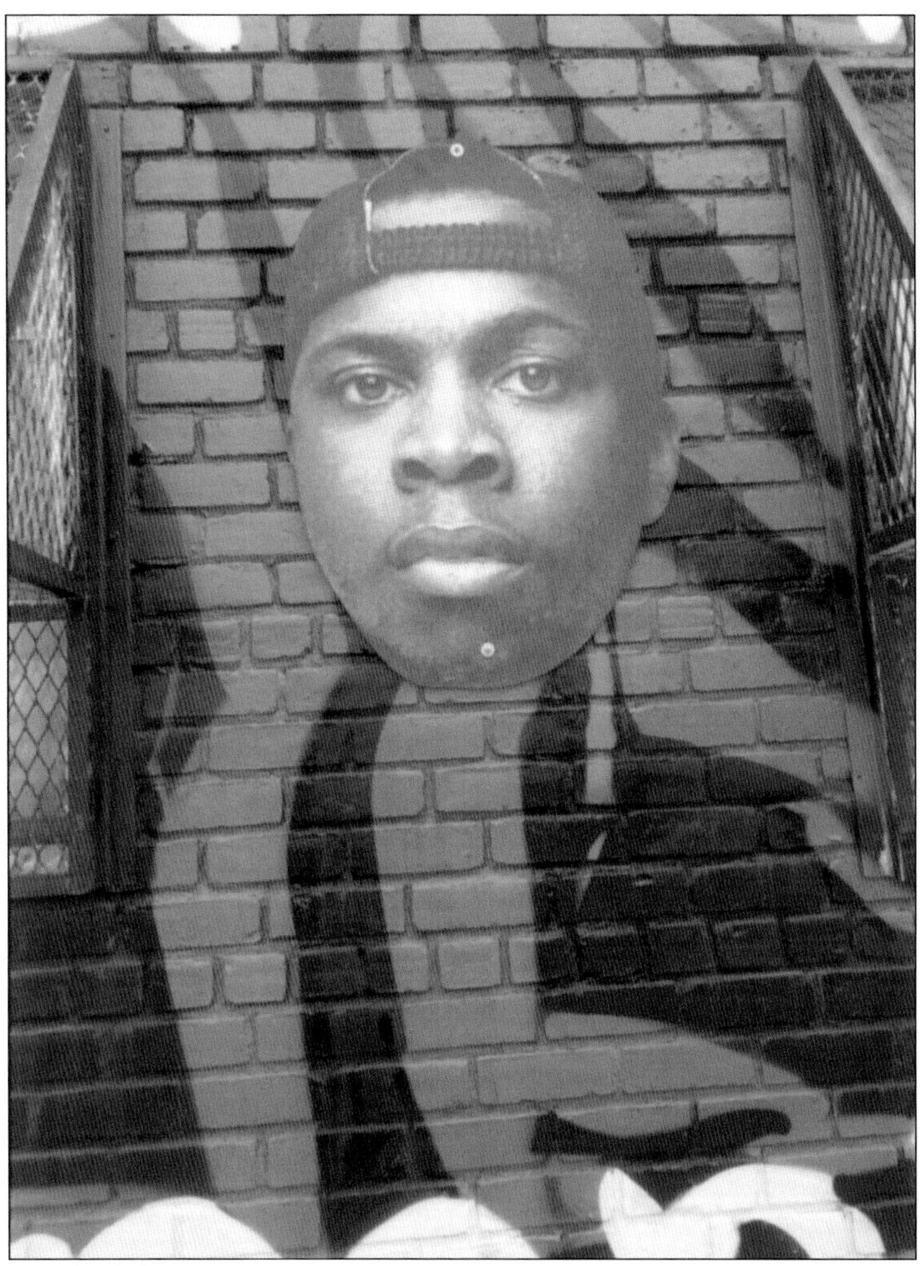

Malik Izaak "Phife Dawg" Taylor was a co-founder of A Tribe Called Quest, an alternative hip hop group formed in 1985. Taylor and two other original members hail from St. Albans: co-founder and producer Jonathan William Davis (Q-Tip) and Jarobi White. A fourth member, Ali Shaheed Muhammad, is a Brooklyn native. The group's first hit was "Can I Kick It?" in 1989, which was praised for its new sound that blended jazz and hip hop. In 1991, the group filmed a video, "Check the Rhime," on the rooftop of Nu-Clear Drive-in Cleaners on Linden Boulevard, which excited local fans. After Taylor died in 2016, a mural by artist Vince Ballentine appeared on the side of the dry cleaner's building as a tribute to A Tribe Called Quest. Community leaders and local politicians worked together to rename the intersection of Linden Boulevard and 192nd St. Malik "Phife Dawg" Taylor Way to honor the popular entertainer. (Photograph by Claire Serant.)

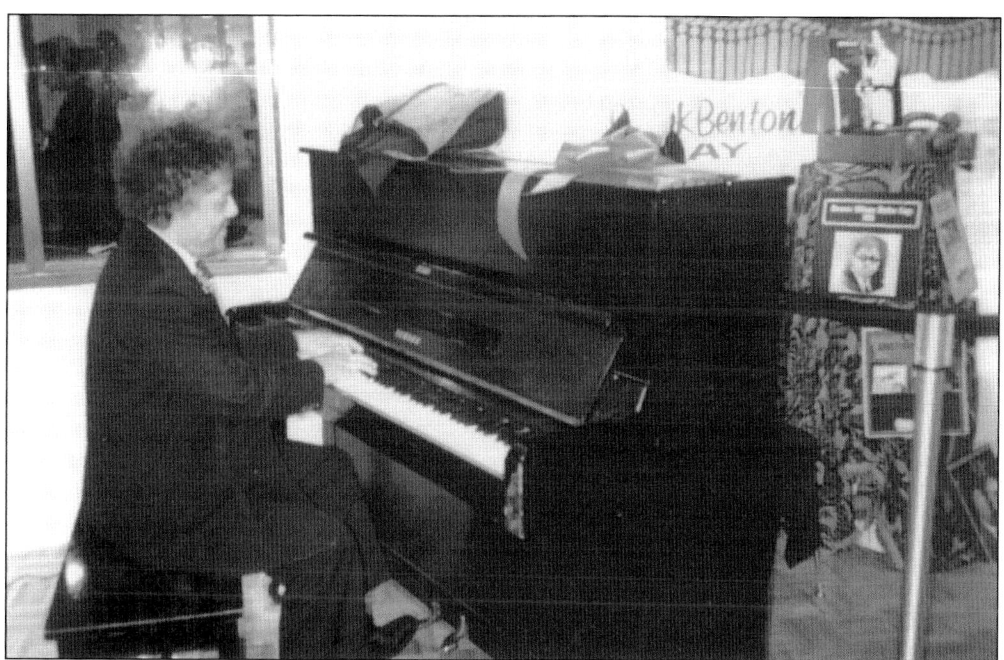

Jazz and blues pianist Bross Elvie Townsend perfected his talent as a Cleveland Institute of Music student. The Kentucky native came to New York City and made a name for himself. He accompanied fellow St. Albans residents such as singer Wynonie Harris and saxophonist John Coltrane on several gigs, to name a few. Despite blindness that occurred in the 1990s, Townsend, who was known for being part of his own trio, the 3Bs, continued to perform in venues around New York City including Flushing Town Hall. This photograph was taken during a Brook Benton Day celebration in Queens. (Courtesy of Lillie B. Crowder.)

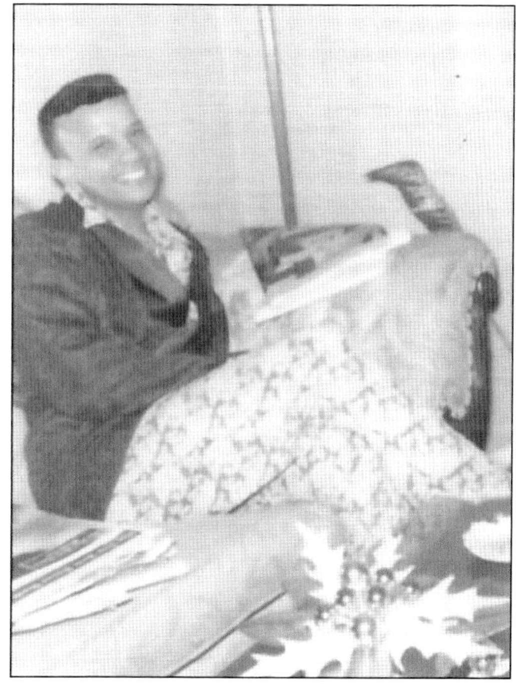

Harold Baron Jackson (1915–2012) was a radio personality and business leader and a pioneer in a field that had few African Americans. The South Carolina native was known for his popular *Sunday Classics* radio show on WBLS-FM and for the Hal Jackson Talented Teen International Competition, which inspired many young women of color to pursue higher education. Jackson started his broadcasting career as a student at Howard University in Washington, DC. When he came to New York City in 1954, he worked on three daily shows at three different stations. In 1972, he and Percy Sutton co-founded Inner City Broadcasting Corp. Jackson was the first African-American installed in the National Association of Broadcasters Hall of Fame, in 1990. Five years later, he was the first African American inducted into the National Radio Hall of Fame. He is pictured in 1957 in the living room of his St. Albans home. (Courtesy of Jewell Jackson McCabe.)

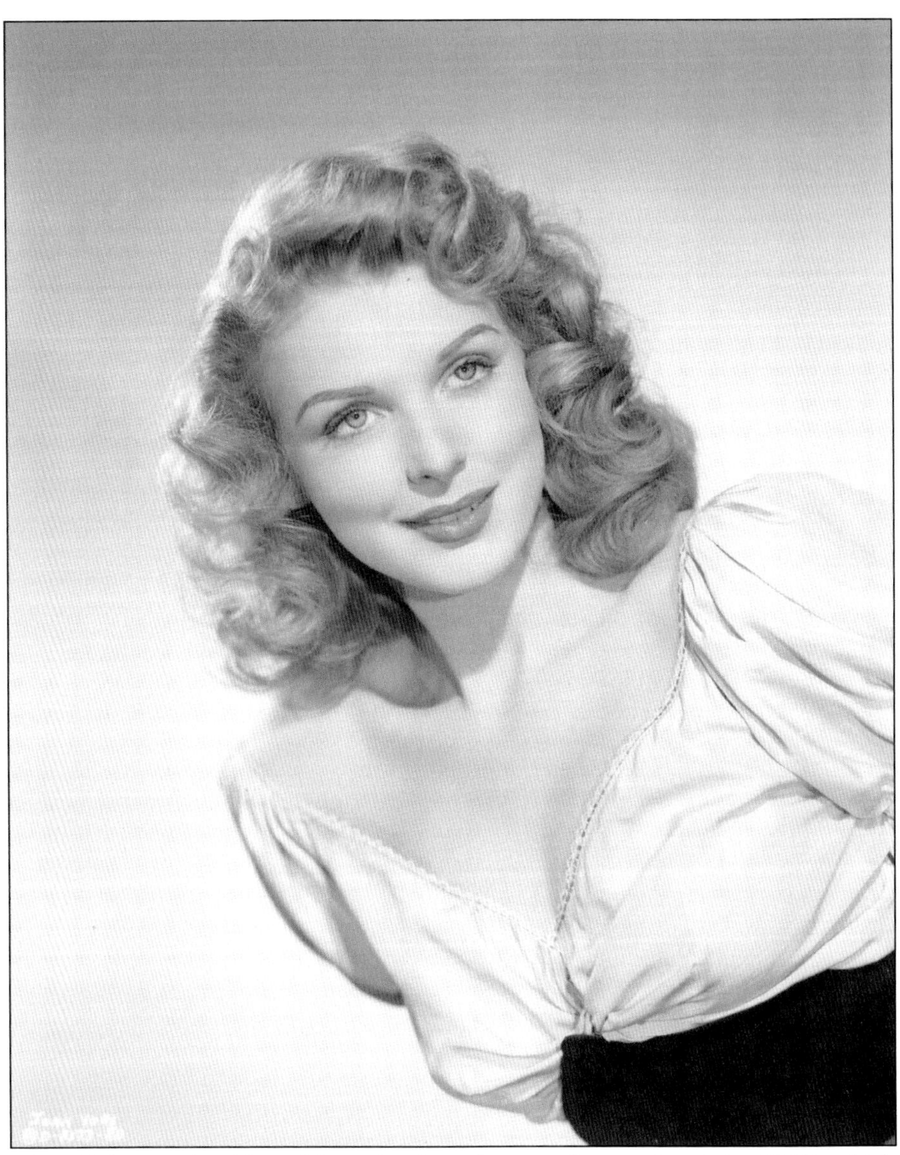

Elinor Joan Vohs was the eldest of three daughters born to Queens electrician William Vohs and his wife, Josephine. The family lived in a modest brick home at 118-31 198th St. in St. Albans in the 1940s. By 16, Vohs, a blond model and dancer, dropped her first name to become one of the youngest Radio City Music Hall Rockettes. Her movie career was given a boost after she appeared in an uncredited role as one of several beautiful women in a scene that actor Ronald Reagan played in *The Girl from Jones Beach* in 1949. The 1950s brought several movie roles such as *Dangerous Inheritance* (1950) and *Sabrina* (1954). Vohs starred with actor Edward G. Robinson and Paulette Goddard in "Vice Squad" in 1953. That same year, a *Brooklyn Daily Eagle* reporter noted that Vohs lived in North Hollywood with her family and was one of the few women in the industry who used her own name professionally. Vohs frequently fought against being typecast in "dumb blonde" roles. She also performed in several television series including *Bachelor Father, Family Affair, Perry Mason, Maverick,* and *My Three Sons*. She married John G. Stephens, a production manager on *My Three Sons*, and had two children. This image is from a 1950s press kit. (Courtesy of C. Robert Rotter.)

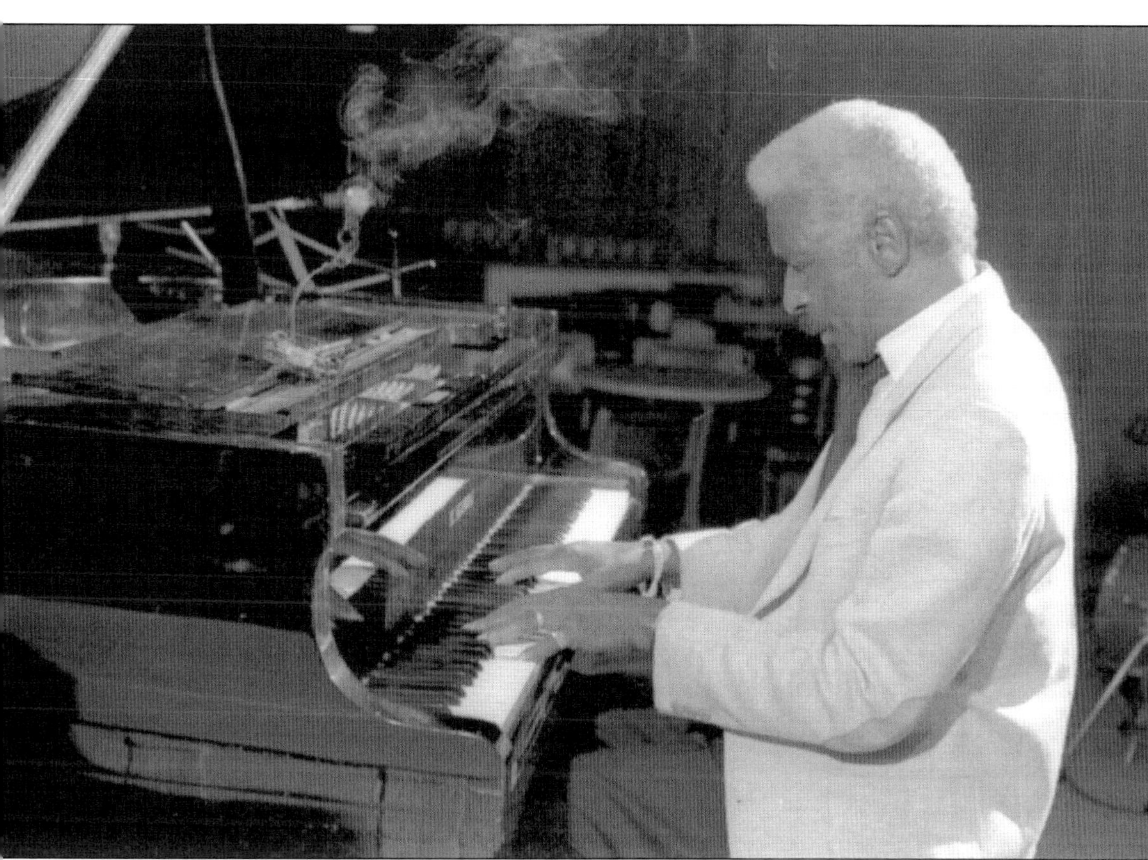

Pianist, composer, and arranger Malcolm Earl Waldron played bebop and free jazz with musicians John Coltrane, Eric Dolphy, and Charles Mingus. The Harlem-born New Yorker moved to Jamaica, Queens, when he was four years old. His Caribbean American parents encouraged him to play the piano. However, by the time he joined the Army in 1943, Waldron was interested in the saxophone. In 1945, Waldron attended Queens College on the GI bill. The music major earned his bachelor's degree in 1949. After playing for local musicians, he formed his own band in 1956. He worked as an accompanist for singer Billie Holiday from 1957 until she died in 1959. Later, he worked with singer Abbey Lincoln and her husband, drummer Max Roach. Waldron spoke four languages: English, French, German, and Japanese. He wrote "Soul Eyes" in 1957, which is widely considered a jazz standard. He often composed songs at his St. Albans home. This photograph was taken in August 1987 during a San Francisco performance. (Photograph by Brian McMillen.)

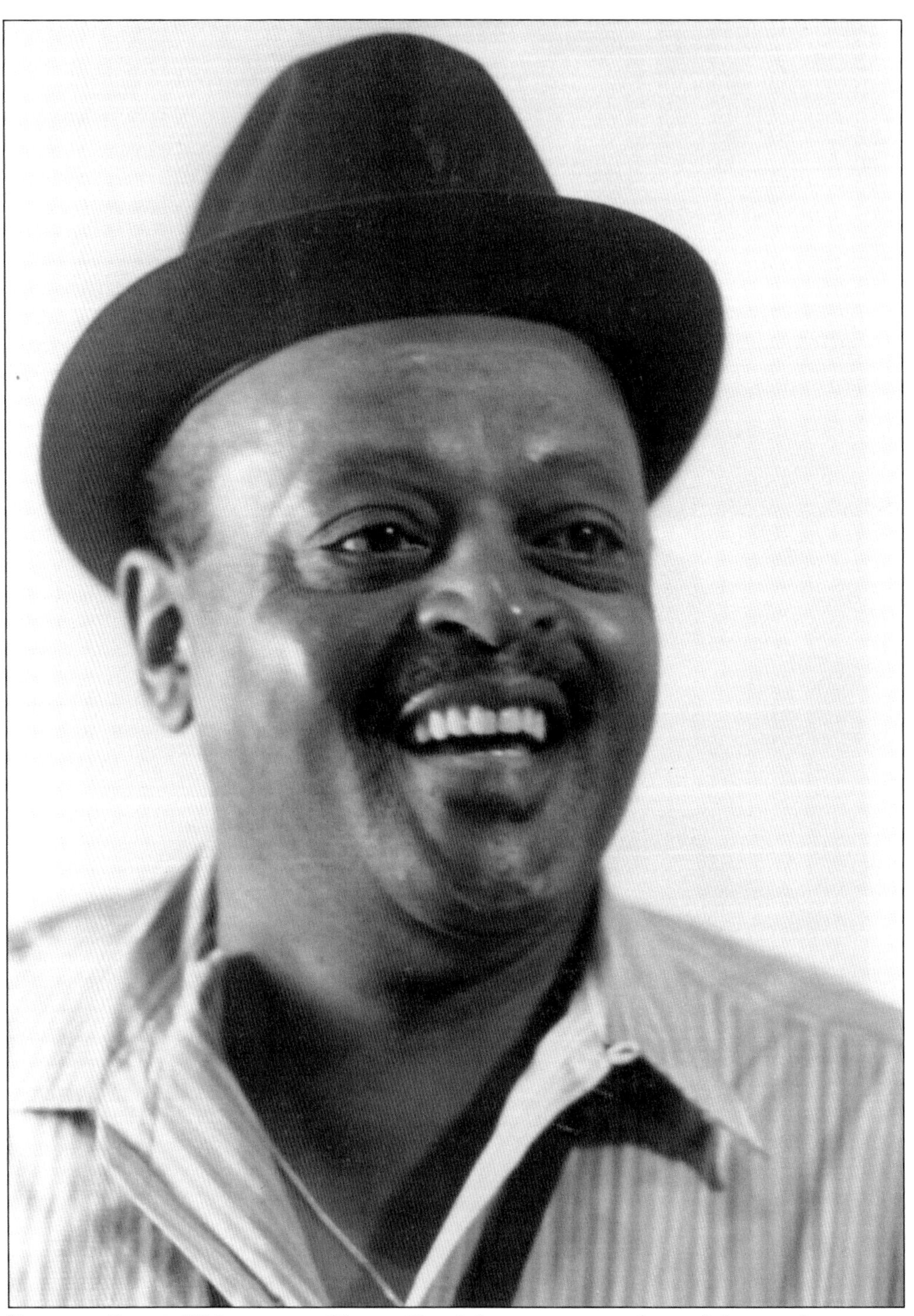

Benjamin Francis Webster was a Kansas City, Missouri, native whose ability to play a tenor saxophone won the admiration of his fans and other musicians. The St. Albans resident performed with Lester Young, the Fletcher Henderson Orchestra, Cab Calloway, Benny Carter, and the Duke Ellington Orchestra. (Courtesy of Lillie B. Crowder.)

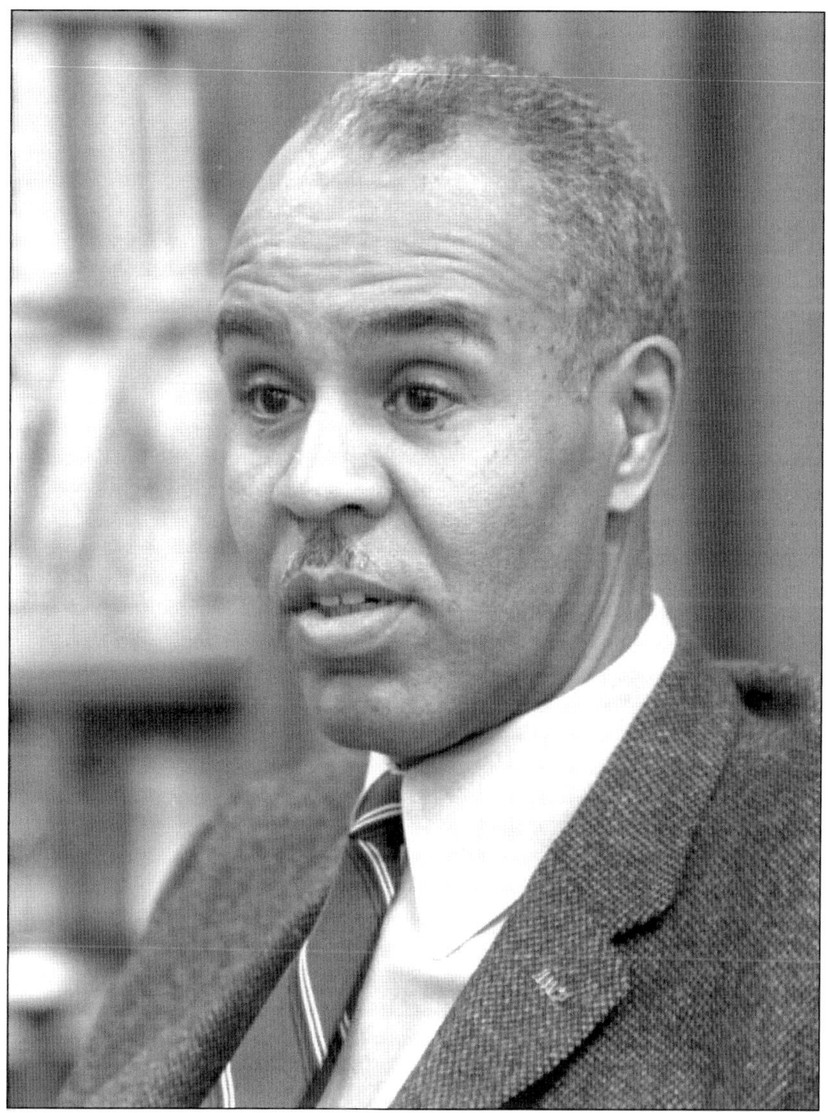

Civil Rights activist and head of the NAACP from 1964 to 1977, Roy Ottoway Wilkins was known for using legislative means to address the economic and social problems that faced African Americans. Wilkins often testified before Congress about the effects of discrimination, limited education, and job opportunities. The St. Louis native graduated from the University of Minnesota in 1923 and worked as a journalist before coming to New York City in 1931. Wilkins became the assistant NAACP secretary under the organization's then-president Walter White. In 1934, Wilkins replaced W.E.B. Du Bois as editor of the *Crisis*, the NAACP's official magazine. In 1955, Wilkins became the NAACP's executive secretary. He played an important role during the civil rights movement and its prominent legal cases such as Brown v. Board of Education, the Civil Rights Act of 1964, and the Voting Rights Act of 1965. In 1967, Pres. Lyndon Johnson gave Wilkins the Presidential Medal of Freedom. Wilkins stepped down from his NAACP top post in 1977. He was later named director emeritus of the organization he spent decades representing. Today, the former St. Albans resident is remembered with the naming of PS 136 on 115th Avenue as the Roy Wilkins School, Roy Wilkins Park on Merrick Boulevard, and the Roy Wilkins Recreation Center inside the park that bears his name. (Courtesy of the Jamaica NAACP.)

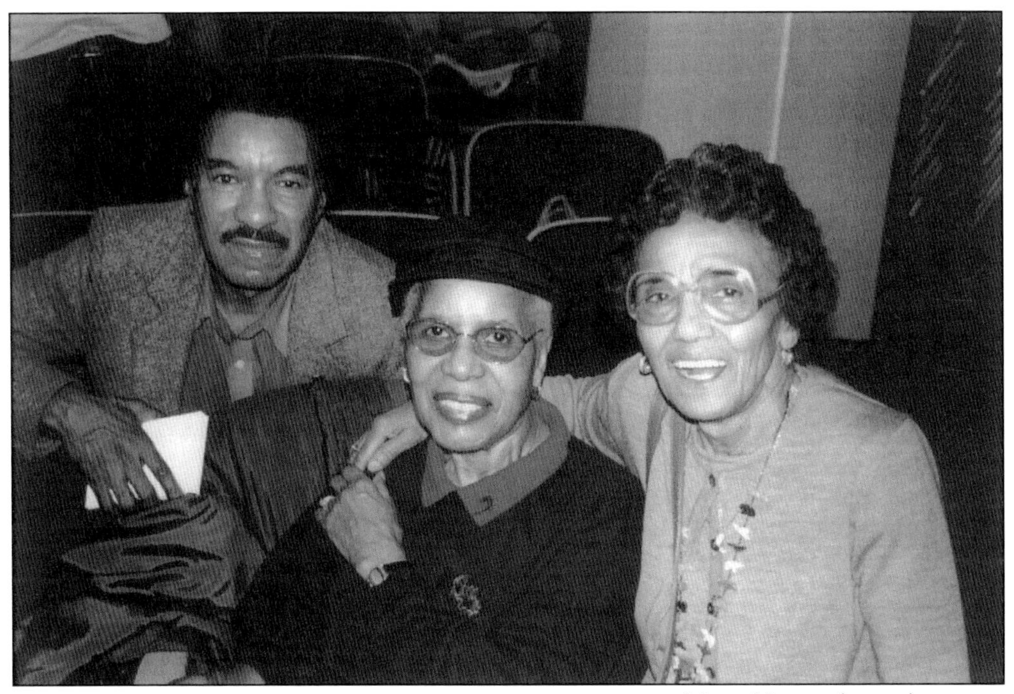

Mona Hinton (center), the wife of bassist Milt Hinton, smiles with musical director and composer Frank Owens and Delores Bell, wife of Dr. Aaron Bell, a double bassist and college music professor. (Courtesy of Lillie B. Crowder.)

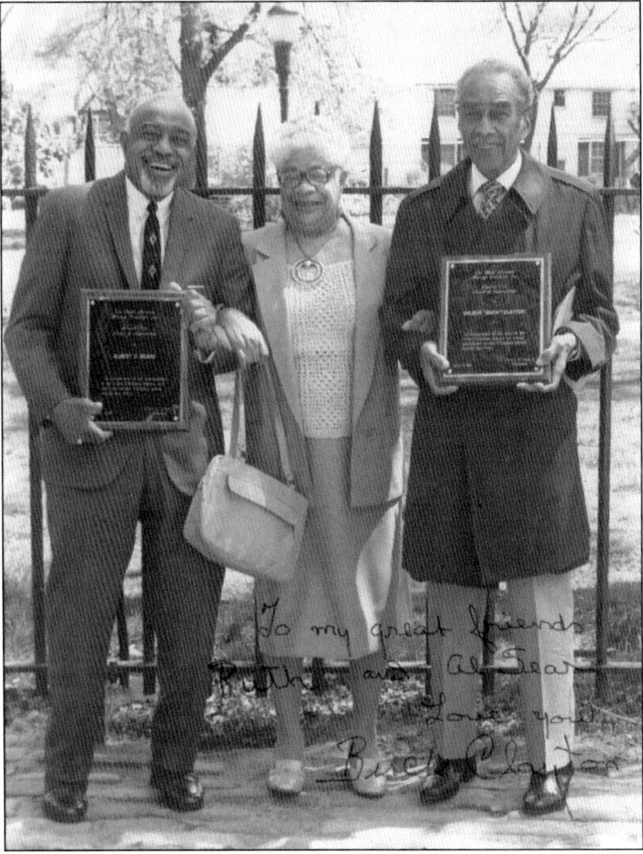

Tenor saxophonist Albert Sears (left) shares a laugh with his wife, Ruth, and longtime friend trumpet player Buck Clayton (1911–1991) in Queens. The musicians pose with awards they received from a community organization. Clayton, a longtime Jamaica resident, also played with Count Basie's orchestra. (Photograph by Nancy Miller Elliott, courtesy of Lillie B. Crowder.)

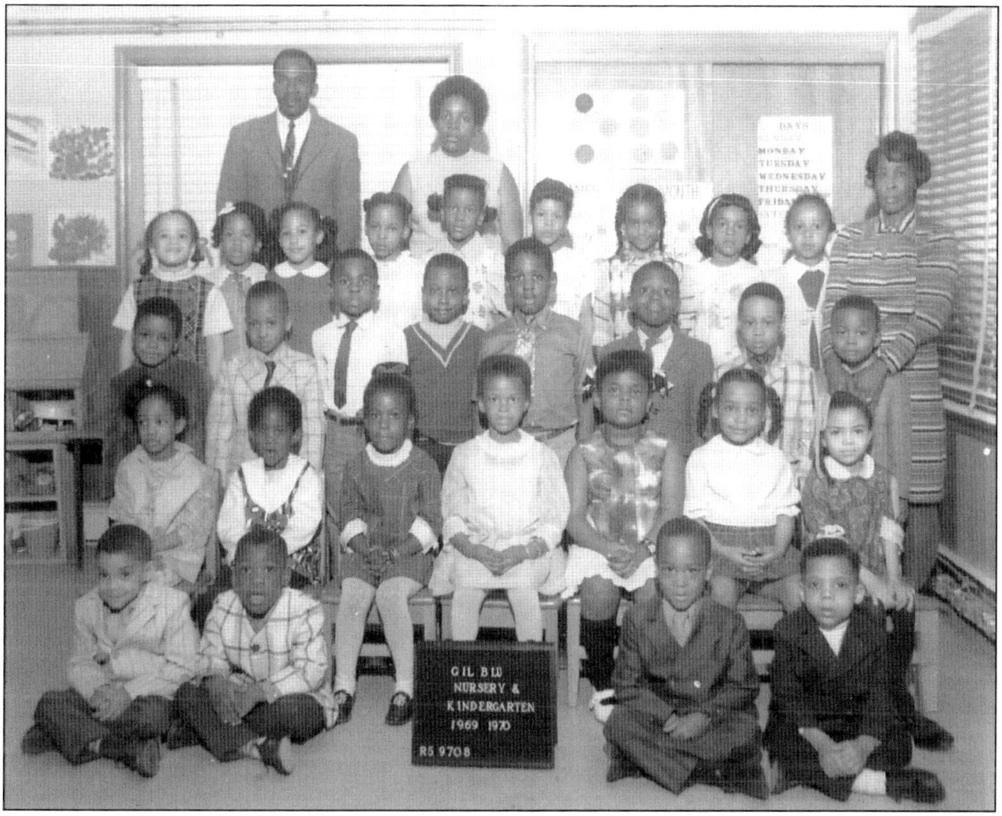

Gil-Blu Nursery and Kindergarten opened in 1967 on Merrick Boulevard. The school, which has educated thousands of southeast Queens students over the years, was started by two Clafin College graduates, Adell Blue and Gertrude Gilford, and Blue's husband, Hugene Blue. Pictured here is a 1969 class photograph with Adell Blue on the far right and her husband on the far left. The Blues moved to St. Albans in 1962. (Courtesy of Pamela Blue-Webb.)

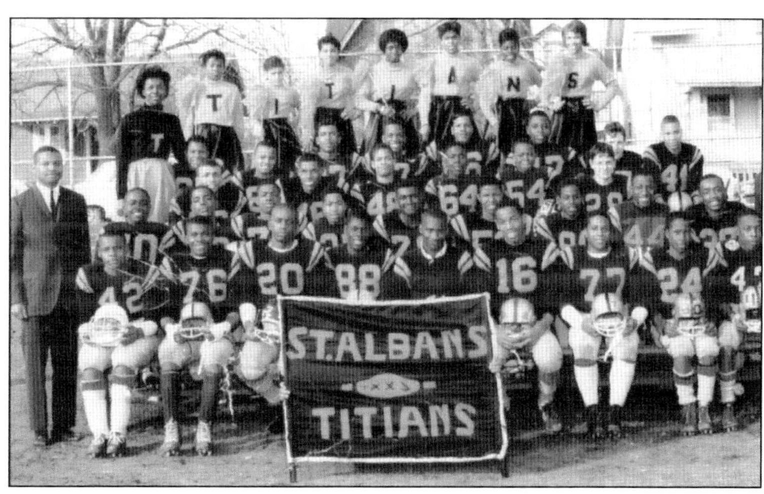

This is a photograph of the St. Albans football team and its cheerleaders. The group, like many sports organizations over the years, utilized Roy Wilkins Park for its recreational needs. (Courtesy of the Presbyterian Church of St. Albans.)

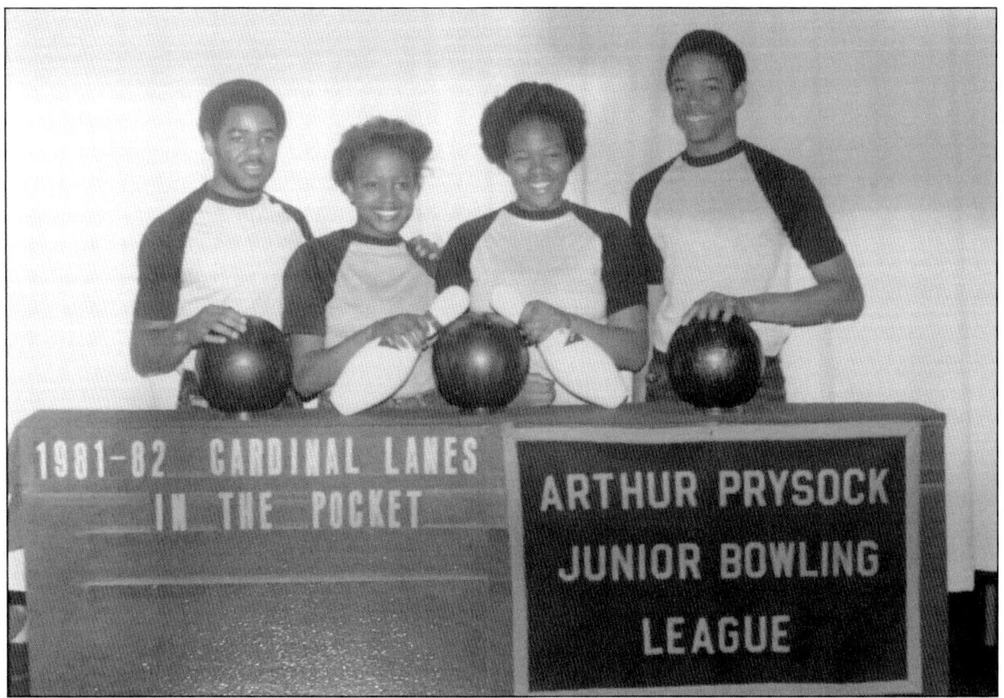

For many years, singer Arthur Prysock sponsored sports teams for southeast Queens youths to improve their baseball or bowling skills. Pictured are four teens standing behind a banner for the Arthur Prysock Junior Bowling League at an event held at Cardinal Lanes in Hollis. (Courtesy of Jean Prysock.)

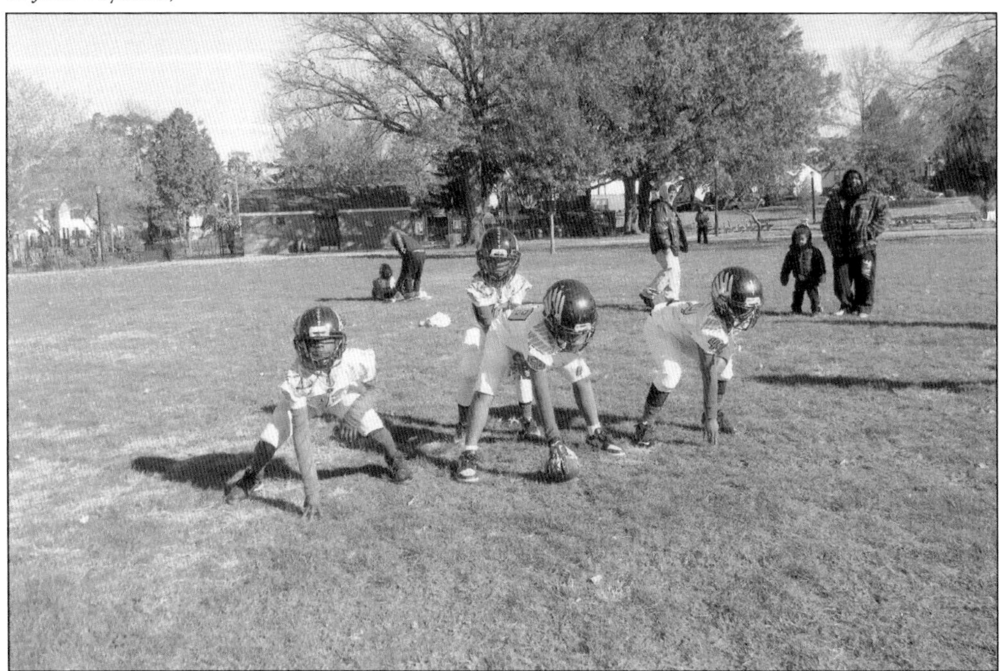

Some members of the St. Albans Trojans football team practice drills under the watchful eye of their coaches at St. Albans Memorial Park in 2016. (Courtesy of Claire Serant.)

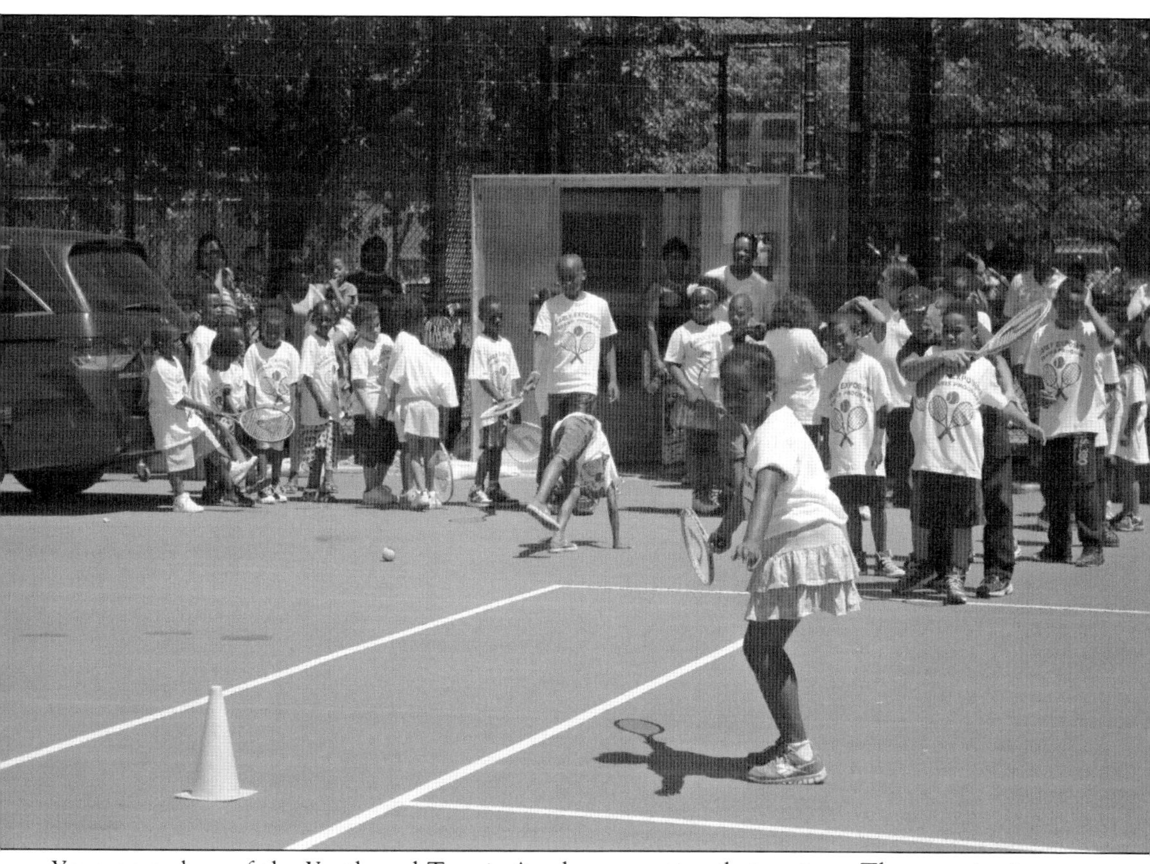

Young members of the Youth and Tennis Academy practice their swings. The organization has taught thousands of children and young adults to love the game. (Courtesy of Dr. Belinda Johnston Briggs.)

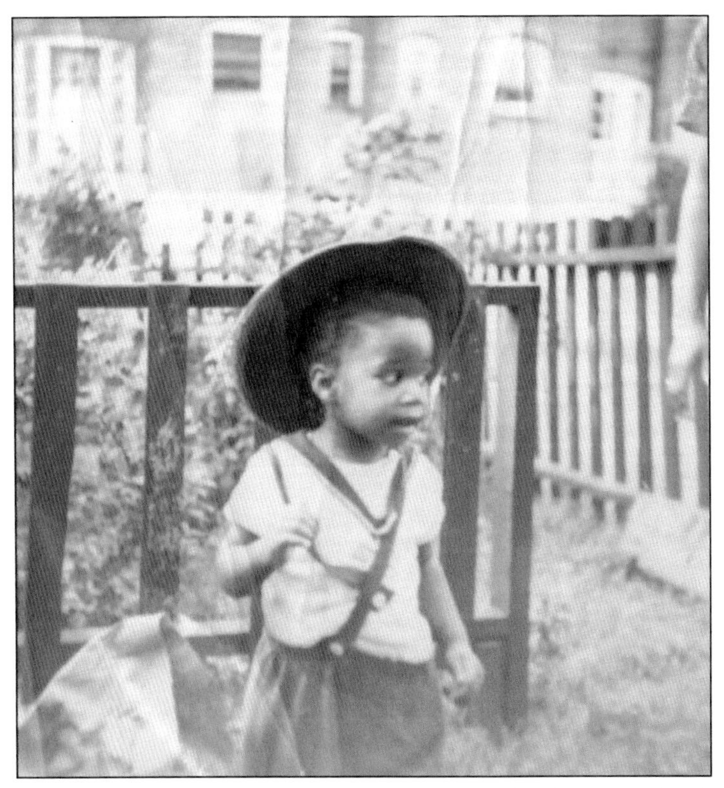

Three-year-old Julian Phillips is pictured at left in the backyard of his parents' home on Ursina Road. Phillips grew up to become an Emmy Award–winning news anchor, co-author of *Discovering Your Hidden Power* with Rev. A.R. Bernard. He is also a motivational speaker and an aspiring chef and restaurateur. He is seen below in 2016 in front of his childhood home. (Both, courtesy of Julian Phillips and Blair Garrett.)

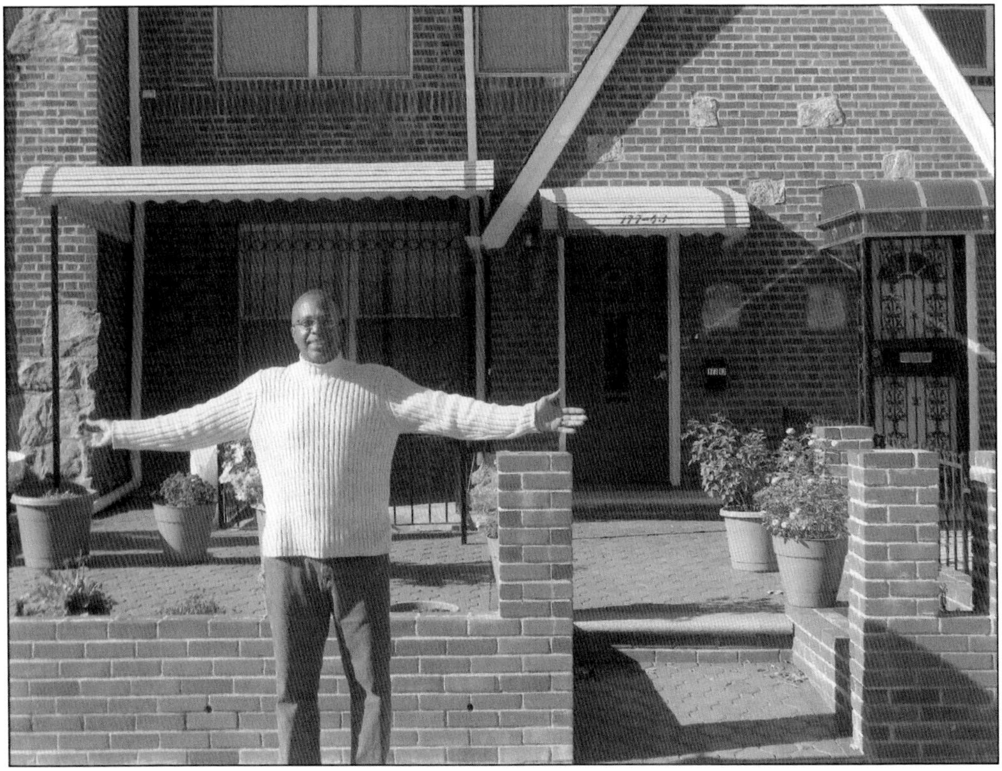

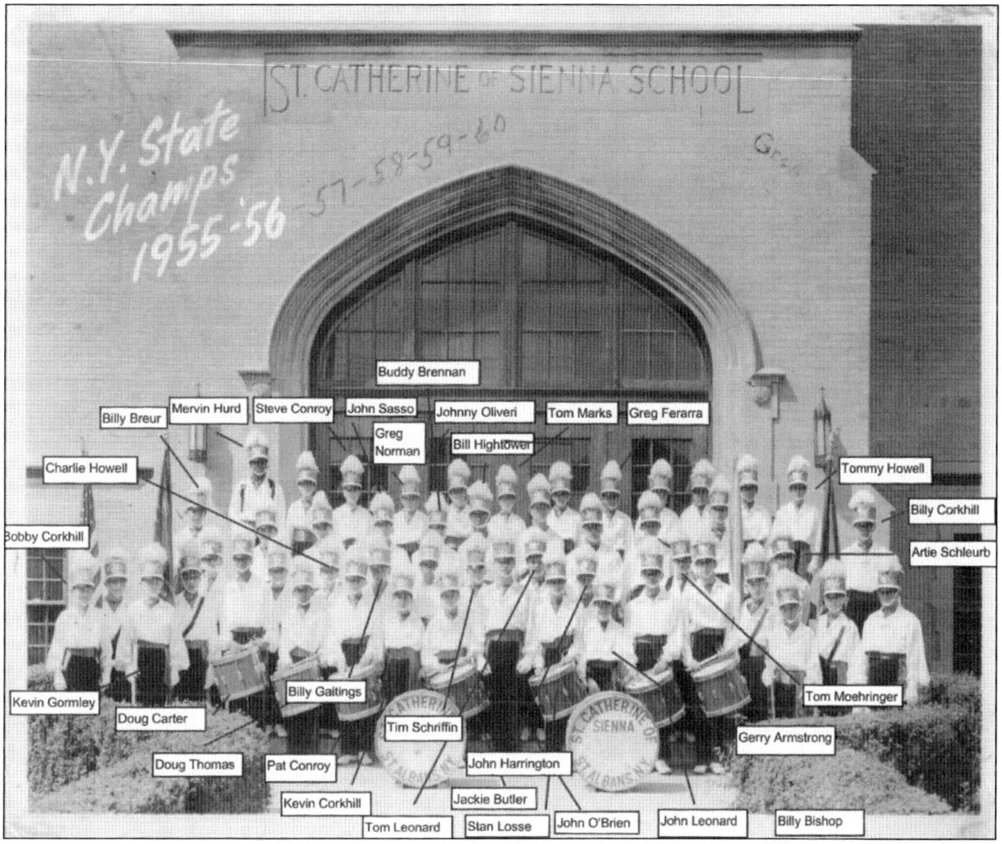

ST. CATHERINE OF SIENNA SCHOOL
N.Y. State Champs 1955-'56-57-58-59-60

Buddy Brennan
Billy Breur
Mervin Hurd
Steve Conroy
John Sasso
Greg Norman
Johnny Oliveri
Bill Hightower
Tom Marks
Greg Ferarra
Charlie Howell
Tommy Howell
Billy Corkhill
Bobby Corkhill
Artie Schleurb
Kevin Gormley
Billy Gaitings
Doug Carter
Tim Schriffin
Tom Moehringer
Gerry Armstrong
Doug Thomas
Pat Conroy
John Harrington
Kevin Corkhill
Jackie Butler
Tom Leonard
Stan Losse
John O'Brien
John Leonard
Billy Bishop

Members of the award-winning St. Catherine of Sienna Queensmen Drum and Bugle Corps gathered for this 1955 photograph. The group were state champions from the mid-1950s through the early 1960s. Drummer Billy Cobham was inspired to play percussion instruments based on his exposure to the Queensmen. St. Catherine of Sienna is located on Riverton Street. Joseph Olivieri was the Queensmen's director. Instructors were Bob Thompson (drums), John Sasso (horns), and Bill Hightower (drill). (Courtesy of Billy Cobham.)

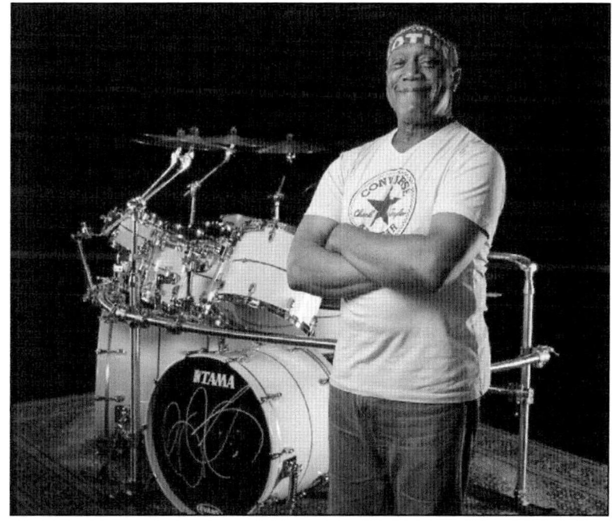

After his Queensmen experience, William Emanuel "Billy" Cobham Jr. attended the prestigious Fiorello LaGuardia High School of Music and Art in Manhattan. He graduated in 1960. The drummer, composer, and bandleader continued his music career performing with famed trumpeter Miles Davis, the New York Jazz Quartet, and the Mahavishnu Orchestra. Cobham is known for his superb technical ability in many genres including funk, jazz fusion, jazz, rock and roll, and popular music. (Courtesy of Billy Cobham.)

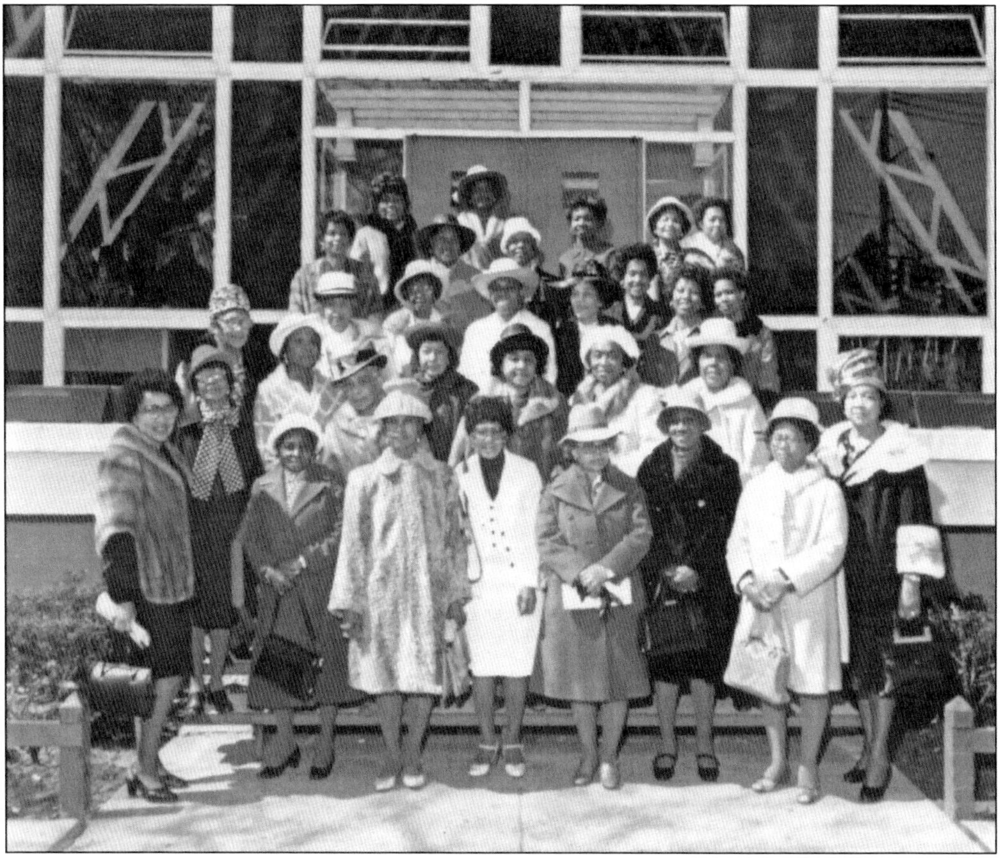

Several members of the Women's Fellowship committee pose outside St. Albans Congregational Church. The edifice is located on Linden Boulevard at 172nd Street and is also known as the "triangle church" for its unique design. (Courtesy of Rev. Henry Simmons and Pat Haskins of St. Albans Congregational Church.)

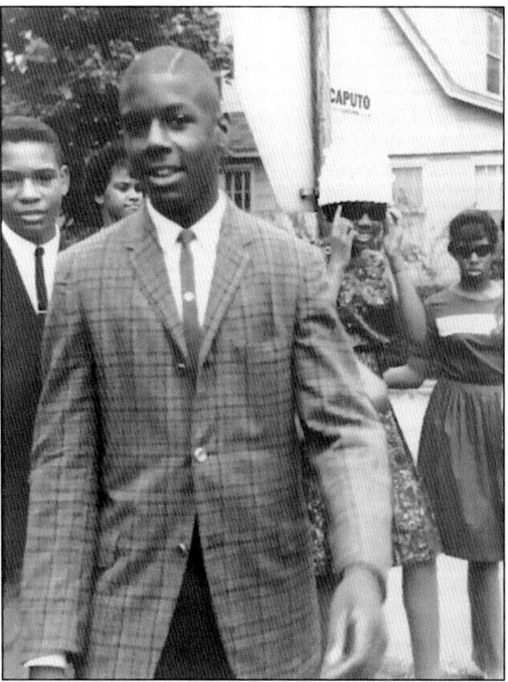

A dapper Richard Clay talks with friends after church in 1962. Clay is the brother of Black Spectrum Theatre founder Carl Clay. (Courtesy of Carl Clay.)

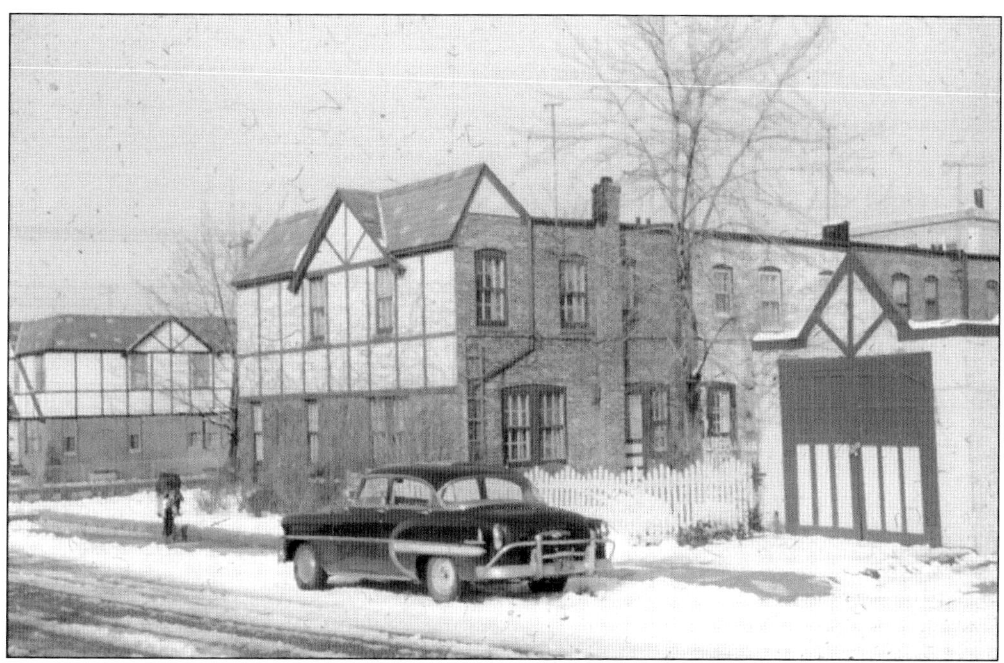

By day, Arthur Golden worked as a social worker. However, the St. Albans resident loved to take photographs in his spare time. Here is a look at 115th Avenue at 200th Street in 1956 after a snowfall. (Courtesy of Joy Golden.)

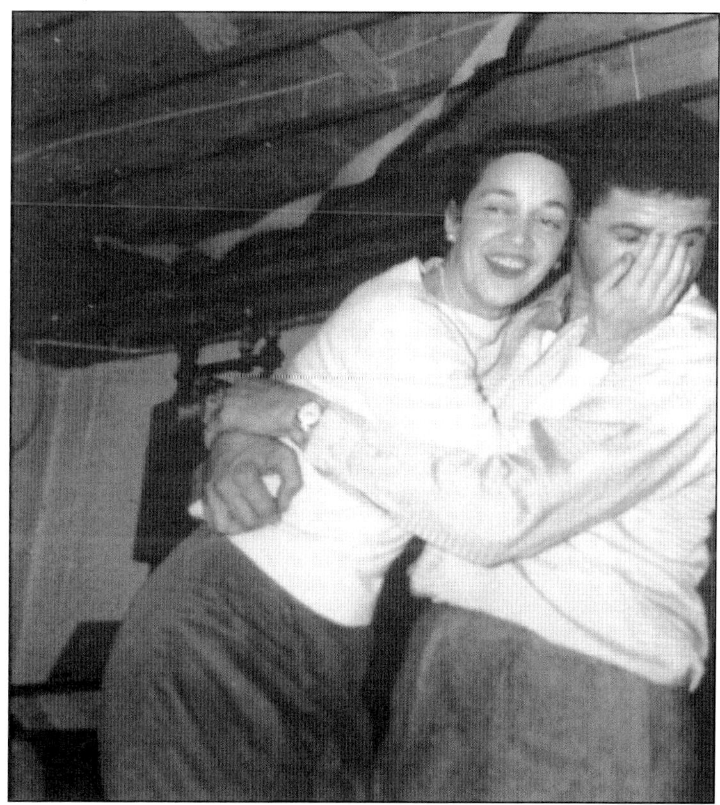

Attorney William Booth and his first wife, Harriet Walker Booth, are pictured in the basement of their St. Albans home. (Courtesy of Gini Booth.)

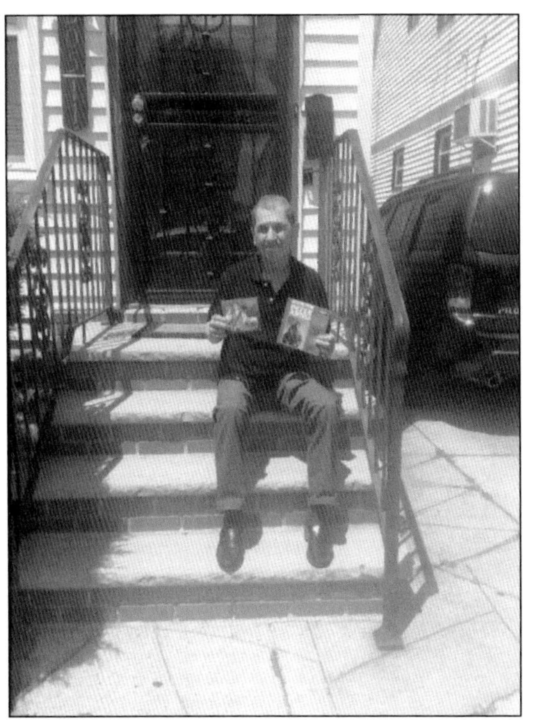

Singer-songwriter Peter Antonio, also known by his stage name Pete Antell, sits on the front steps of his former home at 205-11 116th Rd. The Antonio family lived there in the 1940s through the early 1950s just as St. Albans's demographics began to change. As a 10-year old, Antonio recalled hearing his neighbors whisper, "They're coming," and being confused. His parents, Joseph, a city firefighter, and Carmela Antonio, lived in the modest home with Peter and his four older siblings. The Antonios left St. Albans in 1952 for Long Island, but their youngest son still has fond memories of playing stickball in the street, outings to the St. Albans Theatre on Linden Boulevard to see double-feature movies, and riding the Q4A bus solo to downtown Jamaica's Macy's department store. Peter Antonio returned to his former home in 2016 and met the current owners. He said the single-family homes on the block "looked better than before." (Photograph by Blair Garrett.)

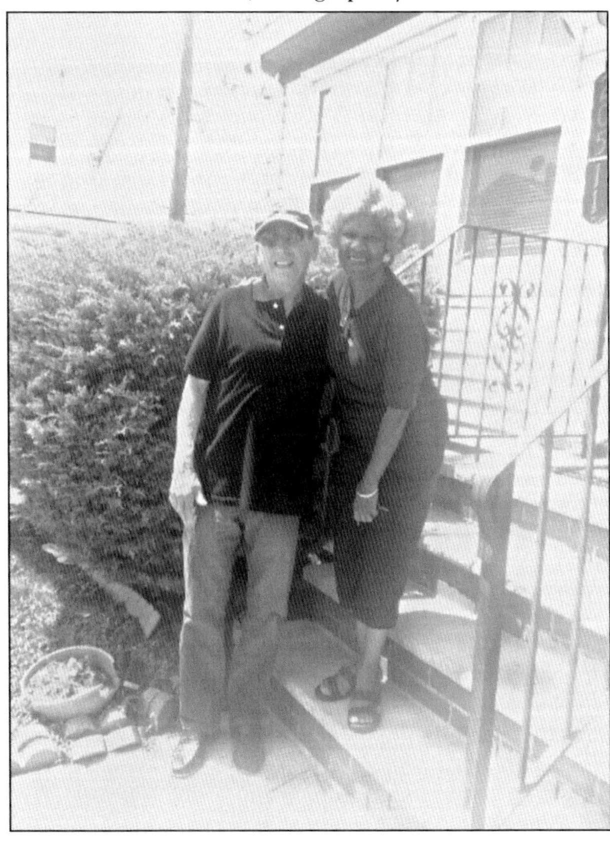

Peter Antonio greets current homeowner Valerie Henry. The pair talked about the neighborhood and shared memories. (Photograph by Blair Garrett.)

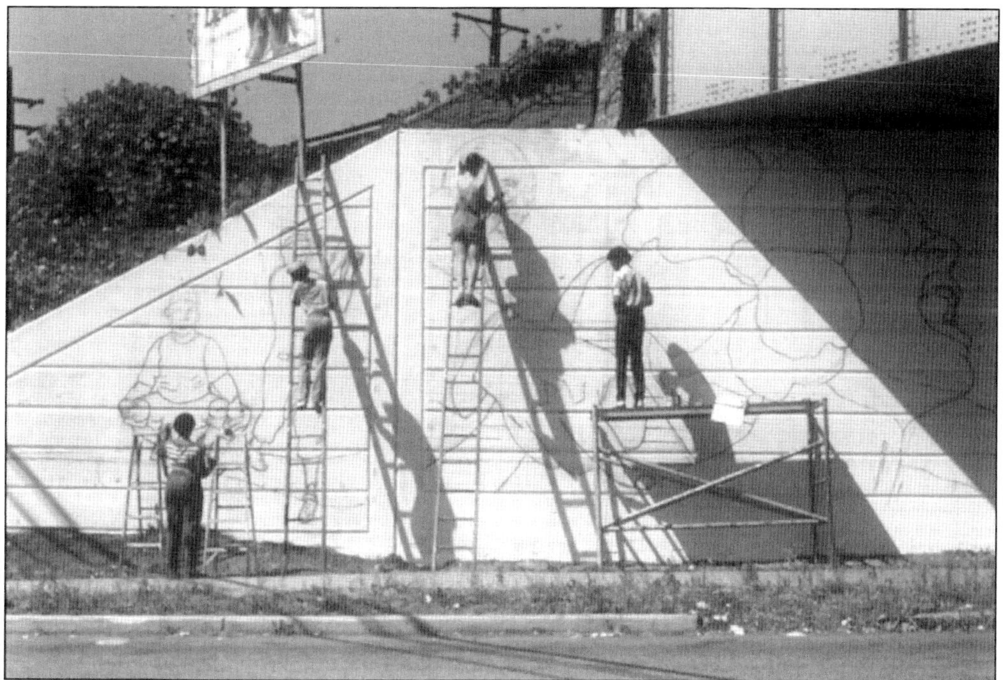

In the summer of 1983, mural artist and St. Albans resident Joe Stephenson and several public school students outlined several images that would appear on a mural near the St. Albans branch of the Long Island Rail Road. (Courtesy of Joe Stephenson.)

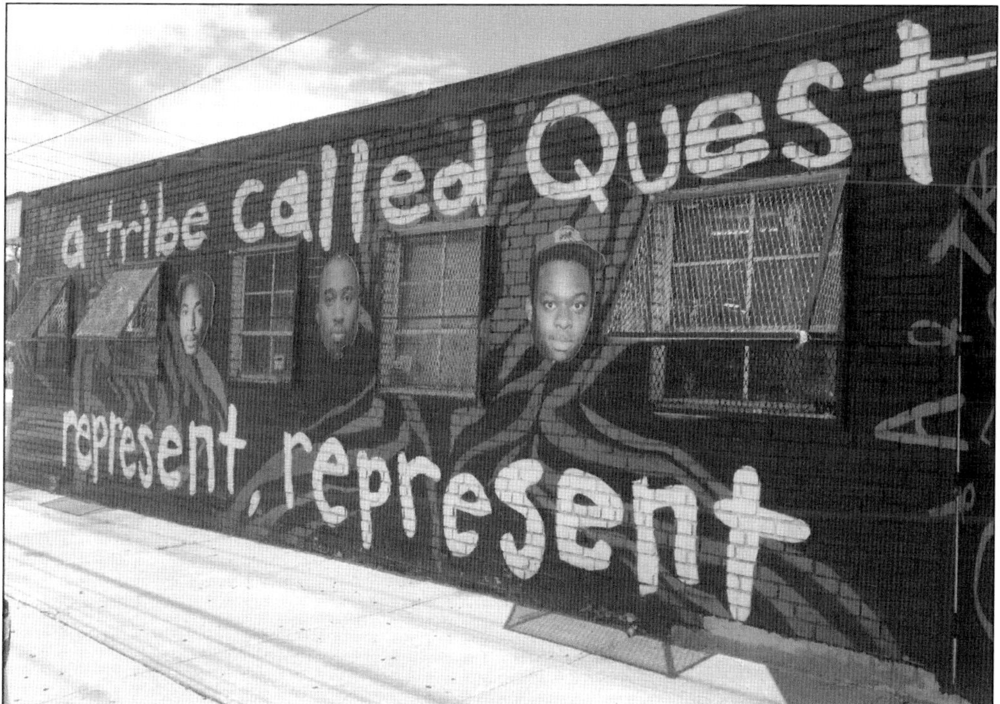

St. Albans's newest artwork honors members of A Tribe Called Quest. This 2019 photograph is a partial view of the mural on 192nd St. and Linden Boulevard. (Photograph by Claire Serant.)

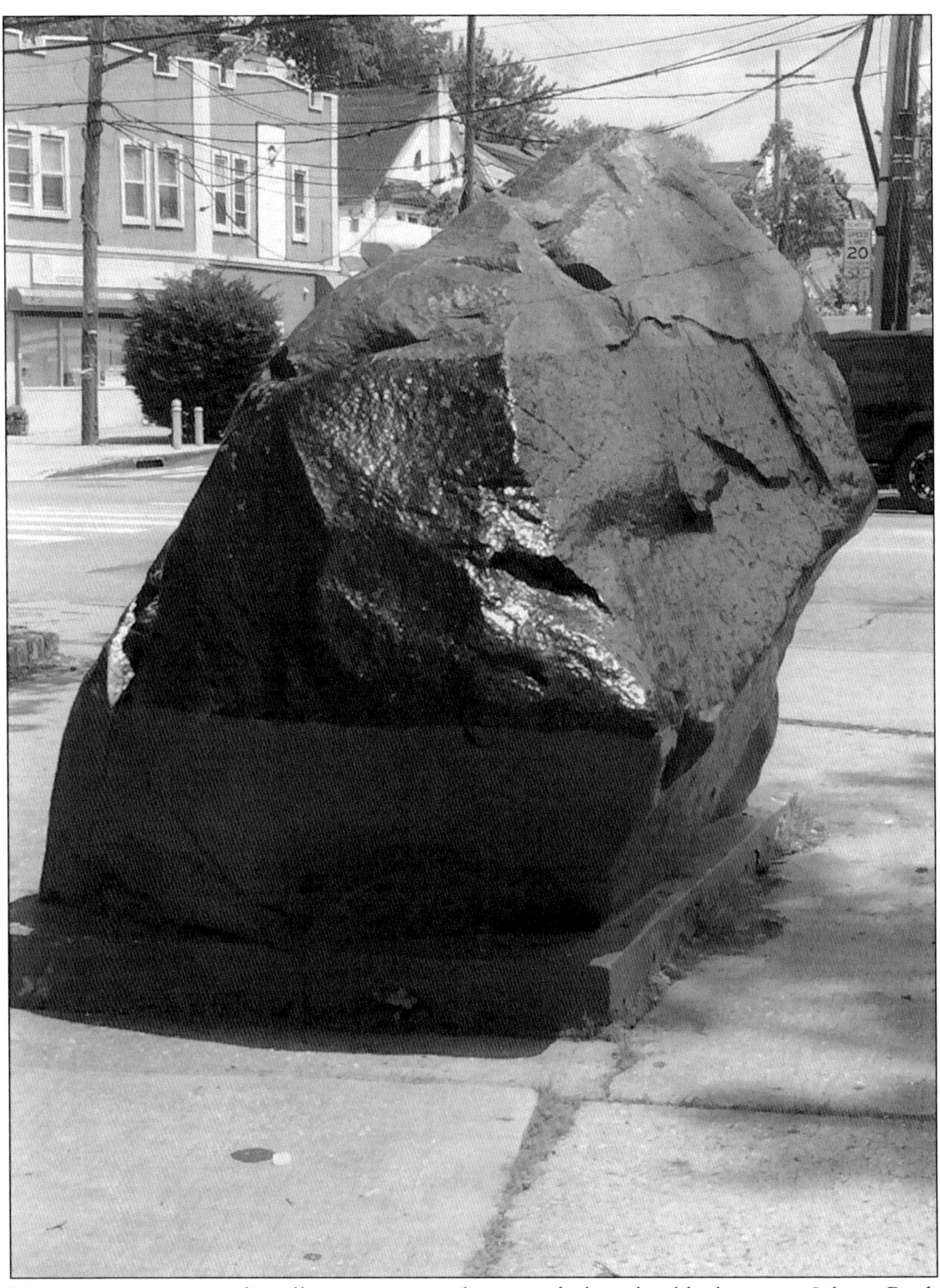

Many years ago, some politically conscious youths painted a large boulder known as Liberty Rock on Farmers Boulevard with pan-African colors to symbolize black power. The rock is a memorial that honors veterans from southeast Queens. It also reminds passersby of the resilience of area residents. (Photograph by Blair Garrett.)

EPILOGUE

St. Albans's story is not limited to the famous entertainers who once lived in the area. The neighborhood represents homeownership and the expansion of the African American and Caribbean American middle class in southeast Queens. St. Albans has numerous churches, such as St. Albans the Martyr, St. Albans Assembly of God, St. Catherine of Sienna, the Episcopal Church of St. Alban the Martyr, St. Albans Baptist Church, Grace United Methodist Church of St. Albans, Maranatha Tabernacle, St. Pascal Baylon, Mt. Olive Baptist Church, Refuge Church of Christ, St. Albans Seventh Day Adventist, Redeemer Lutheran Church, and Beth Elohim, to name a few. Active block associations and other civic groups have contributed to the neighborhood's appeal. During several interviews for this project, current and former St. Albans residents recalled when the community had its own bowling alley—St. Albans Bowl on Dunkirk Street—and when Gloria Jackson's Dance Studio operated on Merrick Boulevard; Ganscap on Linden Boulevard, a must for clothing and shoes; and Berry's Florist and Linda's Hats, to name some of the businesses that brought the neighborhood together. Some older businesses, like Arthur Broadbelt Insurance Company on Farmers Boulevard and the neighborhood doctors, are mainstays.

Newer entrepreneurs have picked up the challenge on St. Albans's shopping streets. For more than 20 years, Frank Williams has operated Thomasina's Restaurant, which caters events for civic organizations and the general public on Linden Boulevard. Naida Njoku, a doll collector, opened the Maria Rose International Doll Museum on Linden Boulevard in 2007. Katie Ballentine has operated Roseland Florist for more than two decades, and the St. Albans Station Florist has satisfied its customers along with the funeral homes, doctors, and other professional offices in the area.

St. Albans's history has not gone unblemished. In July 1968, a major fire at 115-55 Mexico Street killed 11 people, nine of whom were children. At least five others were injured in the blaze. Many of the victims, officials said, were trapped in the home's second story and attic. Fire officials blamed the home's landlord for illegal conversion and occupant overcrowding. Also, a false fire alarm placed by an allegedly intoxicated 19-year-old sailor delayed firefighters' rescue efforts.

In 1981, police officer John G. Scarangella was fatally shot and his partner, Officer Richard Rainey, was seriously injured during a traffic stop on 116th Avenue at 202nd Street. Both officers were assigned to the 113th Precinct. Years later, a portion of Baisley Boulevard near the precinct was named in Scarangella's memory. Rainey died in 2015.

In 2009, 13-year-old Kevin Miller was an innocent bystander who was killed when a gang member fired shots at a rival as Miller walked to a local store. Miller's death stunned area residents. His photograph memorial is still visible on Francis Lewis Boulevard. Those devastating incidents have strengthened the resolve of many area residents who continue to attend civic meetings and watch out for anything unusual in their neighborhood. Social media has helped civic groups post meeting notices and events online to embrace younger St. Albans residents who want to get involved in monitoring quality-of-life issues.

But for St. Albans to continue to thrive, the Rev. Floyd Flake, pastor of the Greater Allen Cathedral, said the community must pay close attention to its housing stock. Properties that are neglected or in disrepair threaten the stability of the entire southeast Queens neighborhood. Unkempt homes and overgrown lawns attract unscrupulous developers and absentee landlords who are ready to take over the weakest property on a block. St. Albans's past has been glorious, and its future remains bright for those residents and politicians who are committed to rolling up their sleeves and continuing the fight.